THIRD WAY DISCOURSE

THIRD WAY DISCOURSE

European Ideologies in the Twentieth Century

Steve Bastow and James Martin

EDINBURGH UNIVERSITY PRESS

Edinburgh University Press Ltd
22 George Square, Edinburgh

Typeset in Sabon by
Hewer Text Ltd, Edinburgh, and
printed and bound in Great Britain by
Antony Rowe Ltd, Chippenham

A CIP Record for this book is
available from the British Library

ISBN 0 7486 1560 1 (hardback)
ISBN 0 7486 1561 X (paperback)

CONTENTS

To our children: Laïra, Esmé and Luis

PREFACE AND ACKNOWLEDGEMENTS

This book surveys the discourse of the 'third way' in modern political ideology. Its aim is to put into perspective recent debates over the notion of a social democratic Third Way by noting the variety and plurality of third *ways* in twentieth-century thought. To do this we conceive the third way, not as an ideology, but as a 'discourse' that operates across the range of ideologies from left, centre and right. Conceiving the third way as a type of discourse, or discursive strategy, enables us to identify specific features that recur in different ideological formations. From this perspective, we believe discussion of the Third Way will be more historically informed and theoretically coherent than it has been. The theoretical basis of our analyses is set out in the Introduction.

In this book we offer only a brief and, for the most part, descriptive sketch of the theoretical structure and historical forms of third way thought. Our purpose is to enable an opening up of debate that, we feel, has been too narrowly constricted to academic analyses of public policy or journalistic glosses. Thus we do not seek to account for each and every instance of third way thinking, nor try to classify the variety of third ways in an intricate manner. Nor do we aim to enter into a normative analysis of third ways as such. These goals are beyond the capacity of any single book. Instead, we have surveyed a wide range of material from the pre- and post-World War Two period, from the left and right of the political spectrum, and have sought to place these in a theoretical context. In Chapter 1 we sketch out the intellectual and political background to third way thought, and in Chapters 2–5 we examine specific examples of third way discourse from New Labour,

Italian liberal socialism, European neo-fascism and, finally, green political thought. These choices reflect our personal research interests but also reflect usefully the different variations in third way discourse across the range of political ideologies. In the Conclusion, we pursue our own interests again in a more speculative manner by setting out how radical democratic politics, too, might be conceived as a type of third way approach on the left. Our explicit point here, as is implied in the rest of the book, is that, for all its obvious deficiencies, third way discourse should not be dismissed as a passing fad. On the contrary, it denotes an important and recurrent strategy in contemporary politics.

For those interested in the division of labour, the Introduction, Chapter 1 and Conclusion were fully co-authored; Steve Bastow drafted Chapters 4 and 5, and James Martin drafted Chapters 2 and 3 (although both authors edited each other's work).

Parts of the book have appeared elsewhere. Elements of the Introduction are to be found in the 'Introduction' to a special issue of the *Journal of Political Ideologies* (vol. 7, no. 3 (2002)) on 'Third Way Ideologies', edited by ourselves and Dick Pels. Chapter 3 is a revised version of an article by James Martin that also appeared in that issue. Other, reassembled parts of the Introduction, Chapter 1 and 2 are to be published as a contribution to D. Howarth and J. Torfing (eds), *Discourse Theory and European Politics* (Palgrave, forthcoming).

For support, advice and helpful input at various stages in the production of the book we would like to thank the following: Nicky Carr at Edinburgh University Press; Dick Pels; Alan Finlayson; Susan Lapworth; Carl Levy; Adrian Little; and Sam Ashenden. Naturally, the responsibility for the content of the book lies solely with us.

Steve Bastow and James Martin
London, 2002

INTRODUCTION
A POLITICS BEYOND ANTAGONISM?

At the start of the twenty-first century the 'Third Way' has come to symbolise the ideology of a revived European social democratic politics. Having rejected socialist statism and the free-market economics of the New Right, leading social democrats claim to have identified an alternative that cuts a path between the dichotomous choice of 'state versus market'. Two of the major parties of the left in Europe – the British Labour Party under Tony Blair and the German Social Democrats under Gerhard Schröder – have proclaimed the Third Way, or in German the 'new middle' (*Neue Mitte*), as an ideology of the 'radical centre' (see Blair, 1998; Blair and Schröder, 1999). It claims to represent a politics based on principle not dogma, a rational answer to the challenges of globalisation and a popular, inclusive alternative to the politics of class and social division that has repeatedly dogged the left. Instead of a supposedly confrontational leftism, doomed forever to protest and never to govern, proponents of the Third Way have announced a politics that claims to have overcome the antagonism between left and right.

The claim to have moved 'beyond antagonism' has proved controversial, for it has become emblematic of a fundamental ambiguity in the whole Third Way enterprise. How can it be 'centrist' and 'radical' at the same time? Doesn't radicalism require opposition to something? If the centre ground mediates the opposition of left and right, are those oppositions still valid? More concretely, in terms of policy options, what exactly is ruled out or in? Not surprisingly, the proclamation of a Third Way in social democracy has initiated a vast debate over the policies, principles and future of the centre-left in Britain and Europe more widely. Increasingly, the contrasting meanings and implications of this Third Way are being debated in academic as well as party political discussions.[1]

However, what is often missed in many of these discussions is an awareness of the variety of ideologies of the third way that span the twentieth century and traverse the spectrum from left to right.[2] Few commentators recognise that third ways claiming to have moved beyond established antagonisms have a long lineage in twentieth-century European social and political thought. Further, current discussions of the social democratic Third Way remain, for the most part, narrowly focused on empirical questions of public policy, few analysts giving much attention to the way the very notion of a 'third' path structures this discussion. Thus the debate over the Third Way has been constrained by its near complete association with the current strategies and policies of social democratic parties, New Labour in particular. Consequently, the fuller implications of a politics beyond antagonism have been narrowed to a limited set of considerations and issues.

In this introductory chapter we explore the 'discourse' of the third way. Understanding the third way as a discourse enables us to think of it as a *mode* of ideological reasoning rather than a distinctive ideology in itself. That way, we can identify common features – what in Chapter 1 we call a 'discursive repertoire' – of third way thought as it appears in a variety of formations such as fascism, liberal socialism and ecologism. These ideologies differ starkly in their analyses, values and prescriptions when expressed as third ways but they share a common claim to have moved beyond the antagonism between rigid ideological oppositions. It is this claim, and the effects it has on various ideological formations, that forms the central concern of this book.

Our first task, however, is to sketch what we understand by discourse and what effect discourse theory has on the study of political ideologies. Having done this, we end the chapter by outlining the substantive analysis developed in the rest of the book.

THE THIRD WAY: LEFT, RIGHT, OR CENTRE?

The Third Way has been difficult to classify. This is partly because it deliberately evades the traditional categories of 'left' and 'right', and is positioned in a 'centre' or 'middle' that purports nevertheless to be 'radical'. At the same time, it has been adopted by parties and advocates of the left who still claim to be working in that tradition.

At first glance, then, the Third Way is difficult to locate in the received ideological spectrum because its proponents claim both to move beyond its strictures whilst, in some way, remaining within it. This problem of classification also has practical implications. Social democrats of the third way repeatedly seek to dissolve or bridge certain policy choices and values: utilising both state *and* market in a governing partnership, emphasising rights *and* responsibilities in citizenship, individual *and* community as the basis of social order, and so on. In abandoning a principled defence of one side of these oppositions over the other, the Third Way exhibits its central claim to have moved beyond ideological antagonism. But moved where? What are the limits to the reliance on the market or the state? When do rights have precedence over responsibilities or vice versa? How can the needs of the individual be reconciled with those of community? For many sympathisers and critics alike, it is not certain exactly whether there exists a new principle 'beyond' the traditional antagonisms that will enable the Third Way to answer such questions. In the absence of a clear point of reference many have accused the Third Way of being fundamentally 'vague and elusive' (White, 2001: 3), eclectically opportunist, or simply facile.

One response to this rather confused picture is to identify an underlying set of motivations that, for reasons of ideological immaturity or political expediency, are not always immediately apparent. If the Third Way can be shown to be intelligible by reference to an *objective* form of reasoning then, it is presumed, its true colours can be discerned. Interestingly, this approach is shared by both proponents and critics alike. Let us briefly examine their arguments.

In his important, early outline, *The Third Way* (1998), Anthony Giddens sets out his view of the Third Way as essentially a 'renewal' of social democratic values of the left under new, globalising conditions. Under these conditions – which include the development of the 'knowledge economy', the growing speed and breadth of telecommunications technology, and the increasing decline in traditional social identities and moral obligations – the traditional values of the left, such as equality of opportunity and social solidarity based around collective needs, are either hopelessly anachronistic or inadequately formulated as policy options. Primarily, claims Giddens, 'old-style' social democracy's attachment to the nation-state as the administrator of a type of social justice is now unfeasible; the state no longer has the capacity to steer a 'national' economy once transnational communications and relations become dominant. Yet, suspicious of markets

and voluntary organisations, unable to grasp the capacity of capitalism to innovate, and indifferent or hostile to the changes in class
identification and political alignments, by the 1970s social democrats
were poorly placed to seize upon the intensifying processes of globalisation as opportunities for the advancement of social justice.

Equally, Giddens goes on, the right-wing, neo-liberal response to
the failings of old-style social democracy has proved insufficient
for regenerating national economies. Market-led strategies destroy
the social basis of stable growth by abandoning the individual to
the vagaries of profit maximisation. Whilst it has contributed to the
expansion of global markets, neo-liberalism's tolerance of vast social
inequalities and, in some instances, its conservative defence of
traditional forms of social organisation such as the Church and
marriage place it outside of any reasonable discussion of social
change. Thus, concludes Giddens, because they were too rigidly
attached to specific forms of economic and social development,
neither traditional social democracy nor neo-liberalism respond with
any degree of flexibility to the challenging conditions of a globalising
environment.

For Giddens, the Third Way represents a transformation of social
democratic ideology to meet these new conditions, whilst retaining the
essential guiding thread of achieving social equality. Globalisation and
the general trend towards a more pluralistic, non-traditional society
disrupt the easy distinctions once grouped around the division between 'left' and 'right' (1998: 37–46). Whereas traditional social
democracy counterposed the state to the market, the Third Way
dissolves the 'dogmatic' assumption of the state's moral and admin-
istrative superiority and looks to both the state *and* the market as
institutional mechanisms for achieving equality. Equally, social democrats must grasp the potential for their general project of emancipation of, for example, voluntary organisations and civic activities,
non-governmental organisations, proliferating differences in individual lifestyle, ecologism, and so forth. All the things that were
dismissed or marginalised under old-style social democracy must be
embraced in a 'more pragmatic attitude towards coping with change'
(1998: 68). Underlying the apparent elasticity of the Third Way, then,
is a positive evaluation of the possibilities for individual and social
emancipation presented by increasingly global economic, social and
cultural conditions.

By contrast, for many critics, especially those further to the left, the
Third Way represents a capitulation to the demands of expanding global

capitalist markets and US-driven policies promoting neo-liberalism. In his trenchant *Against the Third Way* (2001), Alex Callinicos provides an exemplary version of this critique. He disputes Giddens's account of globalisation as a self-driven form of socio-economic transformation and points to the political and economic interests that actively guide it. New Labour's policies, and those of other third way adherents such as Germany under Schröder, as well as former US president Bill Clinton, are in his view little more than cynical rationalisations of a new stage of capitalist imperialism. Despite appeals to pragmatism and a sense of 'community', Blair and others are effectively seeking to introduce private companies into new areas of domestic public service provision and to impose neo-liberal restructuring on the less developed countries as a quid pro quo for international aid. Tony Blair's appeal to ethical standards, therefore, represents 'a "caring" veneer pasted over the relentless com-modification of the world that is the inner truth of the Third Way' (2001: 65). Rather than a policy of pragmatism, the Third Way expresses the 'sincere, indeed dogmatic, belief that private entrepreneurs just are better at running things than anyone else' (2001: 108). The consequence is not a renewal of left-wing aspiration to social justice and human emancipation but the further entrenchment of global inequalities and support for a chaotic and destructive economic system that rewards the few and exploits the many. Thus, in his view (and those of many other critics), the Third Way is essentially an ideology of the right, whose underlying motivation is to conserve the power of capitalist interests.

Although they differ starkly in their evaluation, both Giddens and Callinicos explain the Third Way by reference to external (global) conditions that it more or less accurately represents. The truth and validity of the Third Way is a function therefore of the truth and validity of globalisation. By consequence, their different interpreta-tions of globalisation will produce different interpretations of the Third Way. For Giddens, globalisation represents a wholesale trans-formation in social relations across time and space. Whilst these changes challenge states and economies, they cannot be reduced to changes in the global market but represent a range of issues that individuals must 'reflexively' adjust to in various ways (Giddens, 1998: 30–1). The Third Way is the 'progressive' form that such adjustment can take – that is, in so far as it helps realise values of individual autonomy, equality and social cooperation. For Callinicos, however, globalisation is fundamentally driven by the profit motive of the global capitalist class. The primary issue here is the success with which global markets can be justified to national publics: 'the Third

Way is but an ideological façade behind which capitalism continues on its brutal and destructive way' (Callinicos, 2001: 120).

These interpretations provide a purportedly 'objective' grounding for a classification of the Third Way. What they miss, however, is the way the doctrine helps *constitute* the very objectivity of the world it is supposed to represent. The Third Way automatically positions itself as a more objective account of social conditions than the (first and second) partial views it claims to transcend. The latter can then be dismissed as insufficiently objective, one-sided and therefore limited. Thus the Third Way rhetorically invokes a 'clearing' between these one-sided views in which the full objectivity of social conditions can come into view. For Giddens and Callinicos, however, these social conditions are taken as prior to the analysis that the Third Way imposes; one accepts the analysis, the other rejects it. Although these conditions are important to any assessment of the Third Way, both interpretations fail to see how the Third Way itself is bound up with defining what the objective constraints of the social world are and what it means properly to understand and respond to them. Giddens, for instance, opens his analysis by stating explicitly that 'the term "third way" is of no particular significance in and of itself' (Giddens, 1998: vii). However, we beg to differ.

In our view, the Third Way functions as a 'discourse' that resets the horizons of social objectivity by claiming to transcend received ideological perspectives. In so doing, it resists easy classification along a left–right spectrum. Labelling the doctrine by reference to the analysis of pre-existing social conditions rather misses the point because one key purpose of the Third Way is precisely to redefine the terms by which those conditions are understood. This is not to accept the claim made by some proponents that the Third Way is in some way 'non-ideological'. Nor is it to deny that there are social conditions against which the claims of the Third Way ought to be tested. Nevertheless, the nuances and tensions in the Third Way – and the third way tradition in general – are missed if we treat it simply as a set of postulates to be judged as either true or false and then classified according to a fixed ideological spectrum. In short, as a discourse, the Third Way helps constitute the very conditions to which it claims to be a response.

Below we set out the basic terms and orientation of a post-structuralist theory of discourse. Unlike the approaches taken by Giddens and by Callinicos, this approach understands bodies of thought as complex and contradictory articulations of ideas and notions that help constitute the objective limits of the world. In particular, discourse theory permits us to understand the role of antagonism in setting horizons and providing points of identification for subjects to form identities. As we shall see, these issues are of fundamental importance in understanding the variety of ideological forms third way discourse may take.

DISCOURSE THEORY: A THEORETICAL FRAMEWORK

The theory of discourse we sketch in outline here draws principally upon the work of Ernesto Laclau and Chantal Mouffe, whose analyses developed out of a long-standing criticism of the Marxist tradition which had tended to separate ideological 'superstructures' from an objective economic 'base'.[3] For many orthodox Marxists the base was the ultimate determinant of the superstructure. Thus ideas and values, which Marxists typically lumped together as 'ideology', were often conceived as illusory or 'false' effects of a pre-existing social structure founded on the mode of economic production, whose true workings ideology served to obscure (see Larrain, 1991). In departing from this tradition, Laclau and Mouffe (2001; 1990) rejected the separation of ideas from material practices and developed a theory of discourse for which the material world is partially constituted through symbolic systems that are simultaneously 'material' and 'ideal'; that is, both practical and conceptual. The advantage of this approach is that ideology (that is, ideas, mental representations, symbols, values, and so on) is no longer distinguished as a separate level of social life that can be compared to the objective ('material') world which it is supposed to 'reflect' more or less accurately; rather, ideas and concepts are treated as tools that organise and frame the material world and so give it meaningful shape and content. In that sense, discourse is inextricably linked to struggles and conflicts over how society is organised and not merely a set of passive abstractions floating above the 'real' world (see Howarth, 2000). As we show below, this is of fundamental importance if we are to understand the peculiarities of the Third Way. First of all, we outline some basic principles of discourse theory, then we consider how discourse analysis permits us to rethink the nature of political ideology.

Discourse, antagonism and hegemony

'Discourse' denotes the structured pattern of meanings that frames our perception of, and organises our activity in, the social and natural world. For Laclau and Mouffe (1990), discourse is not a discrete object that can be analysed separately from other activities and objects. Rather, the world is constituted as an objectively intelligible order through discursive relations. Discourse, therefore, constitutes the 'horizon of meaning' within which objects come to have significance. For example, the discourse of 'work' typically involves the identification of a specific set of relationships – between employees and employers – as the core of all other relations. Importantly, these relations are not simply conceptual but material too. Certain physical practices and concrete expectations are entailed in discourses of work. For instance, specific roles and forms of authority are often constructed within the workplace. Likewise, some types of activity and relationship are deemed unacceptable and even punishable by virtue of this discourse (for example, 'pilfering'). Discourse, then, involves simultaneously conceptual and material elements, it denotes the way human relations and activities are rendered meaningful (see Laclau and Mouffe 2001: 108; 1990: 100–12; Torfing 1999: 90–6).

Laclau and Mouffe's theory of discourse follows the structuralist tradition in claiming that social action and meaning are ordered through relations of difference (see Howarth, 2000; Woodward, 1997). Objects, it is argued, do not have intrinsic qualities but are made meaningful through structures of difference that define them by distinguishing and relating elements. Thus a 'worker' can be identified only by reference to an 'employer'. The qualities of a worker do not leap spontaneously from a person but are inscribed on her by a discursive system that invokes patterns of difference that define her. Of course, being a worker is only one way of referring to a person; alternative discourses, such as those that operate in the legal system or at home, will define her in other ways, for example as a 'citizen' or a 'mother'. These other discourses also work by differentiating their object in relation to other elements (non-citizens, child, and so on.). This point underlies a central claim in Laclau and Mouffe's analysis: namely, their 'anti-essentialism'.

Like other post-analytical philosophies, discourse theory rejects the claim that entities have 'positive essences' or core characteristics that give them a 'true' and independent meaning 'outside' of the interpretation given by specific discourses (see Rorty, 1999). Consequently, the identity of all entities is fundamentally unstable or 'contingent' (Laclau, 1990: 109–12). For the social being of an object is radically dependent upon other elements by which it is distinguished, rather by some necessary 'fact' of nature or logic (Laclau and Mouffe, 2001: 75–88; 105–14). Because the elements in this system and the relations between these elements may vary – through social and political struggles, for example – so will the identity of the objects and subjects who bear their meanings. Thus discourse theory starts from the assumption that there are no fully-formed or 'complete' identities or interests that pre-exist social interactions (see also Rorty, 1989). All identities, claims Laclau, are 'dislocated' in the sense that their relational character underscores the absence of an independent meaning (see Laclau, 1990: 41). Individuals occupy a plurality of shifting and overlapping discursive formations (workplace organisation, the home, the legal system) that construct them in relation to others through different discourses; yet none totally subsumes all the others as its 'master principle' (Laclau and Mouffe, 2001: 114–22). Indeed, it is precisely because discourses cannot capture the world fully and finally that we are able to redefine and modify their meanings and related practices. Thus workers have modified the meaning of being an employee through struggles that have changed social relations in the workplace.

If there is no ultimate meaning outside of discursive formations, then how do we judge the validity of any discourse? Without an objective, 'external' (or 'extra-discursive') referent by which to assess specific claims about the world, aren't all discourses equally true? Surely authoritarian bosses can now pass themselves off as fair employers by calling themselves such, even if in reality they brutally exploit their workforce? Marxists (and other critics) often raise this theoretical point to critique post-structuralist thought. However, that is to mistake discourse with conversation or self-description. What it misses is the way discursive meanings are *constitutive* of material relations in society and therefore bound up with bringing into being what they claim to describe. That is, the materiality of social relations is an effect of the way we unthinkingly accept certain meanings as self-evidently true and therefore fully descriptive of an objective 'fact'. Such facts are usually enforced by institutional powers that ensure our compliance; often such powers are taken for granted and seem less threatening as a result.

For example, take the fact that our status as employees does not permit us to remove items from work and sell them for personal profit, even if we ourselves made them. This is a material condition of capitalist relations of production but it is based on a hierarchical distinction between owner and producer that is reinforced in law and policed by rules within factories and offices. The legal discourse and its practical enforcement function to constitute the materiality of the employee–employer relation. We could, of course, completely ignore the law and steal items at will. But that would invoke the authorities to enforce the discourse through punishment. Thus whilst the order of the workplace is discursively organised, it remains materially 'sedimented' in taken-for-granted relations of power. As Daly observes: '*in principle*, nothing stops a person from constructing an object the way they want to except, of course, other people constructing the object in a different manner' (Daly, 1999: 75). It is not some extra-discursive truth that limits the way the world can be constructed but the presence of 'regimes of truth', as Foucault put it, that figure the world in specific ways and make it 'knowable' according to certain criteria (see Shapiro, 1985–6). Challenging discursive regimes requires us to find another discourse against which our challenge can be deemed acceptable (for example, that by stealing we would save someone's life or prevent some dreadful abuse of human rights).

Importantly, Laclau and Mouffe retain a notion of ideology as an illusory appearance: discourses that claim to be founded on an incontestable, authoritative truth – and hence deny their contingency and the power relations they support – are ideological not because they obscure 'reality' but because they obscure the absence of a fully-knowable reality (see Laclau, 1996b). Thus modern medical discourses typically appeal to the authority of 'science' and so reduce the possibility of alternative forms of treatment (and their practitioners) contesting the medical establishment. It is this 'discursive closure' by which discourses are naturalised so as to seem as though they flow freely from reality itself that disguises the historically contingent and partial interpretation they give to the world.

Anti-essentialism, then, forms the centrepiece of Laclau and Mouffe's critique of Marxism, which they claim was mistakenly based on the notion that there was an essence to society, that this essence was economic in form (that is, based on the fundamental activity of human labour and self-subsistence), and that all social identity was ultimately referable to the movement of structured economic relationships. This 'economism' involved the assumption that beneath society's complexities and variations lay the determination of unchanging – purportedly 'objective' – economic laws. Whilst struggles and conflicts in society rage around a multiplicity of issues and divisions, and with varying outcomes, the essential motive force of historical change was an underlying economic 'necessity'. For this reason, Marxists tended to seek out a 'class essence' to social conflicts in order to determine the manner in which various struggles could be referred back to the objective ground of the social: the economic essence (see Laclau and Mouffe, 2001: chs 1–3; Daly, 1999).

Laclau and Mouffe's anti-essentialism, however, rejects the assumption of an underlying objective necessity to society. Indeed, they dispute the very idea of 'society' at all, if by that we understand a unified object to which all social differences can be referred and made intelligible (see 2001: 111; Laclau, 1990: 89–92). If the meaning of social identities is given in the discourses that construct them, then social struggles (and all other social phenomena) cannot be traced back to an economic essence that escapes this discursive construction. Thus we should not expect democratic struggles over women's rights, for instance, to have any intrinsic or necessary connection to class struggles. Nor, indeed, should working-class struggles be expected to be automatically anti-capitalist. There are no essential 'class interests' lurking beneath such struggles giving them an ultimately common meaning. Rather, the character of these social identities are contingent constructions, the outcome of specific discursive linkages that align differences in certain ways (see Laclau, 1990: 4–27). Only when workers and feminists openly identify capitalism as the ultimate cause of the various forms of oppression they suffer – and therefore construct an 'interest' in opposing it – can they be said to be anti-capitalist.[4]

Many Marxists claim that the objective grounding of their analysis proves the intrinsic anti-capitalist interests of workers, whether they consciously accept it or not (see, for example, Wood, 1998). But, for Laclau and Mouffe, appeals to an underlying structure that escapes discursive construction falsely transforms economic relations into an abstract metaphysical essence. All of society can become subsumed within this totalising logic and it becomes difficult to think of social phenomena in their specificity. Of course, that is not to say that capitalism does not produce systematic inequalities, class conflicts and revolution. But the sequence of that logic – the perception of inequality, the identification of its causes, the types of conflict that might emerge – is not the automatic outcome of capitalist structures. It is generated through a series of discursive linkages that may not necessarily be made. Such linkages are more likely to be made, however, in moments of traumatic social change when social identities undergo acute strain. As Laclau puts it: 'it is the dislocation of structural laws which creates the possibility of a revolutionary politics' (1990: 46). That is, it is precisely because structured economic relations disrupt other relations that individuals feel compelled to identify the causes of their hardship and seek ways to transform society. The act of making such linkages is what Laclau and Mouffe refer to as the process of 'articulation', and their being made at all occurs as a consequence of contingent efforts, not as facts of mechanical necessity. The articulation of dislocated identities and experiences around an inclusive discourse of oppression (anti-capitalist, anti-patriarchal, and so on) – that is, the construction of antagonism – is conceived as the formation of 'hegemony'. Let us now consider these two terms – antagonism and hegemony – more closely.

In *Hegemony and Socialist Strategy*, Laclau and Mouffe state that 'antagonism constitutes the limits of every objectivity' (2001: 125; see also Laclau, 1990: 17). What do they mean by this? Put simply, it is through the identification of an antagonist who limits and oppresses 'us' that partial and precarious identities are given a temporary discursive fixity. In this sense, 'objectivity' is symbolically produced through a process of 'objectification': identities are made real by a heightened sense of 'threat'. Antagonism operates to close down the realm of possible differences by asserting a limit, that is, by constructing a barrier or frontier. What oppresses us gives us a determinate sense of our own identity and needs; by stopping us from being fully ourselves (for example, free workers, liberated women), antagonism (for example, with bosses, global capitalism, patriarchy) furnishes the world with a sense of an order yet to come.

Paradoxically, then, it is what negates the being of an identity that 'hardens' the experience of that identity. An antagonism is not simply a logical contradiction (A–not-A) or a physical opposition (A–B); it is a distinctively social, or symbolic, relationship in which one entity is perceived as an intrinsic limit on another (A–anti-A). The presence of an antagonist, therefore, is a threat to the being of the entity; it represents the limit, or negation, of the social as an intelligible order (see Laclau and Mouffe, 2001: 122–7). In millenarian discourses, for example, the world is organised around the antagonistic presence of Evil which constantly threatens to destroy it. The eventual (re)appearance of God, however, will eradicate Evil, judge us for our sins and return the world to its Divine form. Likewise, classical Marxist discourses proclaiming the 'inevitable' overthrow of capitalism looked to the immiseration of the working class and the proletarianisation of intermediate classes as the final, simplifying stages in the antagonism between workers and an irrational capitalist system. In each of these discourses, antagonism alerts us to a potential order underlying social relations; that is, the rationality of particular demands (for example, the demands of Christians, or Marxist socialists) is specified through the presence of an antagonism that currently limits those demands.

How does antagonism work? Laclau and Mouffe refer to the 'logics of difference' and 'equivalence' at work in political discourse (2001: 127–34). Logics of difference highlight the distinctiveness, complexity and particularity of separate discursive elements (worker, boss, and so on). Logics of equivalence, however, unify elements under a common sign (the people, nation, the oppressed). In the identification of antagonism, differentiated demands (over women's rights, wages, conditions of work, welfare) are placed in a 'chain of equivalence' by their subsumption under a single category: what Laclau and Mouffe call the 'simplification of social space' (2001: 130). As equivalential elements, their differences are diminished and they are resignified as common elements of a single identity. Particular demands, types of social identity and practice are blurred and 'run together' as unified 'moments' in a shared opposition. This is precisely the effect that nationalist discourses seek by making aspects of culture, culinary habits, language and geography, and so on, all part of a common struggle to 'liberate the nation'. On their own, these elements are distinctive; as parts of nationalist discourse they become equivalential. Each loses its literal particularity and comes to symbolise a universal quality of nationhood.

At the same time, the logic of difference works in a more simplified way to highlight a single frontier that divides 'us' from 'them'. The antagonist is symbolised by a series of differences that are run together in an equivalential chain: in ethnic nationalist discourses, for instance, the habits, customs and even economic success of the enemy nation are treated as symbols of a common oppressive intent. However, the antagonist is not just another differentiated identity: it stands as the limit of any rational order at all and is therefore conceived as almost unintelligible. Thus antagonists are typically described, for example, as 'disgusting', 'unreasonable' or 'indecent'.[5]

The name Laclau and Mouffe give to the working of this combined logic of difference and equivalence in the formation of social identities is hegemony (2001: 134–45). Borrowed from the Italian Marxist, Antonio Gramsci, hegemony signifies a process of political unification in which distinct demands and aspirations are unified around a common goal. For Gramsci, however, hegemony was a political practice to be accomplished by classes (organised through the political party) rooted in the relations of production. The working class would achieve revolution by hegemonising the demands of various other subordinate social classes and groups in civil society (see Martin, 1998; Laclau and Mouffe, 2001: 65–71). In this sense, he remained broadly within the economistic terms of the Marxist tradition. For Laclau and Mouffe, classes themselves are hegemonic constructions and cannot be accorded an a priori role in the construction of hegemony. There is no intrinsic necessity that economic classes must lead hegemony (which is not to say that classes do not form any part of it).

Hegemony, as Laclau and Mouffe conceive it, is not a fully coherent and harmonious process. The hegemonisation of demands, ideas and values always entails a mutual modification of its components and a holding together of a potentially contradictory ensemble of experiences and aspirations (2001: 135–6). Following Foucault, Laclau and Mouffe are aware of the processes of power and violence that permeate discursive formations. Nationalist discourses, for instance, are often gendered, sometimes racist and therefore inevitably quite selective versions of the national community (see Finlayson, 1998). Hegemony certainly does not mean harmonisation. In any hegemonic discourse, some values and experiences will be preferred over others. No discourse can claim to fully include and domesticate all potential elements and this means that, in principle, all discourses are open to modification and rearticulation. As particular exclusions and hierarchies form into social antagonisms through molecular as well as structural processes of change and conflict, discourses will change as new organising principles (new formations of equivalence and difference) come to dominate (see Laclau, 1996a). These changes might be related to the dynamics of capitalist economies but they will also relate to other discursive formations (of gender, race or religion, for example) that they overlap with and mutually dislocate.

Discourse theory and political ideology

In recent years there has been wide and varied discussion of the nature of political ideologies and how they might be studied (see Freeden, 1996). But what are political ideologies? They are commonly understood to be relatively stable, systematic bodies of concepts and analyses that express particular moral dispositions towards social and political arrangements and that define the range of legitimate choices available. Ideologies are typically expressed in generic form as 'isms': socialism, communism, liberalism, and so on (see, for example,

Vincent, 1992). They are distinguishable by the type of analysis of society that they make, the value commitments they express and the types of arrangements for reordering society that they propose. Of course, there are many different sub-groups of ideologies and even a considerable degree of overlapping between them. However, there is a recognisable set of conventionalised ideological 'families' that have come to define intellectual and theoretical traditions in modern society.

Revival of interest in political ideologies turns on the recognition that, despite proclamations to the contrary in the 1960s, ideology has not come to an end (see Bell, 1988). Instead, the ideological frames through which people interpret and experience their world are recognised increasingly as an ever-present feature of modern social life. A number of approaches to the analysis of ideology have pointed to the way in which the conceptual configurations of ideologies structure the universes of meaning which inform our everyday conduct but are themselves hidden, or covered over, by the 'naturalising' effect ideologies confer upon this conduct (see Lefort, 1986). As such, ideologies are rooted in social relations of power, and seek either to legitimise existing social orders or to delegitimise them. Ideologies – with their partial and value-laden outlooks – thus continue to define the terrain of social and political practices, and the analysis of ideology has come to imply the recovery of the political origins of the practices governing the social and political world.

What is the difference between analysing political ideologies and analysing discourse? There is certainly a considerable degree of convergence between the two concepts. Both the analysis of ideologies and the analysis of discourses refer to relatively stable configurations of representations, concepts and symbols that change over time and are modified according to the specificities of any particular context. Both point to the way social meanings are often partial to specific values, and both are 'political' in as much as they seek to define the sources of social disorder so as to recommend a means of resolution. However, ideologies are typically based around a discursive 'closure', in that they are often presented (by their proponents as well as scholars) as being informed by some underlying necessity (thus producing the naturalising effect noted above). The obvious case in point is the discussion of the Third Way by Giddens and Callinicos noted earlier. It is precisely because both Giddens and Callinicos relate the Third Way to the objective essence of the process of globalisation that the Third Way acts as an ideology in their work. Other ideologies, however, look to 'human nature', 'universal values' or even 'sacred' texts as the foundation that guarantees their objectivity. This guarantee serves to fix the elements of ideological discourse around a supposedly incontestable essence or principle. Discourse analysis, however, focused as it is upon the contingent nature of meaning, seeks to show how such essences are themselves contingent products.[6] Its anti-foundational approach means that it refuses any final closure in a system of meaning but looks to the differential relations upon which such meaning is temporarily constructed.

This refusal underlines a number of differences between the traditional study of political ideologies and discourse theory in practical analytical terms. As Norval (2000: 327) points out, the study of political ideologies has been focused primarily on the major political concepts and the complex formations of ideas formed around dominant political traditions. Such an approach accepts, to a great extent, the divorce of 'ideas' from relations of power within society that is precisely an outcome of the naturalising effect of ideology. It sets limits to the range of issues and concerns under examination, resulting in an inability to fully perceive the ways in which ideologies operate to 'govern' conduct.[7] Discourse theory, however, does not limit itself to dominant political traditions and complex theoretical arguments over the preferred social and political arrangements. On the contrary, the advantage of discourse theory lies in the breadth of ideas, symbols and representations in its scope. For it recognises that the world is made meaningful not simply by political concepts and ideals but also by popular notions, 'common sense' values and often quite irrational prejudices about peoples and their 'innate' characteristics that are rarely formulated as ideologies. As such, it is able more adequately to assess the process whereby ideologies naturalise meaning.

Thus, whilst the study of political ideologies is a highly formal conceptual analysis, discourse theory focuses less on the formal concepts and structure of ideologies than it does on the way this material functions to organise human experience. As Norval indicates, discourse theory is preoccupied with the way the individual subject is given temporary coherence and meaning through discursive mechanisms and how this subjectivity is forged through relationships of power (Norval, 2000). Whereas studies of ideology consider the relatively stable frameworks that organise judgements about the world, studies of discourses focus on how symbolic frameworks get pieced together (or 'articulated') and enable certain types of action in the world. The focus, then, is more on the contingent, open-ended and contestable features of discourse than on the stable, relatively closed and incontestable features of ideologies.[8]

Finally, the study of political ideologies, by limiting the terms of the analysis to specifically delimitable ideologies (that is, the 'isms'), often fails to examine the interrelationship between ideologies. Discourse theory, on the other hand, can help us examine the fluid patterns of thought and understanding shared across ideologies as well as within them. For instance, discourses of economic progress and rationality inform many socialist and liberal ideologies. Likewise, gendered and racial discourses can be found within a variety of ideologies, often without being formally recognised as such. So, whilst we may consider discursive regularities internal to particular political ideologies, we may also find such regularities operating between ideologies, too. Furthermore, elements of distinct ideological families may be deliberately appropriated by being dis-articulated and re-articulated within a new framework, so modifying those elements and giving them a new meaning or significance. Stuart Hall's classic analysis of 'Thatcherism' as a populist combination of neo-liberal libertarianism and conservative traditionalism is a case in point (see Hall, 1988: esp. chs 2 and 4).

What difference do these approaches make to examining the Third Way? If we were to treat the Third Way purely as a political ideology we might look for its recurrent concepts and analytical reference points, perhaps even consider these in relation to their 'parent' ideology, social democracy. We could then proceed to break down the Third Way framework into its constituent ideological elements and review the policy outcomes delimited by such elements. Whilst this approach may bring useful insights, it nevertheless remains limited. First, it overlooks the fact that the Third Way has never been presented as a systematic political ideology. So far, despite the vast amount of discussion on its significance, social democracy's Third Way has – much to the annoyance of its detractors – remained intriguingly vague. Second, the approach neglects the deliberate effort by Third Way proponents to shake off the heritage of ideological continuity and steer a 'new path'.

In light of these two difficulties, the advantages of discourse theory are evident. Since discourse theory is focused on the unstable, often contradictory ensemble of elements that form a discourse, the Third Way's inchoate character is not a problem at all. Nor is the fact that the Third Way seeks to transcend dominant ideological antagonisms a problem, since antagonism forms the very substance of discourse theory's concerns. Finally, discourse theory is uniquely equipped to analyse the variations and discursive patterning in third way thinking across various ideologies, giving attention to how these types differ yet draw upon the same repertoire of meanings.

CHAPTER OUTLINE

Discourse theory is not a substitute for studying ideologies but a useful device that enables a critical, deconstructive analysis. In the chapters that follow, we study different ideological formations by using the tools of discourse theory. Our analyses cannot claim to be exhaustive, either of the range of third ways in modern political thought and practice, nor of all the approaches deploying methods of discourse theory. In many respects, the book focuses on ideas, thinkers and movements that interest us most. Nevertheless, the range of ideologies – social democratic, liberal socialist, neo-fascist and green – allows us to put the case for thinking of the third way as a common discursive strategy in the broad field of political ideology. It also enables us to develop an argument – addressed tentatively in the final chapter – concerning the significance and possible implications of third way thought for radical democrats in the current conjuncture.

To contextualise our studies, Chapter 1 offers an overview of the conjuncture of the inter-war period in which third ways were first articulated. Our point here is that third ways are linked to 'crises' of political ideology that have been diagnosed throughout the twentieth century. Indeed, third ways seek to define and expand these crises by accounting for their objective emergence (for example, as crises of ecology or crises of capitalism) and by offering themselves as routes out of the crisis. Whilst these crises consist in a multiplicity of social dislocations, third ways define them in terms of the exhaustion of dominant left/right options. We go on to sketch what we call the 'repertoire' of the third way, that is, a series of discursive features that acts as a kind of grammar to (often very different) third way arguments.

In Chapter 2 we take up our first substantive study of third ways by discussing the most recent incarnation, namely the Third Way of New Labour in the UK. Many critics have chastised New Labour for the general vagueness of its ideological programme, its apparent break with the traditions of the Labour Party and the lack of obvious intellectual coherence. There are good grounds for many of these arguments but, as we shall see, New Labour's Third Way presents many of the features of other third ways, although in a distinctive form. For New Labour, the strategy to 'modernise' Britain's economy and

society forms the central thread of its Third Way. However, modernisation discourse is crucially dependent on its ability to define the
objective processes underlying social change and convince others of this
definition. For all its efforts to manipulate the media and the public's
perception of its policies, it is not certain that New Labour is able to
disperse successfully the antagonisms brought by social change.

Chapter 3 takes as its object the political ideas of the Italian liberal
socialist tradition in the inter-war period. Whilst only a marginal and
relatively undeveloped ideological formation, liberal socialists were
fully engaged with antagonism because their primary focus was anti-
fascism. Behind this antagonism lay the appeal to an ethic of liberty
that sought to reconcile liberalism's focus on individual freedom with
socialism's principles of community and solidarity. We trace the
development of liberal socialist thought by sketching the ideas of
three of its key thinkers and discuss the role of antagonism in
discursively unifying its principles but also in limiting its success as
a political force after the Second World War.

Chapter 4 examines post-war neo-fascism, in particular the third
way ideas of 'revolutionary nationalists' and 'ethno-differentialists' of
the radical right in Belgium and France. Like inter-war fascism, neo-
fascists assert the principle of nationality as the basis of a third way
between capitalism and communism. However, post-war conditions
provide different antagonisms for fascist-inspired movements to organise around. In this chapter, we outline the key elements of, and
differences between, these groupings and compare them to the *Front
national* of Jean-Marie Le Pen, who continues to have success in
mainstream party politics. However, this success is argued to be based
on a more flexible mobilisation of a third way discourse.

The ideas of the contemporary green movement are analysed in
general terms in Chapter 5. Ecologists have long presented themselves
as defenders of a third way ideal in which capitalism and socialism are
transcended by a new type of society formed around the primacy of the
natural environment. However, it is clear from the start that this third
way exhibits a variety of tensions and important differences of emphasis.
Whilst often conceived as a typically left-wing movement, it is clear that
the discursive framework of third way thought in the green movement
allows for considerable authoritarianism as well as radical democracy.
This slippage, as we note throughout, is a common and disconcerting
feature of a discourse that seeks to place itself beyond antagonism.

In the Conclusion we return to this question of moving 'beyond
antagonism' by focusing on the distinctive problems and possibilities

raised by the various third way discourses. We go on to consider how a radical democratic politics, that expressly promoted by Laclau and Mouffe, can be seen to share many of the same concerns and tropes as third way discourses. Unlike other third ways, however, radical democracy has the distinctive attribute of *embracing* social antagonisms as an ineradicable, indeed ontological, feature of social life. We then suggest, tentatively, that radical democracy can offer a useful approach for thinking through the potential, without repeating many of the dangers, of third way politics.

Notes

1 For overviews of these debates, and contributions to them, see Giddens (2000 and 2001); Bastow, et al. (2002); Béland, et al. (2002).

2 Throughout this book we shall use the lower case 'third way' when referring to the general tradition of third way ideas, and the upper case 'Third Way' when referring to specific doctrines such as that of New Labour.

3 The principal texts of Laclau and Mouffe that we refer to in this chapter are: Laclau and Mouffe, *Hegemony and Socialist Strategy* (2nd edn, 2001; first published 1985); Laclau and Mouffe, 'Post-Marxism Without Apologies' (1990); Laclau, *New Reflections on the Revolution of Our Time* (1990); and Laclau, *Emancipation(s)* (1996a). For discussion of the debates around Laclau and Mouffe's work, especially amongst Marxists, see Smith (1998); Torfing (1999); and Daly (1999).

4 See Smith (1998) for a discussion of the discursive character of political struggles and alliances.

5 Applications of discourse theory to political struggles, and the different 'logics' combined therein, are presented in Howarth, et al., (2000). On the discursive significance of the 'nation', see Finlayson (1998).

6 Laclau and Mouffe's critique of essentialist theorising and the effort to reveal this essence as itself relational (and therefore conditional) owes much to Jacques Derrida's 'deconstructive' approach. See, in particular, Derrida (1978).

7 For a Foucauldian analysis of liberalism as the 'government of conduct' as opposed to a disembodied political philosophy, see Barry, et al., (1996).

8 Bevir (1999) has developed his own 'non-foundational' approach to the history of ideas (and his extension of this work to the analysis of ideology is drawn upon in Chapter 1). However, whilst he recognises the contingent and open-ended nature of meaning, Bevir's approach almost entirely neglects the contexts of power in which ideas change. He tends, therefore, to conceive meaning as the internal, individual experience of ideas. For a critique from the perspective of discourse theory, see Martin (2002).

CHAPTER I

IDEOLOGY IN CRISIS: THE
'REPERTOIRE' OF THE THIRD WAY

Third ways have been pronounced from a variety of perspectives in the field of political ideology in the twentieth century. Considered together, this 'third tradition' exhibits a number of common features, or 'family resemblances', that centre around the motif of 'moving beyond' the established antagonism between left and right (see Bastow, et al., 2002b). That antagonism might be conceived in terms of opposed philosophical principles, models of social and political order, or competing policy options. Whichever form taken, third ways are defined principally by the space they open up between pre-existing alternatives that they purport to both transcend and absorb into a new synthesis.

In this chapter we account for the demand for a third alternative by pointing to the diagnosed 'crises' of political ideology that mark the twentieth century. These crises, themselves the condensation of a variety of social dislocations, mark a moment of rupture in the discursive fabric of social and political conflict in Europe, producing a fertile experimentation of ideas and ideological cross-overs that are not experienced at more stable moments when the parameters of political debate are relatively fixed. Whilst the twentieth century is plotted with numerous instances of ideological crisis of varying intensity, the most productive moments have been those in which a number of intense social dislocations converge. In Europe, such a conjuncture first occurred in the inter-war period (1918–39) when third ways were developed from various quarters. Then the settled parameters of conflict between left and right were disrupted and various efforts were made, often on the margins of mainstream political discourse, to fashion a new politics that synthesised elements of each.

Below, we discuss the origins of third way thought and present a summary of the distinctive features that we refer to as the discursive 'repertoire' of the third way. A repertoire consists in a number of elements or tropes: all third ways, we claim, select from this repertoire, though the meaning of such elements depends on the specific discourse in which they are articulated. The repertoire will form the guiding thread of the later chapters. To substantiate this summary, we provide specific examples of the ideological cross-overs from the inter-war period from different traditions of the third way.

IDEOLOGY AND MODERNITY: BETWEEN ANTAGONISM AND CRISIS

Common to all third ways is the claim to transcend the established antagonism between the 'left' and 'right' poles of the political spectrum, however these are defined in any particular instance. To go a *third* way is, by definition, to reject the first and second alternatives. But the third choice is not just one difference in a series (for example, 1, 2, 3 and so on): typically it is presented as a transcendence of their mutually exclusive duality as the horizon of all ideological difference. The third way aims to define a new ideological space outside the traditional antagonism and, simultaneously, to absorb and reorder elements of those earlier ideologies, thereby creating a new synthesis that is superior to its predecessors.[1] Whilst third ways differ markedly in content, their discursive form as the 'alternative to the alternatives' gives them a distinctive but ambiguous character: they are both outside established ideological discourse and yet inside it; they reject its duality but absorb elements of each in new ways. Thus third ways can be seen to emerge from within the left and right camps whilst often at the same time declaring themselves to be alternatives to that distinction.

As we shall note later, this creates an ambiguous situation in which the third route is presented as new and distinctive but remains closely bound up with the ways it claims to surpass. To understand this situation, we need to place left, right and third ways within the context of social and political modernity. This is because left and right signify opposed, generalised stances towards the contradictory complex of dislocatory experiences associated with modernity, and third ways represent efforts to escape the limitations of this logic of opposition (see Bobbio, 1996: 8–9).

By 'modernity' we understand the articulation of a series of social, political and intellectual transformations that took place from around the sixteenth century onwards. These include: the gradual development of capitalist and commercial economies based on relations of formal exchange rather than hierarchy and ascribed social status; the breakdown of traditional identities formed around kinship and the emergence of individualist cultures; the formation of nation-states based on constitutional (and later democratic) principles; and the ideas of the Enlightenment, which pointed towards the increased control of nature by rational human subjects and the 'progress' this would eventually bring to society as a whole (see Sheppard, 2000: 10–11; Taylor, 1989). It would be wrong to assume, however, that modernity consists in a singular logic of development. On the contrary, these different aspects occurred unevenly across time and space and involved a variety of contradictory experiences and aspirations that the singular term 'modernity' (and narratives about it) cannot adequately capture. For example, the liberalisation of trade and the advent of commercial societies was not seen by all as the harbinger of progress, nor was it necessary that such liberalisation would bring calls for 'universal' democratic rights; indeed, in many instances this did not occur until relatively recently. Likewise, the desire to establish rational, scientific principles of natural and social order contradicted the growing awareness that such principles were man-made and hence fallible (see Blumenberg, 1983).

Modernity, therefore, presents an uneven rhythm of overlapping social and political dislocations, none of which is ultimately reducible to the other. Changes in eighteenth- and nineteenth-century patterns of property ownership, forms of work, relationships with authorities such as the state and church, and so forth produced multiple dislocations in which received social identities were increasingly destabilised and new forms of antagonism and collective identification emerged. As Marshall Berman (1983) points out, the Modern age consists in a contradictory concatenation of ferocious and disorienting change, simultaneously promising increased human fulfilment but destroying the traditional bases of community and order in the process.

'Left' and 'right' constitute opposed dispositions towards these complex processes of change. The terms originate in the seating structure of the French Estates-General in 1789: those who sat to the left of the King were regarded as radicals or revolutionaries seeking social and political change, those to his right supported the monarch in resisting change and comprised conservatives and reactionaries. Since then, left and right have defined the broad space of political antagonism in modern Western societies, although only in the twentieth century were the terms self-consciously applied. It is clear, however, that the terms constitute very broad and loose categorisations for classifying social and political ideals, values, organised movements and policies. The left tends to encompass those who identify the transformations of modernity with the emancipation of mankind from the strictures of tradition, hierarchy and ascribed social status: demands encapsulated in appeals for increased political liberty and formal political equality. This included, at first, the emergent bourgeoisie or 'middle class' of merchants, small property owners and industrialists. The right, on the other hand, included those who regarded modernity, or certain aspects of it (for example, rationalism, equality, democracy, secularism), as fundamentally a threat to social order and human well-being. This often comprised Christian churches, large landowners, aristocrats and many peasants: that is, all those who identify with an older, more stable society in which hierarchy, not equality, and order, not liberty, were central.

The antagonism between left and right consists in the identification by each of the other as a threat to social order: to those on the left, conservative justification of the status quo represents an irrational fear of progress and an obstacle to an emancipated society; to the right, the desire for change (through equality, rights and democracy) undermines the received wisdom and traditional forms of social organisation and community upon which society depends. However, exactly what counts as being on the left or right is less obvious than the simple division implies. Often any particular individual or group can profess beliefs from both 'sides' on different issues: for instance, liberals in the early nineteenth century subscribed to radical views on issues of constitutional controls on government, or greater freedom to exercise their rights to trade, yet steadfastly refused to countenance the possibility of working people having an equal right to participate in government. Conservatives traditionally invoke ideas of community and responsibility to others, yet so, too, do socialists and other groupings on the left who reject liberal ideas that assert the social and political primacy of the individual.

Patterns of political association and belief, then, do not easily 'map' the distinction between left and right. Or rather, the distinction is itself a fluid and constantly changing discourse. As noted in the

Introduction, depending on which dislocations and experiences are in question, different individuals and groups will take different, sometimes contradictory, ideological positions which 'stretch' and modify received discursive structures. Thus in modern European history, the antagonism between left and right has undergone constant shifts as new experiences and conflicts displace older ones and new political subjects are produced. In these shifts, certain ideological elements (such as, for example, 'democracy' or 'liberty') often detach from their dominant ideological constructs and are reappropriated by others; this places them within new ideological frames that modify their meaning and permit new types of social and political alliance.

Changes such as these have led to a frequent blurring of boundaries between left and right and to crises in which the validity of the distinction is put in doubt. After the French revolution, 'radicals' were typically bourgeois liberals (itself a broad category) who sought economic and political liberalisation. At this time, 'socialists' were often as resistant to the industrial and commercial transformations under way as were the traditional landed classes. In its early stages, socialism was primarily a paean to a lost world of community, fellowship and mutual cooperation, not to universal rights and the benefits of industry (Lichtheim, 1969). As the nineteenth century progressed, however, the mantle of radicalism passed from liberalism to socialism. As individual rights to use wealth became institutionalised, individual 'liberty' gradually lost its subversive meaning and became part of the common sense of political discourse. It was substituted, however, by ideas about, and demands for, greater social equality, both in terms of formal freedoms to participate in democracy and for improved material conditions for working people and the poor. Marx and Engel's *Communist Manifesto* of 1848 exemplifies a new phase in political alignments as workers are called upon to view the dynamism of modern industrial society as the first stage in their, and humanity's, emancipation.[2] Thus, as liberals such as J. S. Mill and Alexis de Tocqueville were aware, social equality came to be articulated with democracy, modifying the latter's meaning from narrow political democracy to a more expansive, socialised democracy, so threatening the bases of private property that underscored liberal constitutionalism.

Thus between the mid-eighteenth and mid-nineteenth centuries, left and right shifted from a dominant antagonism between promoters of constitutional change and defenders of the *Ancien Régime*, to an antagonism between defenders of limited constitutional democracies and promoters of further democratisation of the state and economic conditions. The opposition between liberty and order was transformed into an opposition between liberty and equality (see Bobbio, 1996). Even in this new formulation, however, a complex and fluid multiplicity of individuals, groups, organisations, ideas and beliefs were in play, none of which fit easily into a uniform left/right classification. There remained a spectacular variety of ideological formations in European politics and society organised around religion (Catholic and Protestant churches, sects, millenarian movements), regional and nationalist movements, as well as, indeed sometimes fused with, class political organisations. Each of these was organised around its own antagonism and none fit easily into a single category. Thus the dichotomy of left and right was traversed by discourses that gave any specific ideological formation its own irreducible particularity.

Nevertheless, by the end of the nineteenth century, socialism, in its myriad forms, was becoming the dominant ideology of the left in Europe (see Sassoon, 1996). Ever more organised into political parties, trade unions and workers associations, the industrial working class constituted a formidable social force in its appeal to principles of collectivism and social justice. Liberalism, on the other hand, had become markedly more conservative as a political force, seeking to limit the gains of the socialist movement to within the parameters of parliamentary democracy. It is at this stage, however, that ideological differences enter into their first major crisis. For as socialism advanced into the twentieth century, ideological frontiers, and with them political alliances, began to shift dramatically. Conscious efforts were now made to fuse previously antagonistic ideological elements in order to move beyond the supposed socially disruptive exclusivity of dominant ideological frames. Below we shall examine a range of examples of third way thinking from the inter-war conjuncture.

THE INTER-WAR CONJUNCTURE

From the turn of the century until the 1940s, Europe underwent immense intellectual and political turmoil. We can understand this as a confluence of socio-economic, political and cultural dislocations whose culmination at the level of political ideology came in the inter-war years (1918–39). Politically speaking, the dislocations led to the catastrophic collapse in dominance of liberal values and economic and political institutions (see Joll, 1976; Hobsbawm, 1994: chs 1–7;

Brendon, 2000). As the discursive parameters and internal distinctions of left and right fell into crisis, so efforts emerged to define third ways as new spaces from which to exit the sense of crisis. Before sketching some of these efforts, let us first consider the dislocations that produced them.

From the late nineteenth century the values and assumptions of liberalism were put in question by a torrent of philosophical and cultural criticism. As Hughes (1974) points out, the turn of the century witnessed an extraordinary rise in anti-rationalist doctrines that disparaged the myth of progress that underscored the liberal era.

We may start by noting how the framework of science underpinning the Enlightenment belief in humankind's mastery of nature and the inevitability of progress was increasingly called into question by advances made in subatomics and astrophysics by such figures as Mach, Planck, Einstein, Bohr and Schrödinger. Their work 'showed that, beyond the apparently stable and harmonious world of classical physics there lay a "metaworld" or "fourth dimension" that was not describable in Newtonian terms' (Sheppard, 2000: 37). Though not anti-rationalist, such scientific shifts, with their vision of reality as flux and patterns of energy, had a direct influence on philosophy, art and literature, and began to call the rational and orderly discourses supporting political liberalism into question.

At around the same time, liberalism's assumption that human beings were naturally moral and endowed with a power of rationality that enabled them to discover the laws of nature and control it was undermined by discoveries in anthropology, sociology and geology, together with developments in the philosophy of consciousness which brought this certainty of man's rational judgement into question (see Sheppard, 2000: 46). Social change increasingly began to be explained, not in terms of an inexorable process of improvement and increase in human rationality, but as the consequence of the force of the 'will' or 'spirit'. These ideas were developed in different ways such as in Nietzsche's notion of the 'will to power', the 'vitalism' of Henri Bergson, Sorel's notion of 'myth', or Benedetto Croce's 'historicist idealism'. What unified them was a rejection of the positivism and scientism of the nineteenth century: rather than identifying human development with the discovery of natural or even social 'laws' that pre-existed human thought, the 'revolt against reason' looked to the power of the mind and consciousness as the source of creativity. Such ideas opened up a new horizon of cultural and philosophical discourse that replaced the materialism of classical liberalism and Marxism with a subjectivism and voluntarism. Human improvement was not an external consequence of the material world 'out there' but the product of a conscious effort to harness the interior world, both individual and collective.

Anti-rationalism fed into a variety of different, often quite contrasting, political doctrines. What it signalled, however, was an end to the presumption that rationality underlay historical change. In turn, this meant that liberal values such as tolerance, fair play, respect for individual liberty, and so on – values that been assumed to flow from rationality itself – no longer had a 'natural' foundation. Rather, they were the contingent outcome of specific cultural traditions and were not intrinsically superior to other values (see Bellamy, 1992). Thus the crisis of reason helped nurture the sense of exhaustion with liberal society in general, providing justification for alternative conceptions of social order premised on less tolerant, non-individualist values. Such values were central to the fascist (but also revolutionary syndicalist) currents in the inter-war years.

Into this mix was added a series of dislocations within the economic realm. The late nineteenth century marks the decline of the period of international free trade. By the 1930s laissez-faire liberal policy was increasingly discredited, if not extinguished, and protectionist policies widespread. The 'second' industrial revolution at the end of the century saw the rise of new European powers like Germany, as well as increased competition from the US. Capitalism entered what is called by some its 'organised' or 'monopoly' phase, which entails a fusion of financial institutions and industrial enterprises (see, for example, Lash and Urry, 1987). Increasingly, the individual capitalist gave way to the joint stock company; 'ownership' and 'control' were distanced as the authority of managers within the factory was functionally separated from the authority of the financers of the enterprise. Industrial expansion brought changes in class composition, too. Large corporations employed a host of middle managers, clerks, and so forth to run 'offices'; on the factory floor, unskilled workers were needed for production-line work, whilst skilled workers (engineers, technicians) were increasingly important in maintaining machinery.

World war and intensified competition made the twenties and thirties a period of economic volatility. Post-First World War unemployment, the depression of the inter-war years and the stock market crash of 1929 had profound consequences for European economies. The rationality and 'progressive' character of capitalism was severely tested and led proponents of all sides (liberalist, socialist, fascist) to seek an economic system beyond the evident irrationality of laissez-faire. The answers came in different forms of greater state intervention, imperial expansion, autarky, communism and so forth.

Under these conditions, liberal political institutions (parliamentary democracy, constitutions, limited state intervention) were increasingly identified as anachronistic and inadequate. This occurred on a number of fronts. First, the rise of mass politics in the form of workers' parties, trade unions and extended franchise dislodged the traditionally restricted access to power of political elites. More and more, political leaders had to prove themselves in the face of powerful, organised interests. The 'social question' came to the fore as public debate centred on issues of poverty and employment rights (later unemployment). With the rise of mass politics, the role of the state was eventually refigured as a potential agency of intervention and protection rather than mere regulation and minimal interference as in the liberal period. Second, the high politics of the former imperial great powers (Britain and France) was challenged by the more aggressive competitive spirit of emergent powers such as Germany and Italy.

These changes fed into a growing disenchantment with liberal parliamentary democracy. On both the left and right, liberal democracy came to be regarded as insufficient to the economic and political requirements of the age. In the years before the First World War, anti-liberal politics was relatively marginal but, in the wake of destruction wrought by the war, it crystallised into powerful revolutionary organisations. For the left, the Russian revolution of 1917 had announced a decisive break with the reformist parliamentary politics of socialist parties (see Hobsbawm, 1994: ch. 2). Communist parties were founded all over Europe and most took the Bolshevik model of an organised, 'intransigent' (that is, no involvement with parliamentary politics) vanguard as their model. On the right, nationalists rallied around the sense of defeat reinforced by the meagre gains of the Treaty of Versailles.

The effect of all of these events was to disrupt the pattern of left/right ideological positions and to produce experiments from each to transcend the limits of its own discourse. Thus we find third ways emerging from liberal, socialist and conservative camps as each seeks to define a new ideological space beyond traditional antagonisms that, at the same time, absorbs elements of its erstwhile 'opponents'. Let us review these briefly.

Liberalism

We have noted how liberal ideas and institutions came under pressure towards the end of the nineteenth century. However, it would be wrong to suggest that liberal thinkers did not seek to adapt to the changing social and political environment. English 'new liberalism' and French 'solidarism', both from the decades prior to the turn of the century, represent important precursors to the third ways of the inter-war period in so far as they anticipated many of the elements of third way discourse *avant la lettre*.

New liberals recognised the challenge of socialist ideas and movements and the threat these posed to liberalism. Thus they consciously aimed to effect a synthesis of liberal principles and socialist values in a revived version of liberalism that promoted elements of social reform and a common ethical framework (see Freeden, 1978; Clarke, 1978; Bellamy, 1992: ch. 1). New liberals rejected laissez-faire and the idea that liberalism justified self-interested individualism. In the view of thinkers such as Hobhouse, Hobson and Wallas (amongst others), and following J. S. Mill, the liberal promotion of 'individuality' could not be realised without the state taking action 'to secure the conditions of self-maintenance for the normal healthy citizen' (Hobhouse, 1994: 174; see also Freeden, 1978: 32–9). Individuality and social needs were thus conceived as mutually self-sustaining. New liberals aimed to diminish the threat of the socialists' demands for equality by appropriating its appeal to a common ethical framework in which the needs of the whole and not just the individual were attended to. This ethical appeal was separated from any practical economic considerations such as the abolition of private property (Freeden, 1978: 25–32). An ethical stance that rejected the socially disruptive and materialistic doctrines both of Marxism and individualism enabled new liberals to defend holistic notions of 'community' and the 'just society' in which the state (as well as voluntary agencies) was charged with a 'duty' to enact measures of social reform to reduce the pernicious effects of poverty, inequality and ignorance (Ibid.: 52–75).

The new liberals' ideas were heavily influenced both by Hegelianism (on which see Morefield, 2002) and the then current theories of evolution. By adapting Darwin's work in a way that stressed social cooperation, the evolution of the mind and ethics, the new liberals developed a theory of society in which collectivism represented a higher stage of human evolution (see Freeden, 1978: 77–93). Rather than a crude 'survival of the fittest' doctrine, evolution permitted new liberals to justify state welfare and social reform as being bound up with a progressive logic of social development. It also grounded their normative theory in the 'objective' terms of a scientific theory. The new liberals also drew from biology the idea of society as an 'organism', that is, an entity of mutually interdependent parts (Ibid.: 94–116). In this view, individual self-realisation could not be conceived without some sense of the 'health' of the entire organism (that is, society). Thus the efforts of the social reformer could be justified on the grounds that they both enhanced the freedom of individuals *and* contributed to progressive societal evolution (Ibid.: 90–1).

French solidarism, too, drew on evolutionary thought and employed notions of society as an organism (see Bourgeois, 1998). Like the new liberalism, solidarism sought to reaffirm liberal values by stressing its ethical character and reaffirming the debt the individual owed to society. Solidarism came to prominence during the Third Republic and was promoted by such figures as Léon Walras, Charles Gide, Léon Duguit and the Radical party under the leadership of Léon Bourgeois (see Donzelot, 1984: 73–120; Hayward, 1960; Bellamy, 1992: 59–74). The Radicals' doctrine 'was intended to harmonize individualism, corporatism and morality within an essentially liberal framework' (Bellamy, 1992: 63). Rejecting both Marxism and laissez-faire liberalism for their reliance on (individual or class) self-interest, solidarism promoted a moral code of solidarity in which individual and collective interests were to be harmoniously balanced, though without radically transforming property relations. Modern society was conceived as an interdependent whole, a complex organism whose underlying moral foundation was the pursuit of individuality and equal dignity (or 'personalism'). These ideas supported proposals to provide for 'collective welfare', social insurance, free state education, limited forms of wealth distribution and legislation against trusts and monopolies. The solidarists, however, preferred voluntary schemes, mutual societies and cooperatives, rather than the state, as the agency of these proposals.

The sociologist Emile Durkheim is one of the most well-known French liberals influenced by the solidarists' ideas. Like them, he sought to find a way to connect the individual to society without falling into an anachronistic appeal to tradition (see Bellamy, 1992: 75). Durkheim's sociology sought to show precisely how liberal values could be rendered compatible with the modern world. For him, moral rules follow forms of social organisation: thus changes in social organisation elicit new forms of morality. Modern social organisation, with its complex 'division of labour', entailed a highly diverse pattern of interdependence between occupational specialisations. Rather than descending into the anarchy of self-interested egoism or particularism, these parts were tied together by what he called an 'organic solidarity' based around the 'cult of the individual' and an ethos of meritocracy (Ibid.: 78–80). In the modern world, social cohesion was achieved spontaneously through a complex interdependence of social roles, not by the authoritarian imposition of a common value system as such. Social conflicts were therefore 'pathological' interruptions of an essentially cohesive order (Hayward, 1960: 18–33). Like the new liberals, Durkheim believed that a progressive evolution of human sentiments would lead to a functionally integrated and cohesive social order upon which liberal values and demands for social justice could be harmonised (Bellamy, 1992: 84).

Solidarism and the new liberalism both sought to reconcile liberalism with socialist and collectivist principles, overcoming the perceived antithesis between the needs of the 'individual' and 'society', but they differ from later third way thought in a number of crucial respects. First, whilst their proponents regarded themselves as generating a new synthesis of ideas, they also saw their work as building on or rejuvenating liberal principles. This strong sense of continuity with the liberal tradition, especially amongst the new liberals, underscored a notion that liberal ideas were evolving with society, not marking a rupture with it. This point relates to the second: the ethical evolutionary stance remained in tune with the idea of historical progress, bound up as it was with the continued reliance upon rational, scientific knowledge.[3] Third, new liberalism in particular remained an ideology of the intellectual elite, not a 'mass' political ideology. Although it had a crucial bearing on later notions of the 'welfare state', it was not yet a popular ideology that addressed social antagonisms directly in order to hegemonise them. Both solidarism and new liberalism offered a moralisation of capitalism which underscored social, but not political, reform (see Freeden, 1978: 257). After the First World War, this sense of liberal continuity, rational evolutionism and intellectual focus were quite out of step with the widespread sense of historical rupture, social dislocation and the demand for popular mobilisation that characterised the crises of the inter-war years (see Freeden, 1986).

Socialism

Socialist ideas, too, underwent a rapid and complex evolution from the turn of the century onwards, and in the 1920s and 1930s produced some of the first explicit appeals for a third way. This development was the result of a number of dislocations that shattered many of the assumptions of nineteenth-century socialist thinking.

First, the decline of positivism hastened a reaction against Marxist 'scientific' socialism, which still informed most continental socialist parties. The 'revisionist debate' in the late 1890s reflected a sense that the catastrophist vision of Marx was not on the cards (see Laclau and Mouffe, 2001: ch. 1; Hughes, 1974: ch. 3). Instead, as Eduard Bernstein argued, capitalism was proving amenable to political agitation and gradual reform (Sassoon, 1996: 17–26). Second, the First World War destroyed any lingering sense that workers would automatically unite in international solidarity against capitalist imperialism. Instead, working people had largely rallied to the national effort. This generated arguments that internationalism would have to be complemented by efforts at the national level, in turn stimulating tensions within a number of European socialist parties regarding governmental participation (Ibid.: 18–19, 27). Third, the Russian revolution of 1917 both dramatically demonstrated the power of an organised revolutionary movement and made more complex the ideological picture of socialism, eventually leading to the splitting from socialist parties of revolutionary parties based on the Bolshevik model (Ibid.: 31–41). Later, 'actually existing' socialism offered a model of state-led control of the economy, proving for some the power of bureaucratic machinery to rationally control society, for others providing a model against which to pitch more participatory models of socialism (see Schecter, 1994).

Fourth, the traumatic experience of war and the economic and social upheavals that followed in its wake generated a widespread disaffection amongst many workers' movements and socialist thinkers toward liberal democracy. This was exacerbated by the impact of the Depression which, Telò notes, was a decisive turning point in the history of capitalism and of the modern state (Telò, 1988: 11). Together with the poor experience of some parties in power, this led many socialists to look to new kinds of institutions to bring greater equality. Fifth, the transformations in capitalism, noted earlier, gradually produced a trend towards economic 'rationalisation'. This, together with the impact of the war mobilisation, generated a more interventionist, coordinated and planned form of economy, which led many on the left to believe that capitalism was developing forms of control that would enable socialism to control the 'commanding heights' of the economy (see Sassoon, 1996: 50–1). In turn, this facilitated the development of arguments that transition from capitalism to socialism did not necessitate the violent and radical break that was advocated by communists.

Finally, the growing fear of reaction and authoritarianism within European countries exacerbated already present tensions concerning the desirability of left-wing governments within a capitalist system. A number of socialist thinkers came to argue for strategies with a cross-class appeal in order for the left to enter government, on its own or in coalition, simply to prevent their countries from following the Italian or German models.

In these circumstances, socialist thought witnessed a distinctive turn towards 'ethical' as opposed to 'scientific' approaches to socialism. These tended to reject class struggle in the narrow sense of defending class interests and looked to socialism as the principle of a new moral order (see Pels, 2002). Whilst ethical socialism had long been a current of thought within British socialism following the traditions of Christian socialism, these tended to be committed to gradual reforms of the system. On the continent, however, more radical forms of ethical socialism were developing, such as Sorel's revolutionary syndicalism and the 'revolutionary revisionism' (as opposed to reformist revisionism) of Marxism by the Belgian, Hendrik de Man (see Pels, 1987). De Man's work, *The Psychology of Socialism*, was widely influential in its criticism of Marxism's 'determinism, causal mechanism, historicism, rationalism and economic hedonism' (de Man, 1929: 7–8) and its defence of ideas and values that transcended narrow class interests.

A variety of different positions were articulated in the inter-war period, some of which developed a third way socialism that steered between private property and state control as their organising principle. These 'planist' positions were all predicated around the claim that state intervention to produce a managed economy would structurally reform the economic process itself. This argument, as de Man noted, served as a rallying point for a number of diverse tendencies, all having 'in view a gradual transformation of the capitalist regime by means of a series of regulatory interventions which, without abolishing private enterprise, will "direct" it towards the execution of a general "plan" fixed by an authority recognised by the community' (de Man, 1932: 5). In Belgium, de Man authored the *Plan du travail*, which was adopted by the *Parti ouvrier belge* in 1933 (see Pels, 1987; Sassoon, 1996: 66–9).

Similar arguments were made in France by the syndicalist, Barthélemy Montagnon (1929), Bertrand de Jouvenel (1928), Lucien Laurat (1931) and Gaston Bergery's *Front commun* (on which, see Burrin, 1986: 115), as well as elements gathered around George Roditi's review, *L'Homme nouveau* (see, for example, Roditi, 1934). In Sweden, the Hansson government began the elaboration of a 'Swedish model' of socialism, seeking to gradually replace capitalism's hold on a number of social functions, such as the labour market and the mastery of the economic cycle, prior to a second stage of limiting monopoly power and democratising the economy. This, remarks Telò, constituted a ' "model of an intermediary path" between capitalism and socialism of the Soviet type, according to the definition current in the 1930s amongst the European and American political and academic milieu' (Telò, 1988: 29).[4]

The institution of an intermediary path, however, required that socialists enter government. This, it was argued, necessitated programmes broad enough in scope to appeal beyond the working class, uniting working-class actors with other social groups around an 'anti-capitalism' (see, for example, Marion, 1933: 14–16; Laurat, 1931: 41; Déat, 1928a, 1928b) and thus preventing such groups from being attracted by the appeal of the authoritarian right. Consequently, socialist third way theories of the inter-war period tended to call for action within the national framework as a prelude to more internationalist developments. However, despite emphasising intervention at the level of the nation, these third ways tended to oppose state centralism, counter-balancing the authority of the state with that emanating from intermediary bodies representing regions and professions. De Man, for example, called for the elaboration of an 'economic state' alongside the parliamentary political one (Telò, 1988: 30–1).

Of the numerous examples of third way socialism of this period, we can cite that of Marcel Déat, who developed a revised version of socialism from the mid-1920s. Fusing Durkheimian sociology with Marxism, Déat viewed the social domain as an ensemble of institutions embodying both spiritual and material elements (see especially Déat, 1922a and b, 1929c), of which economic institutions played only one, albeit a temporarily leading, role (1929a). He called on socialists to gather together all republican and democratic forces around a 'plan of action' (nationalisation, financial measures, the reorganisation of education, and so on), showing to the middle classes the threat of finance capitalism and that no true democracy could exist as long as such forces were not disciplined (1927a, 1928a, 1928b).

This break with economism led to a reconceptualisation of the state. This was now perceived not simply as an instrument of class domination but as the site of a political contestation with a right-wing authoritarianism promoting economic nationalism on behalf of finance capital (1929d). In turn, this suggested the possibility of a transformation to socialism via the state within a capitalist regime, gradually removing capital from the reins of power. The state could use its resources to 'give direction to the economy instead of submitting to it' (1929f, 1929b). A first step was the occupation of governmental power by socialist parties across Europe, enabling them to impose a socialist rationality upon the production process, and to break the links capitalism had forged with the state (1929e). The occupation of governmental power would be brought about by a gathering of working-class and republican forces enabled 'by making ourselves the defenders of the state and the champions of the collective interest against particular big interests', bringing together 'socialism and traditional democratic ideas' (1927a: 9). This 'socialisation of power' would be followed by the socialisation of profit, through the regularisation of the market, then that of property, at which point the state would be replaced by the democratic anti-capitalist institutions of the cooperatives and trade unions, whose development the state was to encourage in the first two stages (Déat, 1930: 211–12, 224–6).

Conservatism

The inter-war period is best known for the third ways that came to power in the form of German and Italian fascism. Sparked by, amongst other things, a sense of generalised national decline, which was exacerbated by the First World War, and the perceived loss of community brought by contemporary capitalism (to which the comradeship of war seemed to offer a solution), fascists typically posed their aggressive nationalism as a third way between decadent liberal capitalism and divisive Marxist socialism. Here, it was the national community that purportedly transcended the antagonism of left and right. However, in addition to the fascisms of Germany and Italy, there were a range of other fascist and 'proto-fascist' third ways stemming from the conservative right.

In Germany, we might note the 'reactionary modernism' of the so-called 'conservative revolutionaries' that developed largely in reaction to a sense of national decline engendered by the loss of the 1914–18 war, post-war economic problems (culminating in the hyperinflation of 1923), and to the Weimar Republic, which emerged from the chaos of the failed revolution of 1919. Revolutionary conservatism, like Nazi ideology, sought 'a reconciliation between the anti-modernist, romantic and irrationalist ideas present in German nationalism and the most obvious manifestation of means-ends rationality, that is, modern technology' (Herf, 1984: 1). This group of thinkers – including Moeller van den Brück, Ernst Jünger, Oswald Spengler, Werner Sombart, the philosopher Martin Heidegger, the jurist and political theorist, Edgar J. Jung, and the jurist Carl Schmitt – proposed the spiritual re-awakening of a Germanic race and nation made moribund by the forces of modernity, whilst nevertheless embracing the technological forces that modernity had unleashed.

The predominant influence on conservative revolutionary thought was Moeller through his 'spiritual leadership' of the *Juni-Klub*, a nationalist grouping that gathered together a host of young conservatives, formed in the aftermath of Versailles. Moeller lamented the absence of great spiritual and artistic interpreters of modernity, and argued that modern man, particularly German youth, was adrift without spiritual anchor. He sought a new faith, a Germanic world-view that 'would supplant religion and inspire a new state that would retain in a modern industrial society the political and cultural virtues of an idealised past' (Stern, 1961: 194). Arguing that nations were in a Darwinian struggle for survival, and predicting a great imperialist future for Germany, Moeller proposed the cultural rejuvenation of Germany. On the basis of a distinction between culture and civilisation, democracy and the West, Moeller rejected both liberalism, for its belief in man as a good and rational being – for Moeller, men were unequal, inherently limited and irrational – and Christianity in favour of a vision of a closely knit community governed by an elite (Stern, 1961: 194–5).

Moeller's most influential work on inter-war conservative revolutionaries is his *Das Dritte Reich* of 1922 – a book that was originally intended to be called *The Third Party* or *The Third Point of View* – the emphasis in the title, Stern notes, being on the 'Third' rather than the 'Reich', as it fitted in with this search for synthesis (Ibid.: 253–4). He called for a revolution in German culture rather than the material conditions of German life, and strongly criticised Marxism because of its inability – as the product of a nationless Jew – to understand man's spiritual essence in the fatherland. Moeller advocated an organic and corporatist German socialism that would complete the November revolution and alter the republic to make it consistent with ancient German traditions and the eternal laws of human nature (Ibid.: 260–1). The Third Reich, then, was to be a fusion of the 'spirit' of the German 'people', as embodied in its traditions and customs, with the egalitarianism of socialism, transcending both conservatism and socialism in a higher synthesis.

Similar third ways were expressed elsewhere in Europe. This was notable in France through the numerous political activities of the, first monarchist, then fascist, and finally 'republican syndicalist', Georges Valois, and the plethora of groupings labelled the *Jeune Droite* (JD). What marked out Valois in his early monarchist, and then fascist, periods as a third way thinker was his fusion of xenophobic nationalism and anti-Semitism with genuine support for syndicalism. Rejecting both socialism and liberalism, Valois proposed instead a corporative system that was to evolve in the framework of a strong state, above classes and parties, incarnated and led by a king (a figure he later replaced with the fascist notion of a national chief). This was to be brought about by a national revolution 'through which the Soldiers, under the command of a national chief, supported by the intellectual elite of the country, bourgeois and worker, will overthrow the liberal state, will suppress its political, economic and social institutions, and will construct the national State with its own institutions' (Valois, 1924: 162).

The JD comprised a number of intellectuals who, like Valois, had mobilised in the monarchist *Action Française* (AF) but had also become impatient with its immobilism. Members of this group advocated an elitist voluntarism to effect historical change, and rejected liberal democratic politics in favour of a corporate state that would be in touch with 'concrete man'. They also called for a 'spiritual' revolution which belonged 'neither to right nor left', with both capitalism and communism presented as rooted in a materialism that had brought about the degeneration of the nation (see Bastow, 2001; Loubet del Bayle, 1961).

Finally, we should note the 'mainstream' fascist third ways that developed in the inter-war period. These were sparked by the same dislocations that fed into revolutionary conservatism. Like them, fascism rejected both left and right, capitalism and communism, advocating the spiritual rejuvenation of the nation instituted through an organic, corporatist hierarchy, topped by an absolute leader, and a 'total' state that was to concern itself with all aspects of civil society.

Fascists also advocated an aggressive, militaristic foreign policy that paralleled the domestic militarisation of politics. Within such parameters, however, inter-war fascism took an array of different forms. Some versions, for instance, adopted pacifist, anti-war stances (for example, the British Union of Fascists), some based national identity in biology (Nazism), others adopted more 'cultural' forms of nationalism (for example, Italian fascism, Valois' *Faisceau*), whilst still others adopted a confusing mix of the two (for example, the BUF). They did not all share anti-Semitism and the extent of their advocacy of corporatism varied a great deal. Thus commentators seeking to articulate the common features of fascism – what gets labelled 'generic fascism' – have struggled to identify what these features might be.[5] Despite this, it is generally accepted that fascism offered a distinctively third way ideology.

THE REPERTOIRE OF THE THIRD WAY

As a discourse, the third way operates on the basis of a number of distinctive ideas and claims that, however integrated into a specific ideology, persistently reappear. These features organise its content into a coherent narrative by framing facts into a story about the objective world, its current condition and the role of subjects in relation to it. However, whilst the forms of these ideologies concord with this pattern, their content varies starkly since they emerge from different positions within the left/right spectrum. These differences in origin mean that third ways conceive differently the ideological antagonism they seek to transcend, and they employ differing unifying principles according to their specific reading of the crisis from which they emerge.

The elements of the third way discursive repertoire typically include: the claim of 'crisis' in traditional antagonisms; an anti-materialism expressed in the appeal to ethics as the basis of social order; the promotion of a reconciled 'community'; and the designation of a key role for a specific agency (a vanguard or elite) to lead disaffected publics towards a new order. We shall examine these elements in turn.

Crisis

A crisis denotes a moment of rupture in which prevailing conditions are put in question and the possibility for a new order comes into view. Because they pit themselves against a dominant antagonism, third ways can only claim to transcend or move between that division if some space is opened up. The narrative of crisis is therefore designed to articulate the failure of an opposition and present the possibility for its supersession. Thus crisis involves two manoeuvres: the diagnosis of failure and the recommendation of intervention to resolve it (see Hay, 1994).

In diagnosing failure, third way discourses bring together a number of dislocations and present them as moments in a generalised decline. There is, then, no 'necessary' objectivity to the decline; that is an outcome of the articulation of a series of dislocations through the idea of crisis. Particular disappointments, short-term difficulties and accumulated anxieties are metaphorically fused into a single argument pronouncing the 'total' failure of existing institutions and options (see Laclau and Mouffe, 2001: 8–14). These dislocations may include the experience of unemployment, the horrors and privations of war, forms of rapid and unregulated social change, environmental damage, the influx of immigrants, and so on. Taken by themselves, these issues may constitute distinctive policy issues; but taken together, they are rearticulated as symbols of a world increasingly out of control. Often, one problem alone is presented as symptomatic of a wider crisis. The dominant forces of politics are typically denounced as utterly unable to adequately resolve this crisis, being too complicit with the order that produced the problems in the first place. Having produced the crisis, the prevailing options are unable to resolve it.

To pose as a third option requires the other two to be conceived as limited or exhausted in some way. Third ways typically announce the historic end of a period of dominance by two opposed alternatives, which are often conceived in rather closed, stereotypical terms. The crisis supposedly signals the exhaustion of these opposed options. The parties who embodied them no longer represent the experience of 'ordinary' people. Instead, they serve only specific, particular interests, not the interests of the people as a whole. It is in the space of crisis, therefore, that a third way becomes a plausible alternative.

Ethics and anti-materialism

Third ways commonly identify their goals in terms of a renewed ethics. The claim that there is a crisis of the old antagonism opens up a series of problems whose resolution can only be answered in terms of new ethical principles. This contrasts with the purported 'materialism' of earlier doctrines that appeal, for example, to class or individual 'interests' as the source of social order and improvement. These views are typically found in Marxism and liberalism, ideologies whose force derived from their claims about the progressive direction of history. Though they differed in terms of their ideal societies, both Marxism and liberalism saw human emancipation as the outcome of the interaction of forces they conceived as objectively material: the free market of individual needs, or the clash of class interests.

Third ways reject this kind of materialism because it reduces humans to passive subjects of forces that seem to transcend them. Ethical principles, on the other hand, imply a view of subjects as active and purposive, consciously disciplining themselves to moral values that are authentically generated. It is this appeal to moral authenticity, a sense of genuine communal values in which the individual is aligned with the collective, that is lacking in older ideologies. By appealing to base instincts of class or individualism, they have lost touch with the moral bases of social life and are therefore responsible for 'decadent' and divisive behaviour.

Community

This emphasis on ethics is typically accompanied by an appeal to 'community' as an absent order that needs to be made present. Third ways often identify community – a practically cohesive moral order – as something that has been disrupted by the invidious presence of the materialism of earlier doctrines. Of course, all ideologies make an appeal to community of some kind as a future reconciliation of individual and society (see Little, 2002a; Finlayson, 2002a). Third ways follow this tradition but make a distinctive appeal to community as dependent primarily on an ethical transformation in subjects rather than a structural change to socio-economic institutions. This does not mean that institutional reform is ignored. Indeed, precisely because those elements that make up the community are insufficiently represented by the liberal democratic form (a fact usually presented as one of the reasons for the disruption of the community), third ways favour some degree of institutional reform, even if third way theorists do vary in terms of the reforms advocated. However, for third ways the community is first and foremost an ethical ideal.

The specific content of the community may be defined in various ways but, as with all notions of community, it is premised on a sense of a common identity. The communal identity may be a racial or ethnic group, it may be a community of socially-minded individuals or ecologically-aware citizens. Whatever the content, the community is typically represented as what Laclau calls an 'absent presence' (see Laclau, 1996a) – that is, its presence in the discourse is as something that has 'declined' or has been undermined or blocked by certain contingent factors (the arrival of 'foreigners', the misdeeds of a political elite, and so on). Laclau argues that it is precisely this absence or blockage that heightens the sense of the community as a common identity. Discourses of community function by their symbolisation of a presence yet to come. That way, the differentiated components of this community are abstractly related as their individual gripes and issues are symbolically blurred into a generalised claim to sameness.

Agency

Finally, third ways tend to associate the emergence of their new order with the agency of a particular group, individual or elite. Whilst they need not be elitist in the sense of asserting the absolute superiority of particular individuals over others, nevertheless third way discourse gives a certain priority to a creative individual or individuals. This elite is deemed to represent or particularly understand the moment of crisis opened up by the failure of the old antagonism. Because third ways predicate their argument on a notion of ethical, as opposed to material, transformation, proper intervention in the crisis will occur not as a spontaneous movement of impersonal forces (for example, Marxism's 'dialectical laws', or the 'hidden hand' of the free market) but through a full comprehension of the situation and the audacity to challenge the old order. The identification of a leading elite may occur in a variety of ways – charismatic leadership, a revolutionary vanguard, or a socially-minded intelligentsia – but however this leadership is defined, the crucial quality lies in its capacity to symbolise the purposes of society itself, to express a popular will that transcends class and individual interests. The needs of 'the people' are then presented as a unified whole, 'incarnated' in the body of an individual or group that rises above its particular demands and represents the needs of society as such.

This elitism is often complemented by optimism about the historical force of ideas, the mission of 'intellectual' politicians and the style of a new-generational or 'young' politics. Because third way ideologies tend to come to prominence during periods of crisis in which traditional ideas of left and right no longer seem to apply, those preaching a third way doctrine often assume the status of 'missionary'. This ties in with a common emphasis on a 'new generation', 'new order' and youth that is a recurrent feature of third way ideologies. It is precisely because they have no roots in the order that has been dislocated that third way activists can stress their novelty and lay claim to offer a way out from the problems caused by decaying doctrines.

Conclusion

We have argued that third ways represent discursive strategies to overcome crises of political ideology brought by profound social dislocations. These are crises that particular third way discourses themselves articulate through their diagnosis of a particular conjuncture. The discursive elements of the third way repertoire – the focus on ethics, community, agency, and so on – all follow from the very articulation of the crisis itself. This is so in two senses. First, the crisis is the precondition for the necessity of the other ideological elements. It is because there is a crisis that a new ethics is needed. This ethics will provide the practically cohesive moral order that the crisis has shown to be absent, and it will be provided by the very protagonists diagnosing that crisis. Second, the precise way in which the crisis is articulated foregrounds the substantive content of the remaining discursive elements. For example, although the third ways of the inter-war period exemplify many of the characteristic features that we have labelled the discursive 'repertoire' of the third way, we should recognise that different ideological frameworks emphasise significantly different issues and ideas. The similarities between various third ways are at an abstract level that does not make them sufficiently similar to be classified as part of the same 'tradition'. Different ideological frameworks construct crises in their own specific ways and emphasise different forms of resolution: the right, for example, often see the crisis as fundamentally one of national identity and prestige, and the third ways of the right therefore affirm the centrality of the national community as being beyond antagonism. Whilst liberal and socialist third ways also look to community, the idea of community is construed differently.

This brings us to the ambiguity of third ways that we noted earlier. By seeking to go beyond perceived antagonisms, third ways define themselves as both within *and* outside an ideological tradition: we have already highlighted third ways of centre, left and right. Third ways, then, claim to transcend the ideological spectrum, and yet they never manage to do so entirely. Rather, they modify the elements of their original ideological tradition by incorporating those of an other(s).

The effect of this ambiguity is two-fold. First, it is not always clear how to categorise third ways as ideologies since their aim is often to side-step such categorisation. The presence of elements of other ideological traditions in their own framework disrupts our assumption that ideologies are broadly clear-cut and distinguishable formations. Thus, for example, Déat's articulation of socialism with the notion of a national community overlapped with a number of, then contemporary, fascist ideas. The unity of third ways stems primarily from their negative opposition – their antagonism – to earlier ideological divisions that they no longer perceive as appropriate: exactly what they are 'for' is often less important for their proponents than what they reject.

Second, whilst third ways typically promote radical change, the notion of moving beyond antagonism can make them politically ambiguous, as well as difficult to categorise. Third ways invoke notions of social unity premised on ethical rather than primarily material considerations. The danger of this view is that invocations of community can be more or less authoritarian in effect, even when advocated by liberals. This, indeed, is one of the common complaints about New Labour's Third Way. In that instance, the third way appears to promote a politics beyond *any* political antagonism, thus presenting a vision of a reconciled society where no point of view or demand is unable to be assimilated in some way. It is this tendency that perhaps explains Bobbio's claim that the third way – his 'inclusive middle' – always lapses into a form of centrism (Bobbio, 1996: 9). We argue, however, that such a tendency is not an essential part of all third ways but merely one possibility activated within the terms of its repertoire. As we see later, and will specifically argue in the Conclusion, moving beyond a dominant antagonism need not mean eliminating antagonism altogether.

NOTES

1 This reading is similar to Bobbio's, which he labels the 'inclusive middle' (Bobbio, 1996: 7–9). We differ from Bobbio, however, in his reading of the third way as necessarily always propagating a 'centrist' politics. We return to this point later in the book.

2 While Marx was keen to underscore the revolutionary potential of the emergent working class in Europe, he was also, however, acutely aware that classes were only loosely formed as political subjects. In *The*

Eighteenth Brumaire of Louis Bonaparte of 1852, Marx described the shifting allegiances of the bourgeoisie as it oscillated rapidly between liberal republicanism and authoritarian, anti-socialist reaction, identifying with the urban working class at one point and supporting their violent suppression at another. See Cowling and Martin (2002) for Marx's text and discussion of his analysis of class.

3 This is perhaps most clearly seen in Wallas's call for politics to become a science rather than an art, through developing its abilities in quantitative analysis (Wallas, 1948, ch. 5).

4 Telò (1988: 49, n.52) notes that this third way character is reinforced by the fact that the author of the Plan Meidner in the 1970s, the Swedish Social Democratic government's attempt to democratise the economy, explicitly defined the project as a third way. See R. Meidner, 'Our concept of the third way. The socio-political tenets of the Swedish Labour Movement', *Economic and Industrial Democracy*, 1/3, 1980.

5 There are debates regarding whether one can distinguish these forms of fascism from the variants of revolutionary conservatism highlighted above but such arguments are incidental to the task in hand. The list is voluminous but such analysts of fascism as Griffin (1991, 1995, 1998), Soucy (1986, 1995) and Camus (1998) would see the two as essentially the same, whilst analysts of revolutionary conservatism often offer a more nuanced reading of the relationship (see Stern, 1961: 295–7; Dorémus, 1992; Rohkrämer, 1999; Levrat, 1992), though Herf (1984) articulates a close relationship between the two.

CHAPTER 2
NEW LABOUR'S THIRD WAY: 'MODERNISING' SOCIAL DEMOCRACY

To its more venomous critics, New Labour's Third Way symbolises much of the party's character since Tony Blair took over the leadership in 1994 and swept the party to office in 1997: it is prone to announce its novelty and radically transformative intentions and yet, looked at more closely, it lacks theoretical consistency or depth, and its glossy surface hides a rather shallow absence of principle. It is certainly paradoxical that the party most associated with the Third Way in contemporary Europe, despite winning two successive landslide elections, has been unable to define in any precise or elaborate way what its adopted doctrine amounts to. Indeed, the Third Way formed no part of the party's 2001 General Election campaign, though afterwards Blair was happy to announce that the 'Third Way, Phase Two' had begun (see Blair, 2001). This situation contrasts starkly with the feverish atmosphere of 1997–8 when the newly elected government trawled academic journals, seminars and websites seeking out intellectual justification and scholarly legitimation. Then, defining the Third Way, its context, principles and policy implications was a matter of public discussion. Now, more and more, the Third Way is routinely mocked and derided, particularly from the party's left.

To dismiss the idea of the Third Way, as many do, simply as a marketing ploy, a now-redundant effort at rebranding or post-election self-justification, misses the point about a wider effort on the British (and European) left to redefine the terms of social democratic discourse. As Anthony Giddens – New Labour's most favourable academic supporter and chief exponent of the Third Way – indicates, the Third

Way is a 'worldwide phenomenon': 'Labour is not arbitrarily discarding leftist traditions, but reacting to structural changes that every country faces' (Giddens, 2002: 5–6). Whether the Third Way survives as the expression of this effort is a contingent matter; more important is the fact that some kind of third way politics remains on the agenda, even if its precise formulation and popularity varies or wanes.

In this chapter we outline the basic elements of New Labour's Third Way as a discursive strategy. We shall see that this discourse articulates in a distinctive way many of the features of other third way projects concerning crisis, ethics, the renewal of community, and so forth. Understood as a discourse, the various ambiguities and contradictions of New Labour's project seem less disconcerting than many of its critics have implied. Often these critics read the Third Way as a political philosophy rather than a political project; they stress its intellectual coherence and continuity with the past rather than its ability to hegemonise the field of social dislocations in the current conjuncture. Discourse theory, however, permits us to bring this aspect into view. Central to New Labour's hegemonic project, we argue, is a discourse of 'modernisation' that promotes a form of ethical subjectivity designed to mediate the effects of a series of dislocations. That strategy involves discarding earlier antagonisms and recasting social democratic principles in new, sometimes strikingly unfamiliar ways. However, unlike other third ways (which we examine later in the book), New Labour and its sympathisers have proved reluctant to define their project in terms of a new antagonism as such, preferring instead to associate their programme with processes of globalisation they regard as inexorable.

ELEMENTS OF NEW LABOUR'S THIRD WAY

It is not difficult to identify our key tropes in the various publications and speeches in which Tony Blair and his supporters elaborate the ideas that underscore the Third Way. As we have noted, these include: the claim that left and right no longer constitute viable, antagonistic political positions; the identification of a crisis brought by new social and political challenges; the need to tackle these challenges with a return to ethical principles; the emphasis on the renewal of community as a fundamental plank in overcoming socially restrictive or divisive dualisms; and the identification of an agency that incarnates the order to come. Let us consider these elements as they appear in New Labour discourse on the Third Way.

The primary elements of New Labour's Third Way discourse can be discerned in a number of key documents: Blair's Fabian pamphlet *The Third Way* (1998), as well as other of his speeches (Blair, 1996a), the short book of the same title by Anthony Giddens (1998; see also Giddens' other publications following debates on this text: 2000, 2001, 2002), and various other documents published by the party and its supporters around the same time. Whilst these documents were written to different audiences and consequently elaborate at different lengths on different issues, together they enable us to specify the basic elements of the discourse around which New Labour sought to define and legitimise their programme of government.[1]

The Third Way between Old Left and New Right

New Labour's Third Way stands, as Tony Blair declares, 'for a modernised social democracy', a 'new politics' for the British centre-left (1998: 1). As such, it is placed within a distinctive national setting and a recognised ideological tradition. However, from the outset, Blair makes clear his intention to reconcile 'themes which in the past have wrongly been regarded as antagonistic – patriotism *and* internationalism; rights *and* responsibilities; the promotion of enterprise *and* the attack on poverty and discrimination' (Ibid). Elsewhere he talks explicitly of 'going beyond the traditional boundaries of left and right, breaking new ground by escaping from sterile debates that have polarized our politics for too long' (Blair, 1996c: 298).

Immediately, then, we see the discursive effects of the Third Way: the production of equivalences ('*and*' instead of 'or') between elements once divided by the frontier of political ideology (see Fairclough, 2000: 9–12). Values typically considered to belong to the right are now appropriated by the left. As Mandelson and Liddle put it in their 'unofficial manifesto' prior to Labour's 1997 election victory (and, incidentally, prior to the announcement of the idea of the Third Way):

> New Labour does not accept the classic view of the left-right divide, in which both sides are seen to be locked in permanent conflict . . . New Labour believes that it is possible to combine a free market economy with social justice; liberty of the individual with wider opportunities for all; One Nation security with efficiency and competitiveness; rights with responsibilities; personal self-fulfilment with strengthening the family; effective

government and decisive political leadership with a new constitutional settlement and a new relationship of trust between politicians and the people; a love of Britain with a recognition that Britain's future has to lie in Europe (Mandelson and Liddle, 1996: 17).

For Blair, appropriating elements of the right is accomplished by a re-engagement with the liberal tradition with which British social democracy has a historic affinity (see, for example, Clarke, 1978) but from which it has recently been 'divorced' (see also Blair, 1995b, 1996c: 300; and Marquand, 1988, 1999a). Thus he claims that the Third Way 'also marks a third way *within* the left' (Blair, 1998: 1). Liberalism's defence of individual liberty is to be united with social democracy's promotion of social justice. In this way, certain values of the right are modified through a progressive liberalism, so diluting them of their antagonism to social justice (the essential guiding thread of social democracy) and making them amenable to reformulation under a renewed social democracy. Elsewhere Blair has explicitly acknowledged his debt to the new liberalism (examined briefly in Chapter 1) for its effort to reconcile liberty and equality (see Blair, 1995b: 14–15). Peter Mandelson, on the other hand, has more recently emphasised the roots of the Third Way in social democratic revisionism such as that of Anthony Crossland and defends the Third Way as a form of 'modern social democracy rather than centre politics' (Mandelson, 2002: xxviii; cf. Mandelson and Liddle, 1996: 29–30).

The idea of moving social democracy beyond the traditional division of left and right ideology is central, too, to Giddens' arguments. Indeed, he is the author of a book titled precisely *Beyond Left and Right* (1994), and he draws upon the analysis developed there in his own book on the Third Way (Giddens, 1998). For Giddens, 'old-style' social democracy and conservative neo-liberalism have become outdated doctrines, manifestly incapable of responding to the dilemmas of the modern age. He, too, proposes a revival of social democracy, one that reaches beyond the divisions of social class but maintains a commitment to 'radical' change: 'A renewed social democracy has to be left of centre, because social justice and emancipatory politics remain at its core' (Ibid.: 45).

New Labour's Third Way, then, is explicitly claimed to constitute a course through the antagonism between traditional or 'old-style left' and conservative and neo-liberal right but inclined primarily to the 'left-of-centre'. This represents the key trope in the Labour Party's adjustment to what Driver and Martell (1998) call 'post-Thatcherite politics' that has been under way since the party's defeat in the 1983 election (see also Miliband, 1994; Novak, 1998). Both Blair and Mandelson emphasise that the Third Way is not just splitting the difference between right and left but seeks to combine elements of each 'to develop radically new approaches'. Or, in the more ambitious words of Mandelson and Liddle: 'New Labour is a new type of politics. It is about building a new synthesis to which all of the centre and left can subscribe' (1996: 17).

Crisis: the challenge of 'change'

What is it that renders Old Left and New Right obsolete? The answer is almost uniformly summed up by the proponents of the Third Way in terms of the challenge, or crisis, brought by 'social change'. For Blair, social and economic transformations have raced ahead of traditional political ideologies and exposed their failings as programmes of action (1998: 5–7). He summarises these changes in four points: the internationalisation of trade conditions under processes of globalisation; the rapid development of new technologies and their effects on jobs, skills and education (the 'knowledge economy'); the transformation of women's social and economic roles; dissatisfaction amongst European publics with 'unresponsive and often ineffective political institutions' (Ibid: 6). In alerting us to these dislocatory events, Blair constructs a sense of general crisis to which, he argues, neither New Right nor Old Left are able to face up. Whilst statist social democracy 'fitted well with a world' of stable employment, economic conditions and family life, as economy and society changed, social democracy 'proved too inflexible', 'ineffective at promoting growth', 'too inefficient and low quality' in its provision of public services.

In offloading the functions of the state onto the market, the New Right, in Blair's view, brought about much needed modernisation (to trade union law, for example). Yet it, too, remained out of step with the changes in the world (1998: 5–6). The Conservative governments of the 1980s were too dogmatic in their defence of markets and refused to acknowledge the failure of companies, the decline of public services and the widespread social problems brought by both. Ideological rigidity blinded the Tories to their failure to understand and adapt to social change.

Giddens makes similar claims but his analysis is marked by its explicitly sociological reasoning. For Giddens, the underlying dilemma for the old ideologies is how to respond creatively to a series of social transformations, including: changes in time and space brought by globalisation that undermine the capacity of states to manage their economic systems relatively independently of others; the formation of increasingly 'reflexive' social identities and the decline of traditional identities that have led to a greater individualism and sensitivity to questions of autonomy and choice (or 'life politics') rather than class solidarity and collectivist responses to scarcity; the development of an environmental politics at odds with the industrialism of mainstream political parties; the decline of the nation-state as the privileged site of political agency and source of security against 'risk', coupled with the rise of social movements in civil society and international organisations as alternative sites of governance (Giddens, 1998: 27–37, 46–64; 1994: 78–103).

These challenges have 'exhausted' the platforms of left and right, in Giddens' view. For him, both Old Left and New Right adopted 'linear' views of modernisation that dogmatically emphasised the role of one social institution over another in delivering economic growth: the state or the market. These views, he argues, are hopelessly ill-suited to the dilemmas facing 'late modern' societies. Yet it is precisely this comprehension of change that drives the Third Way. Its response to the changing world is 'a more pragmatic attitude towards coping with change' (Ibid.: 68). This response must be a 'modernizing' one that accepts the logic of globalisation as an opportunity but which, at the same time, 'is conscious of the problems and limitations of modernizing processes' (Ibid.: 67). Giddens calls this perspective 'philosophic conservatism' because it seeks to adjust to the 'intrinsically unpredictable energies' of the modern age (and hence is not politically conservative) yet does so with a view to maintaining 'social cohesion' and limiting the disruption such change can bring (Ibid.: 64–8; 1994: 27–30, 247–8).

This view is echoed by Blair when he argues that the failings of Old Left and New Right are overcome in a style of government based on a pragmatic rebalancing of responsibilities of state and market. He outlines four 'broad policy objectives' in which the state takes on a new role: a government that 'enables' (as opposed to 'commands') in a 'dynamic, knowledge-based economy' where 'the power of the market is harnessed to serve the public interest'; a government in partnership with a civil society of 'strong communities' empowered by rights *and* responsibilities; decentralisation and partnership; a foreign policy based on cooperation with international partners. Similar suggestions are made by Giddens (1998: chs 3–5).

These proposals have since been given flesh in the form of (sometimes quite controversial) government policies: the use of private companies to run public services is found in the examples of the Private Finance Initiatives (PFI) taken over from the previous Conservative government; the 'Public Private Partnerships' (PPP) designed to finance the building of hospitals; the delivery of transport services; and the selective handing over of 'failing schools' to be run by private firms. Though routinely accused by the left of enacting policies of privatisation, this is not strictly true because government is closely involved in setting standards and often continues to own or closely regulate. Partnerships with civil society are visible in the areas of both family and crime policy, designed to underscore the responsibilities as well as rights of citizens. Thus the duties of parents to their children – particularly in the instance of family break-up – and of criminals to their victims have been asserted in various measures. Finally, the Labour government has set much store by its positive relationship with its partners in the European Union, its multilateral approach to international politics and its positive efforts in the eradication of debt in the developing world.

The controversy in these policies has arisen because in many instances they abandon traditional social democratic commitments to the role of the state as provider and agency of intervention, and they appear to accept what were regarded as essentially conservative policies and principles favouring the efficiency of the market and mildly authoritarian social policies.[2] In its statements New Labour tends to emphasise the principle organising the relationship (for example, 'partnership') rather than an attachment to any specific institutional means: for Blair, adaptation to social change requires this sense of a common endeavour in which government and society are aligned in a common project that neither Old Left nor New Right could accomplish. Thus we find ethics are a central element of the Third Way's resolution to the crisis of government.

Ethics: 'opportunities for all'

For Blair, 'policies flow from values, not vice versa' (Blair, 1998: 4). Ethical principles are fundamental to New Labour's strategy and in *The Third Way* Blair invokes four key values that the Third Way is set to 'promote and reconcile': equal worth, opportunity for all, responsibility, and community (Ibid.: 3–4). For Blair, as for Giddens, equality of outcome is a dated principle of the left that no longer matches a diverse, pluralistic society where, for the most part, material inequality is not the primary cause of social disorder. In these circumstances, a more classically liberal notion of equal moral worth (that is, regardless of race, age, physical ability, religion, and so on) should be a fundamental principle. The suggestion here is that the central obstacles to human freedom are prejudice and discrimination rather than material inequality (see also Mandelson, 2002: xxxi–ii).

Blair defends the liberal idea of 'opportunity for all'. The left, he claims, 'has too readily downplayed its duty to promote a wide range of opportunities for individuals' (Blair, 1998: 3). Too much emphasis on material equality has inclined the left away from giving people the opportunity to exercise choice in welfare and public services, or to express themselves in arts and culture. This view is similar to Giddens' analysis of the 'new individualism' in de-traditionalised societies (Giddens, 1998: 34–7). Mandelson continues the thread by arguing that British society remains too elitist and lacks a culture of enterprise and risk-taking: 'politicians on the left have mistakenly believed that somehow the actions of the state can fill this gap in values and attitudes among the least well-off in society. But it can't' (Mandelson, 2002: xxxi). New Labour's commitment, then, is to a meritocratic society, one in which individuals can 'take their destiny into their own hands' without the arbitrary obstacles of 'prejudice, racism or snobbery' (Ibid.). This liberal individualism, insist defenders of the Third Way, is not a return to the egoistic individualism of the neo-liberal right but a realistic reflection of social change and economic advance in modern society. Whilst it contrasts with the 'one size fits all' notion of equality of old, it is not to be opposed to solidarity *tout court*:

> If institutional individualism is not the same as egoism, it poses less of a threat to social solidarity, but it does imply that we have to look for new means of producing that solidarity . . . We have to find a new balance between individual and collective responsibilities today (Giddens, 1998: 36–7).

The 'new balance' is identified in the 'ethical principle' that rights are to be matched with 'responsibilities' (Ibid.: 65–6). For the individual must acknowledge that 'in certain key respects, it is only by working together in a community of people that the individual's interests can be advanced' (Blair, 1996c: 298). This demands that we accept our 'mutual rights and responsibilities' in at least two senses: first that government has a duty to give people a stake in the future and, second, that citizens have a duty to recognise their responsibility, individually and collectively, for the consequences of their actions. Whilst the first invokes a notion of social justice administered by the state, the second invokes a more 'communitarian' idea of individual responsibility to others.[3] Blair suggests as an example the responsibility of parents for their children's welfare and education. Rather than assuming the state exists to pick up any fallout from broken marriages, the Third Way works on the basis that parents have a significant role to play. Giddens underlines the point that the principle of no 'rights without responsibilities' should apply 'to everyone' not just 'to the poor or to the needy – as tends to be the case with the political right' (1998: 66).

Community

Vital to New Labour's ethical reasoning is the concept of 'community', both in the sense of concrete local communities and the wider community as a whole (see Mandelson and Liddle, 1996: 19–21; Blair, 1996c; Giddens, 1998: 78–98). These senses encapsulate the combination of 'social liberal' recognition of difference and autonomy, and the social democratic idea of social justice. Communities in civil society are sources of individual success and autonomy, and 'the community' is a principle through which our common obligations as a nation are invoked. Unlike the Old Left, whose 'grievous error' was the belief that the state could replace civil society, and the New Right, who prioritised the market element of civil society, the Third Way looks to voluntary organisations and local communities (appropriately termed the 'third sector') alongside an 'enabling' state. In this sense, civil society has an inclusive connotation that sets it apart from the neo-liberal idea of society as a collection of self-interested individuals: it is both cooperative *and* competitive, consisting of both market relations and non-profit organisations, each of which may serve public purposes (see Blair, 1993). The right's exclusive emphasis on civil society as a free market ultimately led to the 'collapse of community' in the form of unemployment, the emergence of an 'underclass' and overstretched but demoralised public services (Blair, 1996c: 300–1). As we have seen, the idea of a 'partnership' between state and civil society is central to proponents of the Third Way who seek to revive civil society as a socially cohesive realm by deploying the notion of 'stakeholding' (see Mandelson and Liddle, 1996: 19).

It is in promoting the second, but not unrelated, sense of community that New Labour has been more controversial (see Little, 2002a, 2002b). In the wider sense, community refers to a common endeavour in which each person is obliged to play a part; it stands for the principle of social order itself. In the social democratic tradition, this view has traditionally been represented by the idea of 'fellowship', mutuality and interdependence, once expressed in the notion of the 'common ownership of the means of production'. New Labour have explicitly renounced this socialist idea of the 'moralised economy' but retain the moral sense of common endeavour associated with it. In part, New Labour's aim was to reappropriate the term 'One Nation' from the Conservative Party, a deliberate effort to associate Labour with the majority of the country and the Tories with a minority of 'vested interests' (see Blair, 1996c: 299–301). And there remains in the invocation of community a traditional social democratic declaration on the obligation of government to actively promote the shared goal of social justice through certain measures such as welfare benefits and public services (Ibid.: 301–7).

However, the notion of communal obligation is frequently deployed in a highly inclusive but morally conservative sense. For instance, Blair, despite his gestures towards social liberalism, often makes explicit appeal to notions of duty, family and moral rectitude:

> any attempt to rebuild community for a modern age must assert that personal and social responsibility are not optional extras but core principles of a thriving society today . . . It is in the family that children learn self-respect and mutual respect, where they are first taught right from wrong, where they learn to value education and learning (Ibid.: 306).

Here individual responsibility, family and moral awareness are run together as the primary ingredients of a cohesive community, not the shared experiences of work and struggle (see also Mandelson and Liddle, 1996: 20). Although in government New Labour has not sought to enforce a mythical notion of the 'bourgeois family', nevertheless its idea of community as a relationship of individual responsibility often slides towards promoting the idea of a 'normal family' as the moral basis of social order (see Fairclough, 2000: 42–3). This reflects a rather contradictory view of the meaning of community (see Hughes and Little, 1999).

Nikolas Rose (1999: 474–8) has argued that New Labour's notion of community seeks to articulate the notion of the 'community' as a 'sector for government' (Rose, 1999a: 176; see also 1999b: 474–8). This involves addressing the public as essentially ethical beings whose relation to each other is based not on self- or group-interest but on reciprocal ties of obligation, honour and duty. These ties are developed through 'programmes and techniques which encourage and harness an active practice of self-management and identity construction, of personal ethics and collective allegiances' (Rose, 1999a: 176) that underscore the individual's constitutive need to 'belong' to a cohesive order.

One of the most striking examples of this approach is the redefinition of poverty as a form of 'social exclusion'. Rather than structural inequalities causing poverty, the focus is shifted to the absence of attachment to work, family and other virtuous communal resources that ensure individual responsibility (Rose, 1999b: 487–9). Likewise, the government's 'Welfare to Work' policies, designed to compel the unemployed to accept either any work offered or retraining, can be seen as a way of punishing people who refuse to accept their responsibilities to the wider community (see King and Wickham-Jones, 1999). Here the wage 'is a central mechanism for reattachment to moral community with its external responsibilities, its norms of comportment and its psychological concomitants of identity, stability, commitment and purpose' (Rose, 1999b: 489; see also Rose, 1999a: 188–93).

Agency: 'New Labour, New Britain'

New Labour self-consciously marketed itself as the agency of radical change and social renewal, hence Mandelson and Liddle's deliberate overstatement of the approaching 'Blair revolution'. New Labour's impact on public perception, indeed its strenuous efforts to manage public perceptions, was an essential element of its success in the late 1990s. From the rebranding of its public name ('New Labour' is still officially the 'British Labour Party') and the explicit dropping of key principles of its constitution (for example, Clause IV) to the efforts to control the media (for instance, Millbank's 'Rapid Rebuttal Unit' and the crucial role of press secretaries in operating media 'spin'), New Labour has channelled much of its energies into shaping its public image.

In certain respects this merely reflects a growing media-consciousness in contemporary party politics. At the same time, however, New Labour's purpose has been more than just winning a coalition; it has deliberately aimed to associate itself with the process of renewal. This recalls Antonio Gramsci's definition of the political party, what he called the 'Modern Prince', as itself the embodiment of a new hegemonic 'collective will' (see Gramsci, 1971: 125–6; Martin, 1998: ch. 4). Like other proponents of third ways, New Labour sees itself as more than just a party: it is the living symbol of the change it wishes to bring about. Few slogans express this better than 'New Labour, New Britain'. As an agency of modernisation, Labour's newness was to become Britain's newness. Thus, like other third ways, the movement comes to incarnate the ideals it represents (see Blair, 1994), in particular in the person of Blair himself (see Finlayson, 2002b). In his 1995 speech to the Labour Party conference Tony Blair invoked the classic image of 'youth' as the symbol of a reinvigorated unity and purpose: 'I want us to be a young country again. With a common purpose. With ideals we cherish and live up to. Not resting on past glories' (Blair, 1995a: 65).

However, such efforts have provoked resentment from sectors within the party. Many have been unhappy at what they see as the rapid transformation of the Labour Party – the watering down of its commitments, the weakening of the trade unions' influence on policy formation, and so on – from a democratic movement into a vehicle designed merely to campaign on behalf of its leader. Accusations of 'presidentialism' have accompanied Blair's leadership of the party and his personalisation of the party's project. Others point to the detrimental effect of persistent attempts to manipulate the media. Indeed, even Peter Mandelson, widely regarded as one of the key architects of this practice, has now accepted that the party has been 'over-zealous' in giving primacy to its media skills (Mandelson, 2002: xliv).

UNDERSTANDING NEW LABOUR'S DISCOURSE

New Labour's programme, and the various defences of Third Way thinking by Blair, Giddens and others, has come under intense fire, particularly (if predictably) from critics to the left. Typically, the left attacks the Third Way as fundamentally a break with any serious anti-capitalist project and a shameless acceptance of neo-liberalism (Callinicos, 2001). Colin Hay, for example, argues that New Labour's strategy has been to accommodate rather than challenge the 'para-digm shift' that Thatcherism made over social democracy, producing a new neo-liberal consensus on political economy (see Hay, 1997).

Perry Anderson, too, echoes Lenin's critique of parliamentary democracy in claiming that the Third Way represents 'the best ideological shell of neo-liberalism today' (Anderson, 2000: 11). This perspective tends to dismiss the discursive character of New Labour as so much empty rhetoric, a bland surface of cheery ideas behind which lurks the more serious surrender to the machinations of global capitalism.

Others, especially those who identify with the 'progressive' left, tend either to dismiss the Third Way as incoherent nonsense (for example, Toynbee, 2001), as being vastly out of step with the intellectual traditions of the British Labour Party (for example, Hattersley, 2001), or, as Stuart White claims, 'fundamentally vague and elusive' (White, 2001). Even supporters and advisors to the government are apt to dismiss the Third Way as a crude 'balancing act' lacking in inspiration (Leadbeater, 1999: 16–17; Rawnsley, 2001: 154).

Whilst New Labour is unlikely to care much for the critique offered up by neo-Marxists, the charges of incoherence or lack in continuity with the social democratic tradition are more damaging. This is because New Labour prides itself on proclaiming its continuity with the progressive centre-left and of having a reasonably coherent (if, as yet, incomplete) project. Let us consider for a moment the questions of continuity and coherence, for these represent key issues in the reception of New Labour discourse and the various tensions it seeks to balance.

Continuity

Both Tony Blair and Anthony Giddens claim that the Third Way represents a 'renewal' of social democracy, not its abandonment. Nevertheless, the view persists that New Labour has simply adopted policies and principles that are essentially right-wing. The evidence for this view draws upon a number of issues: for example, the replacement of Clause IV of the Labour Party constitution committing it to 'common ownership' of industry (a byword for nationalisation measures); the incorporation of key aspects of Conservative Party policies on crime, education, public service funding, and so on; the refusal to commit the government to renationalisation of privatised public services. Underlying these questions of policy, critics argue, is the acceptance of inequalities brought by a market economy and the necessity for the individual to rely on their own efforts to ensure their well-being, not on 'handouts' from the state. As Roy Hattersley (2001) points out, New Labour is openly committed to a 'meritocratic' society in which individual differences are seen as justifiable (and based on effort) not to equality of outcome. This, in his view, is not continuous with the values of social democracy as he recognises it.

The question as to whether New Labour has 'abandoned' socialism and social democracy was discussed widely in the early years of Blair's leadership and the first term of his government, and it remains an underlying issue on the left in general. It is widely recognised that New Labour draws upon the early twentieth-century tradition of 'new liberalism' to define and defend aspects of its Third Way. As we have seen, Blair explicitly defends his programme as a third way within the left, as well as between left and right. New liberalism's combined support for social reform and the primacy of individual liberty sought to redefine liberty as a positive ethical principle rather than a negative notion, and this finds many echoes in New Labour's discourses: reconciling social justice with individual choice and the market, for example. Added to this, however, are ideas and policies closely associated with the Conservative government, making New Labour ideology, as Freeden (1999) observes, a complex assemblage of different traditions of British political ideology.

But does the presence of themes associated either with Thatcherite Conservatism or new liberalism amount to an abandonment of the social democratic tradition? Early assessments by analysts such as Marquand (1999b) and Vincent (1998) suggested it did. Likewise, for Hay (1997, 1999) New Labour's programme amounts merely to a restatement of a Thatcherite 'consensus'. Such arguments, however, beg the question of how one defines the ideologies to be analysed. This is not simply to point to potential similarities between new liberalism and social democracy (on which see, for example, Clarke, 1978: 139–41) but to the more general argument highlighted in the Introduction: namely, the contingency of ideological formations.

However, as Bevir (2000) points out, identifying an influence or a similarity between different ideological traditions does not constitute a wholesale transformation. In the Introduction, we showed how discourse theory argues something similar. Ideologies are not totally closed or fixed systems in a zero-sum relationship with each other such that the presence of elements from one excludes those of another. Indeed, for Bevir, we should avoid 'reifying' ideologies by assuming they consist in 'core' concepts that remain essentially unchanged over time. Rather, ideologies are 'contingent and changing traditions in which no value or debate has a fixed, central or defining place' (Bevir, 2000: 280). Thus it is mistaken to 'explain' a specific set of ideas by comparing it to a fixed set of principles and drawing a judgment as to how much it approximates its 'original' version. This merely juxtaposes contingent ideas with an arbitrary 'abstract model' posing as the essence of an ideology.

Like discourse theory, Bevir recommends we understand ideologies as open-ended configurations constantly under modification as new problems are faced. As individuals and groups seek to resolve these problems, inherited ideas are influenced and refashioned such that their core concepts are continually modified. For discourse theorists, this is an instance of what Derrida called the 'logic of supplementarity', where new elements are added to a discourse to represent it anew, and in so doing modify the original principles. Thus Bevir claims that New Labour is not 'abandoning' its ideological heritage of socialism or social democracy so much as bringing to it new themes and principles from outside and consequently modifying certain elements of that tradition. Social justice, for example, has now been redefined in light of the recognition of the problems of inflation that undermined post-war social democratic achievements. New Labour, he argues, accepts much of the supply-side economics of Thatcherism that prioritises macro-economic stability not redistribution; this is visible in its rejection of so-called 'tax and spend' policies, and the emphasis it places on efficiency and competitiveness. But if New Labour renounces the primacy of redistribution, it does not abandon social justice. Rather, it 'emphasises the need to secure an efficient and competitive economy as the context within which moves towards social justice can be made' (Bevir, 2000: 290). This may well involve the acceptance of certain inequalities, emphasising individual choice, and so forth, but Labour remains aware of the limitations of the market.

Whilst we agree with the broad thrust of Bevir's analysis, his approach is overly focused on ideas and the intended meanings of human agents (see Martin, 2002). We argue below that we need to consider the wider political effects of discourse, some of which lie outside the realm of human intentionality. Nevertheless, we concur that accounting for New Labour simply by classifying it in terms of the traditions from which it draws overstates the unity of those traditions and refuses to accept the possibility of genuine ideological novelty. It also suggests a rather rigid, uni-dimensional framework of options. Whilst New Labour draws upon various elements of neo-liberalism, conservatism, liberalism and social democracy – both in principle and in practice – many academics and commentators have hurried to provide a global interpretation of New Labour that, arguably, misses many of its nuances, however contradictory. As Kenny and Smith (1997) have pointed out, these views certainly grasp something of the influences on New Labour but they oversimplify considerably and ignore the constraints it faces in changing its principles and in formulating its economic policy.

Coherence

Even if, for the sake of argument, we accept that New Labour is broadly working *from* (if not exclusively *within*) its ethical socialist or social democratic heritage, does its Third Way constitute a coherent doctrine? The charge of incoherence is repeatedly made by critics who point to the absence of any stable principle against which to judge the various aspects of policy. If New Labour's ideology lacks such a principle, then it is open to the charge of cynical opportunism or intellectual eclecticism, both criticisms that challenge its claim to be a new and distinctive ideological formation able to run government effectively. The journalist and commentator Polly Toynbee (2001) exemplifies this view in her charge that the Third Way is a 'butterfly constantly on the wing', unable to be pinned down and classified as a specific political doctrine. The Third Way is all things to all men, shifting in emphasis as the government's mood changes.

What exactly is incoherent about New Labour's Third Way? Powell (2000: 53) argues that 'the third way does not seem to be based on a clear ideology or a "big idea"'. That is, there is no fundamental principle that unites its various claims and policies: 'The third way(s) appears to be based on an "emergent strategy" or "policy-making on the hoof", and used in an eclectic and pragmatic manner' (Ibid). Thus principles of individual freedom and opportunity co-exist alongside those of community and moral order; social justice is pronounced whilst the unemployed are 'compelled' to take low-paid work or training; 'social inclusion' is proclaimed at the same time as 'tough' criminal justice policies; devolved forms of democratic accountability and an emphasis on a 'new politics' of citizen participation are matched by top-down central state intervention in, for example, schools. At the same time as the government rejects 'tax and spend policies', it nevertheless redistributes wealth 'by stealth', increasing support for children of income support recipients and successfully removing a large number of children from poverty (see Lister, 2001: 436).

Furthermore, Powell goes on to assert that, in addition to having no organising principle, many of New Labour's social policies are not even new. Linking welfare and work 'is little more than a more humane version of the "less eligibility" concept of the New Poor Law' (Powell, 2000: 55). Likewise, emphasising the role of civil society and association input into welfare returns to the original ideas of Beveridge, which emphasised voluntary action and self-responsibility for risks facing individuals and families.

For Powell (2000) and Lister (2001), what unifies these 'ambiguous' and contradictory ideas and actions is not a new ideological principle but a political attitude of 'pragmatism and populism'. New Labour's Third Way 'has pragmatism at its heart' (Powell, 2000: 53) in as much as it seeks to adapt to the changes of the Thatcher governments rather than overturning them, distinguishing only those reforms that worked from those that failed. Lister claims that this pragmatism is reflected in the selective approach New Labour takes to social reform, dealing with 'social problems' as discrete issues demanding 'organisational solutions' rather than attempting a systemic understanding of the wider causes and effects of poverty and inequality. Such problems are 'targeted' by agencies such as the Social Exclusion Unit and solutions are generated on the basis of a 'managerial calculus of economy and efficiency' (Lister, 2001: 433), not as part of a more concerted and principled attack on inegalitarian social and economic structures (see also Temple, 2000).

New Labour's populism, it is argued, consists in its effort to formulate policies that appeal to popular attitudes and sentiments, usually those that 'grab' newspaper headlines. More often than not, these involve an appeal to the reactionary common sense of the so-called 'ordinary man in the street'. Policies claiming to be 'tough on crime', that tackle welfare 'scroungers', or appeal to the values of 'hard-working people' reveal an effort to speak to the public via the language of tabloid newspapers (Powell, 2000: 54). As Lister points out, use of authoritarian language and notions of welfare 'dependency' seeks to 'woo', not challenge, the public; it starts out from the assumption that the public are essentially conservative and reactionary and policies need to adjust to this mindset. Thus the Third Way is constrained to work within parameters that are fundamentally conservative, hostile to those on welfare, asylum-seekers and immigrants, and so on. This prevents more imaginative and 'progressive' ideas from emerging, ideas that might challenge the public and radically transform structures of power (Lister, 2001: 428–31).

This apparent lack of coherence suggests that New Labour's Third Way has failed to develop into a new synthesis of left and right, that is, into an ideology that is not simply a negation of Old Left and New Right but stands for a positively new ideological framework. This, indeed, is the view set out by Driver and Martell (2000). They argue that 'the third way involves the combination rather than transcendence of Left and Right' (2000: 154). The novelty of New Labour's Third Way is not its claim to have invented an entirely new programme but rather to have combined or mixed principles traditionally associated with the 'closed ideological systems' of left and right. This involves a pluralistic and pragmatic approach to policy-making, one that remains broadly within a distinctively British centrist tradition. Driver and Martell point out that this novel mixture offers opportunities for new ways of formulating policy that would not have been possible in the Old Left version of social democracy: for instance, the combination of social justice measures with economic efficiency. Yet, they also indicate that there are intrinsic 'pitfalls' in this approach. New Labour can find compromises between once opposed options but it cannot resolve their tensions (Ibid: 155). Whilst the Third Way 'often appears rhetorically to . . . reconcile . . . irreconcilables', New Labour 'is also aware that different interests remain at work and that tensions remain permanent features of the political and policy-making landscape' (Ibid). In particular, the egalitarian outcomes of social justice are difficult to reconcile with the 'inegalitarian dynamics of the market'. Indeed, for Mouffe, abandoning the distinction between left and right for the elusive 'radical centre' has created 'the illusion that, by not defining an adversary, one can side-step fundamental conflicts of interest' (Mouffe, 2000: 111).

Driver and Martell's argument suggests that within New Labour's Third Way there are important decisions to be made on key issues. Lacking any final ideological standard, the Third Way must work pragmatically, assessing the opportunities available at any given moment on any given issue. Unlike the critiques by Powell, Lister and Mouffe, this view looks more positively to the possibilities that remain open within Third Way discourse. New Labour's pragmatism is often read simply as conservatism by its critics but it may also be understood as holding opportunities for alternative emphases, different combinations of policy, and therefore different 'ways' to move beyond the old antagonisms, some of which veer more to the right (like Blair's) and others that stand more to the left (like Giddens') (see White, 2001).

GLOBALISATION, GOVERNMENT AND THE THIRD WAY

On this reading, then, New Labour's Third Way defines a very broad, fluid conceptual space that permits a variety of options unthinkable within the terms of earlier left/right discourses (see Fairclough, 2000: 50). This discourse might be tentatively continuous with Labour's ideological heritage; it might be so loosely constructed that political pragmatism rather than clear principle gives it the only internal coherence it has. Yet, arguably, it constitutes a workable space within which the government can define its objectives, despite its admittedly blurred boundaries and tentative formulation.

Yet debates about the uncertain continuity and coherence of Labour's Third Way, however they are resolved, to a great extent miss the point. Often these debates reflect a concern on the part of politicians, commentators and academics to register their own preferred ideological commitments, which they tend to assume are more continuous with a radical tradition and more intellectually justifiable than New Labour's. But continuity and coherence are only part of the issue. For all its intellectual awkwardness and contradictions, New Labour's Third Way is fundamentally a *political* discourse, one whose purpose is not simply to appeal to intellectuals but primarily to manage a broad coalition of interests unified around a programme of government. Inevitably this is an exercise in rhetorical inventiveness, manipulation and audacity, as different, sometimes deeply contradictory, demands and expectations are brought together under one umbrella, or 'big tent' as New Labour often calls it.

What this means is that Third Way discourse should be understood, and analysed, as part of a hegemonic strategy for social and economic governance, that is, as an intellectual/policy framework designed to coordinate the relationship between state, economy and society in a period of unprecedented change. We shall sketch our analysis of this perspective below and point to some of its limitations. As we shall see, New Labour's discourse reveals itself as a distinctive, if deeply problematic, effort to define new kinds of subjects for a global age it conceives as objectively present.

Managing change

New Labour Third Way discourse seeks to articulate a strategy for social and economic governance in response to a series of dislocations that have emerged in recent decades. Many of these have been identified by Giddens, and were mentioned earlier in this chapter, but they also formed the focus of the vision of 'New Times' produced by *Marxism Today* in the 1980s (see Hall and Jacques, 1989), which focused on novel social forms based on flexibility, consumption, the knowledge economy, and so on. We shall return to such dislocations in the Conclusion but, in sum, they involve: a growing commodification of social life; the emergence of a generalised distrust of 'grand narratives'; a weakening of the state brought about by factors such as globalisation; and a 'crisis of identity' involving the pluralisation of social subjects. The Third Way is New Labour's response to these dislocations, articulating a programme which, as Finlayson notes, 'requires a restructuring of the relationship between the state, the economy and citizens' (Finlayson, 2000: 187).

Such a programme rejects 'old-style' social democracy which, it is argued, was premised on a 'Fordist' accumulation strategy based on mass production and consumption, the integration of organised interest groups into policy-making, and large-scale state intervention and provision of services. The role of the state was to balance the different interests and provide the conditions for stable growth based on mass consumption. Thus the welfare state and various social policies removed the insecurity of poverty and illness and enabled working people to purchase consumer goods; likewise, social democratic policies prioritised full employment and provided a stable regime for large-scale industry to grow (see Jessop, 1994).

The dislocations noted above, however, signal a revised role for the state and new relationships between state and citizens. Fordist mass production increasingly exhausted its markets, new forms of technology have rendered obsolete the industrial factory and enabled diversified products, and citizens in industrial democracies are demanding greater choice and quality than the 'one size fits all' norm of the Fordist era. These conditions, it is claimed, have led to the emergence of a post-Fordist economy.[4] This is a highly competitive economy; it is intensely dynamic, seeking constant innovation in both product and production process, and needy of flexible work skills in order constantly to adapt in the face of ruthless competition and a permanently shifting market. Leaps in computer and micro-chip technology have made knowledge a fundamentally important element of this economy, or 'knowledge-economy' (see Leadbeater, 1999). For innovation, greater consumer choice and competitiveness in production all rely on the ability of individuals and companies to utilise knowledge and skills effectively.

For Finlayson (2000), New Labour's self-appointed task is to embrace these new conditions and help companies and citizens adapt to their demands, promoting a new society based on their forms. In many respects this strategy accepts the legacy of the Thatcher governments, yet, at the same time, New Labour's 'project' is more ambitious. Whereas Thatcher's reforms to trade union laws, privatisation, internationalisation of the economy, and so on, opened the way to a greater movement in the market, their social costs were enormous in terms of unemployment, social division, rising crime, and so on. For Thatcher, the social disruption caused by the switch to the free market was met, in Andrew Gamble's phrase, with the 'strong state' (Gamble, 1988). For New Labour, however, marketisation sits alongside a more benevolent state, yet one equally committed to ushering in the new economy. Unlike Thatcher's, this state accepts responsibility for ensuring some degree of social cohesion and solidarity. The state does not renounce its responsibility to the citizen but takes an active role in integrating the citizen into the economy and the wider society (see, for example, Blair, 1996b).

Like the Thatcher governments before it, New Labour seeks to place the burden of responsibility on the individual and firms to take the risks under these new conditions. Unlike the neo-liberal policy, however, the state has an active role in encouraging, exhorting and, where necessary, actively assisting citizens and companies to do this. This explains some of the contradictions in its Third Way discourse: neo-liberal emphasis on individual choice is conjoined to the solidaristic language of community and responsibility because adaptation to the market is to be achieved without the fallout of social disruption and breakdown. As Finlayson summarises:

> New Labour's distinctiveness lies not so much in its attempts to change British politics or society, as their predecessors tried to do, but in its greater potential for bringing about such change while maintaining the legitimacy of the social order (Finlayson, 2000: 178).

In order to manage change peacefully, New Labour addresses the public through moral categories that emphasise common purpose, mutual obligations and shared responsibilities. As we have noted already, the emphasis on ethics and community is a key element in all third ways. New Labour, however, seeks to develop this ethical community not in order to halt or slow down social change so as to protect a mythical community 'under threat' but to *enhance* that change. For critics, such exhortations jar uncomfortably with the liberalising effects of marketisation and the social and economic inequalities that ensue. Yet in New Labour's project moralisation is not a façade masking its real intentions simply to adopt free market policies. On the contrary, and perhaps even more insidiously, the purpose is to generate a new culture in which individuals think of themselves as self-regulating subjects responsible for their own personal innovation as products on the labour market. As Rose suggests, New Labour's emphasis on education, re-skilling and, ultimately, work promotes a specific conception of the individual as 'an entrepreneur of his- or her-self, striving to maximize his or her own human capital' (Rose, 1999b: 483; see also 1999a: 142). The Third Way, then, is the ideological framework for generating this new 'ethical subjectivity' in line with the 'new economy' and other changes in social conditions. It is the ideological codification of a 'technology of governmentality' in which subjects are disciplined and shaped in such a way that they freely govern themselves in accordance with internalised assumptions and expectations (see Finlayson, 2000: 193–8).

The limits of modernisation

'Modernisation', then, is the linchpin of New Labour's Third Way discourse. Under the category of modernisation, social change is managed by a creative, if seemingly disorderly, assemblage of elements from traditional social democratic, liberal and conservative ideological discourses. But what makes this Third Way compelling is not so much the finish of its 'philosophy' but its capacity to hegemonise a variety of anxieties and concerns, reinscribing them within the story of modernisation. In this way, criticisms of the theoretical coherence or continuity of New Labour can to some extent be transformed into its supporting evidence; extolling the contradictions of its policies or its 'betrayal' of certain radical traditions or interest groups sometimes plays into New Labour's modernisation narrative. For it is precisely these 'enemies' of progress, these 'forces of conservatism' who refuse to accept the changed conditions of the modern world that New Labour claims it has left behind.

What we find theoretically problematic about New Labour's discourse of the Third Way is not any apparent contradiction between its discursive elements. Nor is it any absence of continuity with cherished versions of 'social democracy'. Rather, our problem stems from the essentialism with which Labour seeks to fix the contours of its programme, seeking to endow it with an 'objectivity' that limits the political horizon of change and fails to acknowledge the possibility that antagonisms continue to exist.

At the root of modernisation discourse is a notion of social and economic change brought about by processes of globalisation (see Fairclough, 2000: ch. 1). For New Labour and its supporters, modernisation consists in adapting to the irrevocable changes brought by globalisation, specifically the intensification of competition across the globe brought through new technology. The generation of flexible labour markets, the emphasis on education, re-skilling and 'life-long learning', partnerships with the private sector, and so on, are all policies inscribed within the idea of enhancing the structural competitiveness of the British economy by recognising and adjusting to the changes brought by globalisation. Globalisation, then, is the symptom and modernisation is the cure. In this discourse global changes are invoked as the horizon of all possible action; like it or not, globalisation takes no prisoners. 'Adapt or die' is the implicit, often explicit, demand and this accounts for the urgency New Labour attaches to its programme of modernisation.

This view is endorsed, too, by Giddens' sociological reasoning. For him, globalisation is encapsulated in the notion of a 'runaway world'. Under such conditions, it is necessary to catch up and, where possible, control a constantly moving environment. Whilst Giddens denies that we are entirely passive in this emergent global environment, nevertheless his analysis implies the necessity of individuals and states inscribing themselves within its inexorable logic, adapting our moral and political understandings to its course.[5] Thus elsewhere Finlayson has argued that 'the third way derives its arguments from a sociological assessment and not a philosophical one' (Finlayson, 1999: 277). This leads to the possibility of 'a dangerous solipsism' where:

> The intellectual justification for policy is an interpretation of our present socio-economic context, where that context is the source of both the conditions for economic transformations and their legitimacy (Ibid.: 278).

Giddens' analysis provides us with little room to consider alternative ways of thinking about globalisation because the conditions of thought have themselves been objectively defined (see Rose, 1999b: 471–2; 2000: 1396–97). This encourages us to think of economic and social change as non-political (that is, essentially incontestable) and therefore enforces a closure on political discourse (see also Mouffe, 2000: 118–27).

Thus, as Raco (2002) points out, the emphasis on the irresistibility of globalisation effectively rules out alternative ways of thinking about changes in the economic structure associated with global transformations. In his analysis of economic policy documents, New Labour persistently deploys concepts of 'risk' and fear to promote economic restructuring. New Labour 'define reality' by selectively alerting citizens and companies to risks that accompany the emergence of the knowledge economy. By forecasting the potential likelihood of economic decline, the government deliberately cultivates anxiety and insecurity about the unpredictability of change and in so doing invokes a need to assert control over reality, to render it more calculable and oneself more prepared. Thus companies are encouraged to adopt forms of e-commerce, agencies such as the 'Performance and Innovation Unit' are deployed to promote new ways of working, and 'Regional Development Agencies' endeavour to enhance the competitive advantages of distinct regions and communities ('place competitiveness') (see Raco, 2002: 30–5). These efforts therefore define change as an inevitable condition and exhort citizens and companies to become part of that change in order to survive: 'Change is seen as a mechanism for overcoming the risk of failure, so that discourses of success and the capacities for accepting "change" go hand in hand' (Ibid.: 31).

But the selective deployment of risk frames change in such a way that it is difficult to justify any other course of action than to adapt. For Raco, this 'partial and selective' analysis disqualifies alternative ways of conceiving global changes and, therefore, alternative forms of adjustment. For instance, it overstates the significance of high-tech, high-skilled global industries and deliberately downplays the more mundane but nevertheless significant role of manufacturing industry. By stressing the discontinuity between the 'old' economy and the 'new', it marginalises economic activities that employ low-skilled labour (the decline of which accounts for a good deal of 'social exclusion'). Strategies for economic renewal are framed in terms of a preference for globally competitive industries that employ the skilled middle classes. Yet these strategies do not recognise the inherent unevenness of economies in a global environment. Indeed, globalisation is conceived as a unilinear process of increased competition that renders obsolete any alternative that stands in 'its' path.

CONCLUSION

In his comparative historical studies of socialist and social democratic parties in contemporary Europe, Donald Sassoon comes to the conclusion that there is a general ideological 'convergence' amongst these parties (see Sassoon, 1996, 1999a, 1999b). Like its sister parties in Germany, France, Italy and elsewhere, New Labour has had to come to terms with conditions that demand a wider range of options than permitted by the broad model of social democracy after the war. Whilst these parties differ in emphasis and style, they all now accept reduction of inflation as a primary goal; the independence of their central banks; the necessity of greater private involvement in the provision of public services; and the need to overhaul the welfare state. Similarly, these shifts to the right have been accomplished with a distinctively social democratic emphasis on the need for further regulation of business practices, minimum wages and an appeal to collective goals and standards (Sassoon, 1999a: 8–11). Thus New Labour's Third Way might be regarded as little more than a version of this converging pattern in specifically British circumstances (see also Giddens, 2001).

Such a view is certainly plausible. But we should be careful not to downplay the possible variations and alternative emphases that may be made within third way discourse. The terrain of the third way – its appeal to ethics and community, and so on – is not by necessity a conservative one. We noted in Chapter 1 the 'revolutionary revisionism' of Hendrik de Man and other 'planists', and in Chapter 3 we shall discuss the anti-fascist third way of liberal socialism. Whilst both these inter-war third ways sought alternatives to the choice of *either* state socialism *or* free market liberalism, they did not abandon a commitment to radical change in property ownership and political participation. Of course, it would be absurd simply to try to revive these currents of thought. But they do suggest a greater degree of manoeuvre on the third way on the left than both proponents and critics of New Labour tend to suggest.

Whilst we have argued that New Labour tends towards a discursive closure around the notion of globalisation and the project of modernisation that ensues from this, it remains uncertain that this closure can successfully displace the dislocations and emergent antagonisms with which it is intended to deal. These antagonisms (concerning work, skills, ethics, rights, and so on) constitute a vital, though challenging, source of mobilisation for the left. However, New

Labour's evident unwillingness to openly embrace antagonism (see Mouffe, 2000: ch. 5), and its acceptance of the neo-liberal status quo reduces its sensitivity to these experiences and its capacity to recruit subjects for the left. We shall suggest in the Conclusion how a radical democratic project, one that accepts the ineradicable nature of antagonism, might be conceived as an alternative form of third way politics for the left.

NOTES

1 Norman Fairclough provides an extensive textual analysis of New Labour's 'political discourse', including the Third Way, in his *New Labour, New Language?* (2000). Much of this excellent work parallels our own, although our conception of discourse differs in certain respects from his linguistic model of 'critical discourse analysis'.

2 For Giddens' largely positive appraisal of Labour in power, see Giddens (2002).

3 One might note the similarities with the position of the new liberals here. Hobhouse, for example, was fully supportive of the notion that the individual had responsibilities but argued that such responsibilities had to be counterbalanced by rights granted by the state in order to enforce social and economic justice (see Hobhouse, 1994: ch. 8).

4 A 'post-Fordist' economy does not entail the total loss of the 'Fordist' industries. For a discussion of post-Fordism and its weaknesses as a theory of social change, see Kumar (1995: esp. ch. 3).

5 Giddens' reasoning is, therefore, not unlike that of Durkheim (sketched briefly in Chapter 1). This partly explains Levitas' argument that a 'New Durkheimian Hegemony' is in operation under New Labour (see Levitas, 1996).

CHAPTER 3
ITALIAN LIBERAL SOCIALISM: ANTI-FASCISM AND THE THIRD WAY

Recent discussions of a third way in British Social Democracy often highlight the influence of the 'new' or 'social' liberalism of the early twentieth century on this nascent ideological formation. Alongside thinkers such as G. D. H. Cole or R. H. Tawney – whose 'ethical socialism', fashioned in opposition to Soviet statism, took on board elements of liberal thought – their combination of individual liberty and social justice is commonly presented as the quintessentially British contribution to the creative synthesis at the heart of the third way (see Wright, 2001). Both L. T. Hobhouse and Cole referred to the potential advantages of a 'liberal socialism' over the supposedly more drastic options of economic liberalism or state socialism (see Hobhouse, 1994: 80; Cole, 1972). Liberalism, it was believed, provided an ethic of individual autonomy and self-realisation, whilst socialism looked to the extension of freedom to the wider population through mechanisms of collective provision and economic self-management. Together, each could overcome the limitations of the other and remould society in a manner conducive to the realisation of individual freedom in an inclusive social context.

The effort to combine or even synthesise liberalism and socialism is not, however, an exclusively British phenomenon. Liberal socialism was also a distinctive, if relatively marginal, current in inter-war Italy. Unlike its British counterpart, which had a considerable impact upon its proponents, Italian liberal socialism was deeply influenced by the oppositional position it took in relation to the fascist regime in Italy. Anti-fascism was an integral element of the new outlook and signified a frontier that separated off the failed political ideologies, practices and institutions of the past whose miserable culmination was fascist authoritarianism. It was this frontier, rather than a sense of societal evolution common in its British counterpart, that enabled a reworking of liberal values around socialist demands for economic justice into a new, purportedly 'revolutionary' doctrine.

In what follows, we discuss some principal features of Italian liberal socialist discourse – that is, the broad set of conceptual elements that form its general 'field of reference' – by surveying the ideas of three of the major figures in its early development: Piero Gobetti, Carlo Rosselli and Guido Calogero. Although they wrote at different stages in the development of the fascist regime, each presented liberty (*libertà*) as an ethical principle upon which a new civil order was to be built. That ethic, which they argued had been historically absent in Italy, could encompass socialist demands for economic and social justice. It is the attempt to overcome the dichotomy between liberty and justice that places the Italian liberal socialist tradition as a candidate for third way theory, although only Calogero explicitly and consciously made this association. We shall argue, however, that anti-fascism is crucial to this enterprise and the manner in which this is articulated explains both the success and relative weaknesses of the liberal socialist tradition.

ITALIAN LIBERAL SOCIALISM

From the 1920s until the mid-1940s Italian liberal socialism was predominantly a political philosophy discussed at the level of principle rather than concrete political proposals. This reflected the stark fact that the fascist regime, under which all of its proponents lived (and some died), simply did not allow for practical political and policy alternatives. Liberal socialists developed their ideas at a distance from concrete questions of governance, often in exile, sometimes in prison. At root, liberal socialism articulated two basic principles: liberty and equality (or social justice). This involved the disassociation of each from any specific set of social and political arrangements. Separating off liberal values from laissez-faire economics minimises their distance from socialist principles. Likewise, socialism must be detached from any strict association with the abolition of private property or class dictatorship if it is to adequately incorporate liberal principles.[1]

In Italy this was enabled by the relative weakness of liberalism and socialism as autonomous ideologies rooted broadly in popular experience. The predominantly agricultural economy and the lateness of its industrialisation meant that Italy, as a whole, was not fertile soil for 'progressive' ideologies except in the developed northern regions. Italian capitalism lagged far behind the economies of Germany and Britain, and its expansion was premised on considerable state protectionism. Nor was Italy's system of political representation a huge success for liberal politics. The vast majority of the public had little or no contact with their representatives – full male suffrage was not introduced until 1918 – and parliamentary politics rapidly degenerated into a widely discredited system of patronage and corruption. Lack of public legitimation was underscored by the official *non expidit* of the Catholic Church, which refused to endorse participation by Catholics in parliamentary elections.

Equally, Italian socialism was a largely northern political organisation with little support from, or interest in, the wider conflicts of the nation, particularly the underdeveloped south. Officially a revolutionary party adhering to crude Marxist revolutionary principles of a positivistic bent, the Socialist Party nevertheless cooperated with the parliamentary system. Its reformist leaders ensured the party remained ambiguously opposed in principle to the liberal state and yet in practice complicit with it. On its margins, however, existed a diverse but influential syndicalist tradition with a powerful critique of the limitations of the liberal state (see Levy, 2000).

The failure of liberalism or socialism to hegemonise Italian political life was viewed by some radicals as the principal reason behind the rise of fascism.[2] Neither liberal nor socialist values had succeeded in extending their influence across the (mostly peasant) population. When the widely discredited liberal institutions fell into crisis after the immense dislocations of the First World War, there were precious few who sought to defend them.

Liberal socialism has its origins in the reaction by educated intellectuals to the emergence of fascism in the 1920s. Whilst its early precursors, such as Gobetti and Rosselli, developed their own idiosyncratic, 'heretical' doctrines within the traditions of liberalism and socialism respectively (and both deeply influenced by syndicalist ideas), later proponents, such as Calogero and Aldo Capitini, aimed to develop a more systematic theoretical framework as the basis to the Partito d'Azione (Action Party), the left-liberal anti-fascist party formed in 1942. Let us consider each in turn.

Piero Gobetti

Piero Gobetti (1901–26) was a Turinese intellectual and radical liberal.[3] He died tragically young following a beating by Mussolini's fascists but had already developed a distinctive liberal anti-fascism in the 1920s (see Vanek, 1965; Urbinati, 2000: xv–lvi). Whilst no socialist, Gobetti's liberalism – which he styled 'revolutionary liberalism' in his newspaper of that name – approached revolutionary socialist activities with an inclusive liberal ethic. This later earned him the appellation 'liberal-communist' (see Revelli, 1994). For Gobetti, Italy's political unification in the 1860s had failed to produce a dynamic liberal society centred on the value of liberty. It was necessary, therefore, for the proletariat to complete this task.

Gobetti's contribution to the formation of liberal socialism lies in three central and related themes in his work: his redefinition of liberalism as an emancipatory ethic not strictly attached to the bourgeois class or the free market; his sympathies with the workers' movement as the contemporary liberal agency able to bring about a new order along with its own distinct class of leaders; and the role of anti-fascism in announcing a definitive break with the past. Whilst there are difficulties in uniting these elements together, Gobetti's work nevertheless stands as a touchstone for many later liberal socialists who, though differing in style and emphasis, continued to deploy his themes. It is to these themes that we now turn.

The 'heretical' character of Gobetti's liberalism stems from his disassociation of liberal values (for example, individual liberty, autonomy, self-realisation) from the bourgeoisie and the institutional separation of private and public spheres. Liberalism was understood by Gobetti not as a juridical or constitutional set of arrangements but as an ethical outlook, a 'faith' based on a conception of liberty as self-emancipation (see Gobetti, 1919a). This libertarian outlook was premised on a philosophy that repudiated any transcendent point of view that might lock human subjects into a predetermined schema and block what he called the 'vivifying potency of the spirit' (Ibid.: 76). Gobetti derived his philosophy in great measure from the humanist idealism of Benedetto Croce. Croce had set out to construct a 'historicist' or immanentist philosophy that would serve as a cultural and moral foundation for Italian society. There were, he argued, no moral or epistemological truths outside of the particular conceptions constructed by individuals within history.[4] This should not lead to a total relativism or nihilism but ought to encourage individuals to find their own sense of purpose and moral value in the circumstances they confront individually. History was the ceaseless creativity of humans, irreducible to the outworking of some 'higher' rationality or law-like process. Croce's historicism encouraged others to reject preconceived notions of historical development and to draw faith from the ability of human subjects to creatively mould the world around their own designs and in the face of their own specific dilemmas.

Croce's philosophy led him to a moderate, often conservative liberalism that separated off cultural and moral questions from those of politics and the state (see Bellamy, 1991). However, his followers were less restrained in their adoption of his 'austere' humanism and regarded his emphasis on creativity as having more directly political implications. In the first two decades of the century, historicism was joined to a radical, sometimes 'anti-rationalist' agenda amongst young intellectuals eager to promote cultural and political renewal and so generate a more cohesive and robust civil life (see Jacobitti, 1981; see also Roberts, 1981). In the years immediately following the First World War, Gobetti identified with the call for cultural renewal inspired by Croce and his followers, particularly the romanticist editor of *La Voce*, Giuseppe Prezzolini (see Bagnoli, 1984: 35–45; Bobbio, 1986: ch. 2). Gobetti was later to describe his own vision as a form of 'Protestantism', a new creed that would reshape the individual's relation to the rest of society (see Gobetti, 1925). Yet, unlike Croce and Prezzolini, Gobetti's demand for cultural renewal was always directly linked to political reform (see Gobetti, 1919b). He was deeply influenced by the criticism of the liberal state led by the socialist historian Gaetano Salvemini (see Bobbio, 1995: 86–90). Salvemini called for democratic reform to be initiated outside the official party system, which he regarded as entirely discredited, and this chimed with Gobetti's sense that cultural and political renewal must come from the wider society.

The content of Gobetti's liberalism was more inspired by his economics tutor at college, Luigi Einaudi, than by Croce. This is especially visible in Gobetti's emphasis on conflict as a source of historical progress. Like Salvemini, Einaudi was a trenchant critic of the liberal regime's political system, with its compromises and efforts to absorb potential enemies in order to offset social conflict (see Bobbio, 1995: 81–6). A free-market liberal, Einaudi identified in the open clash of economic interests the dynamic that built strong economies and disciplined social groups. Gobetti's liberalism drew from Einaudi's view of the progressive role of conflict and free play of social forces (Gobetti, 1922c). The Italian bourgeoisie had failed to permit conflict to run its course by parasitically attaching itself to the state and forging compromises in parliament to diminish conflict. Unlike Einaudi, Gobetti did not regard the proper role of the state as consisting in a 'neutrality' over and above conflicting social forces. On the contrary, the outcomes of conflict were new forms to embody the demand for liberty, and these operated within the 'public' as well as the 'private' sphere. Thus even Marxism could be conceived as a liberal doctrine in so far as it inspired workers to 'create history' and formulate a new sense of group autonomy (see Gobetti, 1924a; Bagnoli, 1984: 97–9).[5]

Gobetti's sympathies with the workers' movement and his argument that they embodied a new liberal sensibility stem from his experience of the famous Turin factory council struggles and his contact with their intellectual leader, Antonio Gramsci.[6] The factory council struggles of 1919–20 involved workers taking over the operation and management of the factories. Gramsci argued that this form of protest prefigured a whole new type of participatory workers' state centred on the production process and he expounded a novel theory of workers' democracy that contrasted with the reformism of the trade union movement and the Socialist Party.[7] Gobetti was profoundly inspired by the movement and Gramsci's argument that it could be conceived as a new form of state akin to the soviets in Russia. Like many young intellectuals, Gobetti had been deeply influenced by, and was sympathetic to, the Russian revolution. Similarly to Gramsci, he saw the factory council as the basis for a new type of autonomous worker and citizen; self-management of the factories appeared to produce a new psychology that disciplined workers and raised their awareness of their collective responsibilities. For Gramsci, these features were best understood as a new form of state; for Gobetti, by contrast, they indicated the proletariat's role in supplying new national leaders, or what he called a new 'aristocracy' (see Sbarberi, 1999: esp. 41–7). Following Gaetano Mosca, Gobetti argued that classes were the breeding ground for an elite to guide society with a distinctive programme of reform and to disseminate a new culture and ethic. With the historic failure of the bourgeoisie in Italy, this task had now fallen to the workers (see Gobetti, 1922a and 1922b).

The failure of the factory council movement following the defeat of the occupations in September 1920 signalled the end of working-class militancy and the beginning of full-scale fascist reaction in Italy. For Gobetti, the change in political atmosphere required a new kind of campaign, one aimed at a longer-term cultural transformation. Following his obligatory military service, in 1922 he began editing a new review, *La Rivoluzione liberale* (Liberal Revolution), with the express purpose of encouraging the formation of a new political class able to bring the wider populous into the state (see Bagnoli, 1984: 23). To enable this, he published analyses of the character of political forces in contemporary Italy and undertook a critical examination of Italy's historical legacies.[8]

Gobetti started to develop his own theoretical critique of fascism, understood as a dangerous threat to social and political freedom and therefore to be opposed vigorously. In his analysis, fascism did not represent a break from the old post-Risorgimento order but a deformed legacy of it. It was strictly continuous with the regime's longstanding tendency to avoid conflict, to erase autonomous political struggles rather than let them openly challenge and transform society (Gobetti, 1924b). Fascism, he argued, was the 'autobiography of a nation'; that is, it contained within it the dismal story of Italian social and political life since unification (Gobetti, 1924c: 213). 'The true contrast', he argued, was not between freedom and dictatorship but 'between freedom and unanimity' (Gobetti, 1924b: 227). The liberal ethic, embodied in the conflicts and clashes of ideals between classes, was always threatened by the conservatism of the ruling bourgeois class; fascism merely followed its logic to a greater extreme. Thus Gobetti's anti-fascism sought to distinguish, not between liberal and authoritarian regimes but between those forces that promoted the expansion of liberty and those that sought to crush it. Under this classification, socialism (of the radical 'autonomist' variety witnessed in the factory council struggles) lay within the remit of revolutionary liberalism.

It has been widely noted by Italian scholars that Gobetti's ideas do not add up to a concrete programme of political action. Gobetti was interested neither in practical questions of organisation nor in elaborating a political theory focused on the internal workings of institutions (see Revelli, 1994). His ideas remain abstractly 'intellectual', undeveloped, somewhat pessimistic and more of an 'inspirational' character than directly instructive. Various questions arise as to how the elements of his thought fit together. In particular, his identification of the workers' struggles in Turin as the embodiment of the demand for liberty was at odds with the movement's own aspiration to develop an integrated socialist order based on rationalised production. Gobetti's emphasis lay on the independence of the councils from the wider socialist movement and not on the vision of an 'organic' state that Gramsci proposed.[9] As Vanek points out, Gobetti was essentially a liberal in his outlook and his attachment to the revolutionary workers' movement was always from the perspective of a libertarian (see Vanek, 1965). His emphasis was on liberty conceived as an ethical disposition, not on equality as such.

If Gobetti was not, strictly-speaking, a liberal socialist, he was nevertheless a crucial precursor to its proponents. In particular, his conception of liberalism as an ethical disposition, the opening this permitted him to the workers' movement and the role of anti-fascism in aligning the two, are key components in later liberal socialist discourse.

Carlo Rosselli

Carlo Rosselli (1899–1937) was the first proponent in Italy of a distinctive theory labelled 'liberal socialism'. His book, *Socialismo liberale*, was written in 1929 during enforced internal exile by the fascists and was first published the following year in France (and in French) after his escape.[10] A politically active anti-fascist, Rosselli succeeded in bringing together a number of intellectuals and militants in a series of campaigns both in Italy, France and, with the outbreak of civil war, Spain. He was co-founder of the movement (and journal) *Giustizia e libertà* (Justice and Liberty), which organised its own brigades in the anti-fascist war in Italy in 1943–45 and which was at the root of the Partito d'Azione. Rosselli, however, was brutally murdered with his brother in France in 1937 at the behest of Mussolini (see Bourdrel, 1970: 213–15).

In *Liberal Socialism*, Rosselli laid out the analytical framework for what he called an 'ideological renewal' of socialism in the context of a major 'intellectual crisis' for the left (Rosselli, 1994: 3). Liberal socialism, he argued, was the general form that European social democratic and socialist parties were currently adopting and whose basic principles he sought to make explicit (Ibid.: 83–4). Socialism was *heir* to the legacy of liberalism, not its antagonist. Increasingly, social conditions had permitted the workers' movement and socialists to take up the defence of individual liberty but on a wider scale than had the bourgeoisie. Socialism, he argued, is a philosophy of liberty extended to all individuals, not a privileged sector of society. The task at hand, he suggested, was to adapt socialist thought to the new realities of the twentieth century by making explicit its relationship with liberalism.

Rosselli devoted considerable space to attacking Marxism as both an intellectually inadequate and practically insufficient doctrine that had rendered socialists unable to properly rise to the challenges of the new century.[11] Here he was directly influenced by Hendrik de Man's *The Psychology of Socialism*, which castigated Marxism for its failure to grasp the role of values in human conduct. Thus, for Rosselli, Marxism was a deterministic doctrine that vastly overstated the importance of economic factors in historical development. Marx had much of value to offer socialism, in particular a realistic understanding of social change, but his legacy was a mechanically materialist and reductionist doctrine that failed properly to understand the role of 'human will' in political struggle.[12] By subsuming all social phenomena within the contradictions between the forces and relations of production, Marx understood politics only in terms of class struggle. This was itself merely an extension of capitalism's *homo oeconomicus* (Ibid.: 76). Marxist thought, by consequence, had left socialism bereft of its own ethical framework and with a tendency to doctrinaire and messianic proclamations but little in the way of practical political engagement with the working masses (Ibid.: 48). The revisionist debate at the turn of the century, he argued, had initiated an important break with the semi-religious worship of Marx's teachings and imported a long-needed critical spirit into Marxist discussion. But the revisionists had not gone far enough: realising that their critique of Marxism implied that socialism was not a necessary outcome of historical development, they quickly retreated in order to retain their support of the workers' movement (Ibid.: 58–9, 31–2).

Now, however, it was time, in de Man's phrase, to 'overcome' Marxism. Social conditions were such that its core beliefs and arguments were simply anachronistic (Ibid.: 54). The greater organisation of the workers within trade unions, their engagement with practical problems of governance, the extension of the franchise, the growing influence in parliament by workers parties and a 'more rational', less anarchic, form of capitalism rendered Marxism's hostility to the bourgeois world much less compelling (see Ibid.: 64–77, 92). It was possible now to envisage a peaceful transition to socialism in a way that Marx could not (Ibid.: 67). Socialists therefore required a doctrine – an injection of ethics'(Ibid.: 77) – that permitted them to confront practical problems, to win support from a wider constituency than their own class, to replace the bourgeoisie as the protagonists of a new civilisation. This, he believed, was why socialism must take up the legacy bequeathed by liberalism.

Like the other 'planists' outlined in Chapter 1,[13] therefore, Rosselli articulated a form of socialism that, through a fusion with the values of liberalism, offered a mode of transition to socialism from within the capitalist system. However, Rosselli's explication of the principles of liberal socialism was indicative rather than detailed. Liberalism was defined as an ethical attitude, a set of values or 'faith' focused on the principle of individual liberty.

> Liberalism . . . takes the inner freedom of the human spirit as a given and adopts liberty as the ultimate goal, but also the ultimate means, of shared human life. The goal is to arrive at a condition of social life in which each individual is certain of being able to develop his own personality fully (Ibid.: 85).

Liberalism was not, therefore, a fixed set of political or economic institutional arrangements but an evolving value system. It was 'historicist and relativistic', being endlessly refashioned in different historical circumstances; an 'eternal becoming and overcoming' (Ibid.: 87). All forces that sought to transcend the present circumstances could be liberal in that sense. Thus the proletariat was liberal in so far as its cause was essentially one of freeing individuals from the constraints of the present (Ibid.: 89; see also 91). The bourgeoisie no longer represented a liberal force (Ibid.: 87). Its conception of liberty had become fixed and stale; it no longer expressed the principle of liberty but rather a spirit of conservatism and reaction.

Socialism, on the other hand, sought to extend liberty to all. The socialist demand for social justice and equality was not merely some levelling principle; rather, it aimed to eradicate the constraints on individual self-realisation imposed by the iniquities of capitalism:

> Socialism is not socialization; it is not the proletariat in power; it is not even material equality. Socialism, grasped in its essential aspect, is the progressive actualisation of the idea of liberty and justice among men (Ibid.: 78).

The individual, he pointed out, was the basic unit of society, this latter designating 'an aggregate of individualities' (Ibid.: 79). The liberal recognition of the individual permitted socialists to fashion a new civility that respected individual rights and difference. This had vital implications for the manner in which a socialist politics was conducted. Whereas for Marxist socialists the end (socialism) was everything and the means (revolution) of merely instrumental significance, for liberal socialists the 'means must not only suit the end . . . it must also be permeated by it' (Ibid.: 81).[14] The liberal emphasis on constitutional 'rules of the game', on toleration and dissent can allow socialist practices to be informed by liberal and democratic principles in such a way that the new society can be harvested from within the struggle to change the old.

Rosselli said little in depth about economic arrangements under a liberal type of socialism but he did indicate the possible plurality of forms including markets, state nationalisation, guild- and union-led associationalism. No one type of economic organisation, he argued, could exhaust the principle of liberty (Ibid.: 124–5). Rosselli's revisionist view of capitalism meant he did not oppose socialist collectivism to capitalism: private property, he suggested, need not be entirely abolished but it must lose its hegemonic position. Indeed, from the point of view of production, capitalist and socialist 'rationalized' industry did not differ starkly (Ibid.: 67). What difference there was lay primarily in the sphere of distribution and 'morality'. The evidence from Russia, he pointed out, undermined any utopian ingenuousness about politically directed economies. Soviet statism, with its bureaucratic and authoritarian tendencies, had shown the danger of a single vision of a socialist society (Ibid.: 69). However, modern socialism's 'liberal' character lay not in its practical programme but in its character as a movement; that is, its ongoing application of universal moral principles to reality. For Rosselli, the best example of such a movement was the British Labour Party, with its various associated membership, lack of ideological rigidity, 'typically English empirical mentality' and 'love' for 'concrete problems' (see Ibid.: 121, 127–8).

Fascism, argued Rosselli, had created the conditions for Italians to move beyond their historical disregard for liberal values. Invoking Gobetti's characterisation of fascism as the 'autobiography of the nation', he claimed the political system had been constructed on compromise not moral values. Mussolini represented the return to a monarchical rule that, eventually, would force Italians to grasp the 'myth' of liberty and forge themselves into a modern liberal nation. The Italian revolution, he claimed, would be a liberal revolution.

Guido Calogero

Perhaps the most sophisticated attempt to define liberal socialism in Italy was undertaken by the philosopher Guido Calogero (1904–86).

Building on the ideas of Rosselli, Calogero coined the term *liberal-socialismo* (or 'liberalsocialism') to define the unity of liberalism and socialism rather than the conjunction of two separate components implied in *socialismo liberale*. Both Calogero and Capitini were founding members of the Partito d'Azione and sought to make liberalsocialism its doctrine.[15] Calogero also explicitly defended liberalsocialism as a third way doctrine, arguing that it represented a new ideological programme for a 'post-fascist' order.

Calogero belonged to a generation of Italian intellectuals who, as he recorded himself, became inspired by anti-fascism as the regime declined in the late 1930s.[16] Both he and Capitini responded to a 'spiritual crisis' amongst young intellectuals who felt profoundly alienated from Mussolini's war in Ethiopia in 1935–36 and the 'race laws' of 1938. In the late 1930s, as teachers at the University of Pisa, Calogero and Capitini set out philosophical principles for a renewed spiritual life based on the idea of man as a moral subject. In this they were greatly inspired by Croce's defence of liberal values in the late 1920s and 30s, which outlined liberalism not as a political ideology but as a 'total conception of history', that is, as the principle that historical progress depended on the free initiative of autonomous, human creativity. Ideals that fitted this principle, such as those of liberalism, would enable an increase in freedom whilst those that did not (in Croce's view, communism and fascism) were authoritarian. Croce's philosophical defence of liberalism presented it as a civil ideal, or lay religion, to reconcile individuals to their historical circumstances.[17] Later generations of intellectuals, however, took it as the basis of a humanistic revolt against fascism in favour of restoring political liberty, uniting individual and collectivity in a single moral framework with freedom at its core.[18]

Capitini had developed an openly religious outlook based on Christian principles. Calogero, however, sought to develop what Bagnoli calls a 'civil doctrine' based on idealist philosophy, particularly the 'actual idealism' of Giovanni Gentile (Bagnoli, 1996: 156–7).[19] Drawing on Christian personalism, Calogero argued that moral doctrines involved self-abnegation. The onus on altruism made morality a matter of deeply internal motivation rather than the recognition of external, 'transcendental' principles. It was this subjectivism that Calogero brought to his conception of liberalsocialism in the early 1940s.

The central thread of liberalsocialism was the identity of liberty and social justice. For liberty to be conceived as a shared moral good it had to be combined with social justice, that is, by definition it had to be a shared liberty. Socialism and liberalism conceptually converged at this ethical juncture. As Calogero put it in the 'First Manifesto of Liberal-socialism' in 1940:

> At the basis of liberalsocialism stands the concept of the substantial unity and identity of ideal reason which supports and justifies socialism in its demand for justice as much as it does liberalism in its demand for liberty. This ideal reason coincides with that same ethical principle to whose rule humanity and civilization, both past and future, must always measure up. This is the principle by which we recognize the personhood of others in contrast to our own person and assign to each of them a right equal to our own (Calogero, 1940: 199).

Considered alone, liberalism conceives of liberty without justice, whilst socialism promotes justice but without individual liberty. These were precisely the failings of pre-fascist liberalism, Marxist socialism and communism. Properly conceived as a unity, however, 'liberal-socialism' conjoins liberty and equality as an autonomous ethical ideal with none of the issues of which term qualifies which other. As an ethical principle, rather than merely a pragmatic compromise between separate systems of thought, liberalsocialism had a normative force consonant with Calogero's earlier work on self-abnegation as the essence of morality. Conceived as a moral ideal, individual liberty could not be rationally conceived except in terms of a value for others whose liberty, therefore, one must also will: 'The political liberty to which every true democrat aspires is always his liberty measured up to the liberty of others, it is not a personal liberty but a universal one, it is a liberty for everyone. It is, to put it another way, a *social liberty*' (Calogero, 1944b: 79). As such, liberty and justice were conceptually inseparable.

Calogero defended liberalsocialism as a coherent and autonomous political philosophy based on sound ethical principles. In so doing, he distinguished liberalsocialism from Rosselli's liberal socialism (see Calogero, 1944c: 67–70). The latter, he argued, had laid the foundations for the doctrine but had aimed primarily at unifying the anti-fascist movement. By consequence, he had not adequately synthesised its conceptual components. Indeed, Rosselli had only succeeded in defending a liberalsocialist economic order based on the idea of 'two sectors', collectivist and market-based, which owed much to Hendrik de Man. This was not, however, a 'true and proper liberalsocialist ideology'(Ibid.: 69). To achieve this required a 'logical integration' of liberalism and socialism such that liberty and justice were conceived as being identical. It was this ethical unity that truly distinguished liberalsocialism from its conservative liberal and Marxist socialist precursors as a new and genuinely democratic ideology. Whereas these other ideologies have compromised with democratic ideals in order to achieve their (one-sided) goals (that is, *either* individual liberty *or* social justice) and, as a consequence, will eventually reach a crossroads at which they will resume their 'normal', one-sided path, liberalsocialism chooses 'a third way: the way of the union, coincidence and indissoluble co-presence of justice and liberty'(Calogero, 1944b: 77). Liberalsocialism's third way accepts democratic values without qualification; it constitutes a 'new and coherent synthesis' of the liberal and socialist traditions that will serve as the basis for a new republic.

In his two manifestoes for liberalsocialism Calogero laid out what he saw as the guiding principles and political programme of the new *Partito d'Azione* (see Calogero, 1940 and 1941). In each manifesto liberal political institutions aimed at defending rights were combined with arrangements designed to promote social justice. They included a democratic republican constitution guaranteeing liberal rights, freedom of the press and the franchise, as well as provisions to ensure commitments from political parties to liberal and democratic principles in order to underwrite party competition free from political and economic privilege. The manifestoes also recommended the collectivisation of certain public goods such as transport, communications and energy, as well as state programmes of reform in education. Large agricultural and industrial enterprises were to be nationalised and forms of collective worker management to be encouraged on the principle of a 'dual economy' (see also Calogero, 1943). Supporting these proposals was a foreign policy based on peace and cooperation between nation states, a rejection of 'nationalism, racism and imperialism' and the extension of economic and political rights on an international scale. Finally, at a domestic level, the new party was to promote a 'Freedom Front' of all parties of liberalism and socialism who wished to see a new democratic republic.

The *Partito d'Azione* brought together a wide variety of radical intellectuals and it played a prominent role in organised anti-fascism and the resistance movement during the civil war period of 1943–45 (see Novelli, 2000). It was also one of the parties of the Committee for

National Liberation that participated in the constituent assembly organised after the war to frame the new constitution for post-war democracy in Italy. However, although the party earned itself a reputation as a defiant anti-fascist organisation and played a key role in constitutional debates, it never achieved the popular support it required to be a major force in post-fascist politics. In part this was because it simply could not compete at an organisational level with hostile communist and Catholic parties who mobilised support through the trade union movement and Catholic Church respectively.[20] In addition, the party itself never fully agreed either what kind of movement it was or what its founding principles should be. Even its supporters, like Norberto Bobbio, regarded Calogero's liberalsocialism as somewhat 'doctrinaire' (Bobbio, 1995: 151). Certainly, Calogero's moralism at times verges on the sanctimonious, exemplified in his claim that liberalsocialism 'is merely a form of practical Christianity, of service to God brought down into reality' (Calogero, 1941: 226).

The religious tone of Calogero's thought stems in part from the secularised Christian personalism he developed in the 1930s. In Sbarberi's view, the influence of Gentilian actualism on his liberal-socialism is visible in the manner in which the altruistic ethic extends from within the subject rather than from between subjects. This produces what Sbarberi regards as a noticeably monistic form of ethical reasoning where the moral value of liberty is 'identical' to, rather than merely balanced with, justice (Sbarberi, 1999: 108–9, 114). Such a view, he argues, contrasts starkly with Gobetti's and Rosselli's pluralism, which identified moral conflict as the source of the progress of liberty.

ANTI-FASCISM AND THE THIRD WAY

At the levels both of conceptual ordering and political engagement, Italian liberal socialist discourse was intrinsically anti-fascist. The fascist regime was both anti-liberal and anti-socialist in so far as it sought to dismantle the organisational form of these ideologies (parliament and trade unions respectively) and recast their elements into a programme that was 'neither left nor right'. By consequence, as Norberto Bobbio points out, for many of its proponents 'anti-fascism as a whole could be neither purely liberal nor purely socialist, but had to be both' (Bobbio, 1995: 147). Their shared antagonism, therefore, was perceived to position liberals and socialists as common enemies of fascism and therefore brought them into the same contested space.

But this does not entirely explain the movement towards conceptual realignment that liberal socialist discourse advanced. To do that requires more than a common awareness of isolation; rather, fascism must be regarded as symbolic of a wider failure of social order such that liberal and socialist identities cannot themselves avoid being transformed by it. In that sense, anti-fascism constituted a discursive frontier that signifies more than mere opposition to a specific author-itarian government (what conservative liberals such as Croce con-ceived as a mere 'parenthesis' in history) (see Roberts, 1987: 226). This points to what Ernesto Laclau has identified as the crucial role of 'antagonism' in the formation of a collective identity (see Laclau, 1990: esp. 17–41). An antagonist is not just a partial limitation on an identity but signifies the impossibility of identity *as such*. The enemy consists in more than just its literal content and indeed symbolises the threat to *all* social order. Thus for liberal socialists fascism was understood to be the highest expression of moral and political degeneracy; it represented the culmination of all the failings of Italian political life: the failure to develop into a modern democracy, to accept political conflict as part of a just order, to eliminate the Machiavellian distinction between force and persuasion as the high arts of politics, and so forth.

Gobetti's comment on fascism as the 'autobiography of the nation' became powerfully emblematic of the liberal socialist view that the regime was more than a temporary diversion; on the contrary, it exemplified the totality of ills to which Italy had been vulnerable for centuries. Faced with the full scale of Italian degeneracy in one regime, an alternative order had to be total in its response (see Bobbio, 1995: 147). Thus the regeneration of a civil order could only be conceived as a revolutionary act (for Gobetti and Rosselli a 'liberal revolution', for Calogero and the *Azionisti* a 'democratic revolution').[21] As such it had to leave behind it the old oppositions and antagonisms whose lack of resolution had paved the way for fascism: namely, Marxist socialism and conservative and free-market liberalism.

Furthermore, liberal socialist anti-fascism was structured around a moral critique of the failures of pre-fascist political culture and institutions. The limitations of these lay principally in their inadequate intellectual and cultural horizons, which oriented them away from liberal values. Thus a new, anti-fascist outlook had to be based not on materialist principles (whether those of the individual or of a class) but, more profoundly, on a renewed spiritual activity, an intellectual and moral reformation at individual and collective levels. Thus liberty was the core of a belief system that functioned like a religion, tying the individual and the community in an indissoluble bond. Gobetti's notion of a new Protestant reformation and Calogero's secular Christian ethic exemplified this view well. Both followed Croce's example in defining liberal values as more than a political ideology; it was a whole belief system able to underwrite a renewed civil order.

Thus a specific kind of moral anti-fascism was key to liberal socialist discourse, despite the evident differences of emphasis and style in the views of its proponents. Fascism negated liberty and, therefore, 'liberty' was the central value of 'revolutionary liberalism', 'liberal socialism' and 'liberalsocialism'. How liberty was expressed varied for each writer, of course: for Gobetti, it was a cultural and political value disseminated by elites; for Rosselli, the issue was more about redefining socialism as political project; and for Calogero, liberty was a moral principle expressed in an ethics of altruism. None of these views automatically overlap or necessitate any of the others; yet by hinging the total reform of Italy as a whole on the extension of the principle of liberty, they enabled, in various ways, a socialised liberalism to present itself as a revolutionary creed able to supplant traditional ideological divisions and, in the case of Calogero, to be presented explicitly as a third way doctrine.

Nevertheless, liberal socialist discourse never crystallised into the political ideology its proponents had hoped it would after the defeat of fascism. There are a number of reasons for this. Principal amongst them must be the general vagueness and indeterminate boundaries of the discourse itself. Moral anti-fascism delineated an ethical terrain between Marxism and traditional liberalism but it left considerable scope for variation. This brought it under fire from traditional liberals, socialists and Marxists for being an unstable, eclectic mix of principles that lent itself to a variety of (sometimes dubious) political positions.

The charge of eclecticism and instability in its principles derives from the 'family resemblance' between the liberal socialist third way and other third way doctrines of the period (that is, with political programmes that defined themselves as alternatives to capitalism and communism). We have already noted in Chapter 1 how third way doctrines all draw on the same repertoire of terms. Each of these terms can be found in the discourse of liberal socialism. This articulated a clear break with the past – earlier political forces having failed to establish the conditions in which freedom could flourish – and was reflected in the claim that liberal socialism was 'revolutionary'. This 'revolution' was to be a spiritual or ethical one. Hence the emphasis on ethical values and spiritual renewal, and the transcendence of class divisions by a renewed moral community. This was to be a national community,[22] albeit a liberal one as opposed to that advocated by fascists, represented by a new state that would balance individualist and collectivist economic systems. Finally, liberal socialism presented itself as the privileged agent of this revolutionary transformation. Liberal socialists typically combined revolutionary zeal with an emphasis on skilled members of the proletariat (Gobetti's 'new aristocracy') as leaders of the wider movement or on an informed elite (Rosselli's anti-fascist vanguard in *Giustizia e libertà*) to bring into effect the revolutionary changes necessary. Liberal socialists believed that a national community was yet to be formed and argued that a 'second Risorgimento' began with an elite who would educate the public and raise it to a new form of civilisation.

The fact that these emphases were shared with other forms of third way discourse explains both the aversion by traditional liberals and socialists and the fact that, despite its intrinsic hostility to fascism, liberal socialist discourse retained certain affinities with variants of fascist ideology. This reflects, perhaps, the 'dark underside' of third way thought (see Pels, 2002). These affinities arose partly because liberal socialists were both contesting and seeking to reconfigure some of the same ideas and notions as were fascists. Thus liberal socialists are often accused of being rather elitist or overly intellectual in their outlook, partly because they tended to assert the need for extending social justice as a point of principle but at a distance from the actual organisations of the working classes. Moreover, although liberal socialists differed from fascists in the type of nation they sought to develop – fascists saw this as a strictly national community, liberal socialists understood it as a liberal nation – for both, however, a Mazzinian conception of revolutionaries forging the national community was central.[23] The emphasis on a new form of integration between individual and community is also a common point of reference. For both fascists and liberal socialists, the materialism of Marxism and liberalism, their supposed reduction of the individual to a form of economic agency, had to be replaced by a more moral or spiritual emphasis on values. The individual self was simultaneously a communal self, inescapably linked to the wider society through its capacity for moral agency. Yet fascists, too, saw themselves as proponents of a cohesive moral order beyond class and egoistic individualism, where the individual would be reconciled with his/

her communal existence *from within* and not exclusively through coercion.

If the family resemblance with more authoritarian discourses (deriving from the common repertoire of third way tropes upon which liberal socialism drew) accounts to some extent for the failure of liberal socialism to hegemonise anti-fascist forces, it is possible, also, that the centrality of anti-fascism explains its failure to develop into a 'mass' political ideology after the war. After 1945 anti-fascism no longer united the political parties of the Resistance. War-time unity rapidly gave way to peace-time disagreement over the nature of the constitution, the type of reforms to be enacted, and so on. The Cold War antagonism between 'East' and 'West' soon supplanted anti-fascism, forcing it to compete with the virulent anti-communism of the Catholic Church and ruling Christian Democrats. Consequently, anti-fascism was reduced to a nostalgic ideology and an intransigent 'spirit' of the Resistance that would return intermittently on the left in the following decades.[24] Only in recent years, as the Cold War itself dissolved and the question of political reform of Italy's corrupt state and society emerged, has the significance of anti-fascism and the liberal socialist tradition returned to political and philosophical debate (see, for example, Rusconi, 1995 and Bosetti, 1989).

CONCLUSION

Antagonism, explains Laclau, refers us to the intrinsic negativity of identity, the way what we 'are' is founded upon an exclusion of what we 'are not'. It also highlights the contingency of shared identities, that is, the way they are bound to specific historical conditions despite their claim to embody 'universal' principles (Laclau, 1990: 18–21). We have argued that anti-fascism tells us much about the character of liberal socialist discourse in inter-war Italy. That antagonism radicalised liberalism, enabling an ethic of liberty that, in principle, could be extended to socialist thought and practice and that underscored a revolutionary politics. The anti-fascist frontier marked a radical rupture with traditional ideological formations and placed liberal socialist discourse in a similar space to many third way ideas of the inter-war period. Yet occupying that space also marked out its weakness: namely, its attachment to a moral critique, inspirational to politically committed intellectuals but with little popular force beyond its own historical conditions. Contemporary third way theorists, who, by contrast, have been accused of promoting an illusory 'politics without adversary' (see Mouffe, 2000: ch. 5) – that is, a limitless ethical inclusivity without a clear antagonist – are yet to learn that the price of genuine political engagement is, eventually, the uncomfortable realisation of the limits, and therefore historicity, of discourse.

NOTES

1 Thus Virgilio Mura has defined the 'common element' of the liberal socialist 'general field of reference' as 'the combination of principles based on a *non-free-market liberalism* with principles based on a *non-Marxist socialism*' (Mura, 1994: 13) (italics in original).

2 A point made famous by Gramsci but also shared by Gobetti. For a brief comparison, see Bellamy (2001: 265–9).

3 For biographical details, see Bagnoli (1984: ch. 1) and Bobbio (1986: ch. 1).

4 Our understanding of Croce's ideas has been greatly influenced by Roberts (1987) and Bellamy (1991, 1985).

5 On the significance of conflict in Gobetti's liberalism, see Urbinati (2000).

6 For comparative analyses of Gramsci and Gobetti, see Spriano (1977) and Sbarberi (1999: ch. 1).

7 On the factory council struggles and Gramsci's theory of them, see Schecter (1991). Gramsci's views are collected in Gramsci (1997).

8 Gobetti collected and reissued his articles from this period in book form in 1924. See the recent republication (Gobetti, 1995) and the excerpts in Gobetti (2000).

9 On the illiberal connotations of Gramsci's conception of the factory council, see Schecter (1990) and Sbarberi (1986).

10 See Rosselli (1997), English trans. Rosselli (1994). The French first edition of the book is *Socialisme libéral*, trans. Stefan Priacel (Paris: Librairie Valois, 1930). For Rosselli's biography, see Pugliese (1999).

11 The first five out of the eight chapters of *Liberal Socialism* are devoted to the critique of Marxism.

12 Besides the obvious influence of de Man in Rosselli's critique of Marxism, there are also strong parallels here with the new liberal critique of what Hobhouse labelled 'Mechanical Socialism' (see Clarke, 1978: 65).

13 Rosselli participated in the first international plan conference in mid-September 1934 at the Abbaye de Pontigny in France, alongside de Man and a host of French planists such as Laurat, Belin, Robert Lacoste, André Philip (Horn, 2001: 248–9).

14 Again clear parallels can be drawn on this point with the new liberals, who argued that the end of a more progressive, democratic society could not be divorced from the means for realising it, and hence castigated Fabian socialists such as the Webbs for their opportunism (see, for example, Clarke, 1978: 143–5).

15 For an account of the development of Capitini's and Calogero's views, see Bagnoli (1996: 153–76).

16 For his own record of the origins of liberalsocialismo, see Calogero (1944a).

17 Croce's later views on liberalism are well represented by his essay 'Liberalism as a Concept of Life' in *Ethics and Politics* (1946). On Croce's liberalism, see in particular Bellamy (1985, 1992: 140–56) and Roberts (1987: ch. 5).

18 As Calogero put it himself, when talking of Croce's influence on young intellectuals in the 1930s: 'From him they learned to love liberty, not just as an egoistic right of privilege but as the duty to achieve an ever more ambitious liberation of men from any force of bondage' (Calogero 1944a: 192).

19 For an assessment of the influence of Gentilian actualism on Calogero's thought, see Sbarberi (1999: 78–114, particularly 78–93).

20 For a discussion of the origins of hostility from the left, see Pugliese (1999: 155–64).

21 Claudio Novelli (2000: ch. 1) argues that the otherwise disparate intellectual strands of the Partito d'Azione were unified primarily by the view that fascism was symptomatic of Italy's general cultural and political failings.

22 Indeed, in the 1930s Rosselli had himself endorsed the views of the French neo-socialist leader, Marcel Déat, in his emphasis on the nation as the terrain of struggle upon which contemporary socialists should fight (see Rosselli, 1933; on this episode, see Pugliese, 1999: 142–50).

23 On the Mazzinian notion of an enlightened elite educating the people into a new national consciousness and its influence on fascism, see Gentile (1982: esp. 3–29).

24 On the shifting meanings of anti-fascism and anti-communism, see Lepre (1997). On the role of the Resistance in left discourse in Italy, see Gundle (2000).

CHAPTER 4
NEO-FASCISM AND THE THIRD WAY

Fascism is far from being a homogeneous ideology. The very difficulties that have beset attempts to define a 'generic fascism' testify to the extraordinary heterogeneity of fascist discourse (see, *inter alia*, Payne, 1980; Griffin, 1991: 1–55; Griffin, 1995; Thurlow, 1999). It has long been accepted, however, that fascism constitutes a third way discourse. For example, the scholar George Mosse claims that fascism was 'a revolution attempting to find a "Third Way" between Marxism and capitalism, but still seeking to escape concrete economic and social change by a retreat into ideology: the "revolution of the spirit" of which Mussolini spoke, or Hitler's "German revolution"' (Mosse, 1979, cited in Griffin, 1998: 145; see also Mosse, 1999: 7). Likewise Ze'ev Sternhell argues that fascism consists in an ideological synthesis of nationalism and socialism, exemplified in the formula 'nationalism + socialism = fascism' (Sternhell, 1976: 333).[1] For him, fascism was an anti-materialist revolt, rejecting 'the rationalist content of liberalism and Marxism' and opening the way for the development of 'a third revolutionary option between liberalism and Marxism' (Sternhell, 2000: 150). Indeed, the very title of Sternhell's analysis of fascism in inter-war France, *Ni droite, ni gauche* (Neither Right, Nor Left), exemplifies his understanding of fascism as a third way discourse (Sternhell, 1983).

It seems clear, then, that the variety of 'fascisms' of the inter-war period articulated different versions of a third way discourse. However, it does not logically follow that all neo-fascist movements of the *post-war* period constitute third ways.[2] Moreover, even if they do, these are not necessarily the same kinds of third way found in the inter-war period. The complexity of this issue is shown by the fact that

attempts to define fascism in the post-war period have led to definitions so broad that they encompass a wide variety of sub-groups. A
first question to be asked, therefore, concerns the extent to which post-
war neo-fascism, in all its rich varieties, can be claimed to be a third
way discourse. The second question concerns the types of discourse
they are.

The variations in post-war neo-fascism stem from its responses to
very different social, economic and political conditions than those of
the inter-war years. Not the least of these was the obvious fact that the
actions of the Nazi regime had brought the extreme right of all stripes
into disrepute. Beyond this, however, a number of other factors played
a key role in the transformation of post-war fascism: notably, the
sedimentation of liberal democracy in the aftermath of the Allied
victory and through the emergence of the Cold War; the strong levels
of economic growth and related general affluence that characterised
the first decades after the war; and the process of decolonisation and
turn away from militaristic forms of imperialism, which fed into a
demilitarisation of society. Such changes fed into the development of
new variants of fascism, although crude reproductions of inter-war
varieties could still be found.

More recently, further shifts in the European social, economic and
political context have sparked a new set of developments. As we noted
in Chapter 1, and again in the discussion of New Labour, these relate
to a generalised crisis of left and right ideology as it developed in the
post-war period, which, in turn, is connected to: the crisis of the
regulatory capacity of the nation-state; a series of dislocations in
identity; a generalised distrust of 'grand narratives'; the ever-increas-
ing commodification of all aspects of social life; and a disillusionment
with mainstream politics – seen as increasingly disconnected from
peoples' everyday lives. These shifts have fed into a further transformation of neo-fascism. This is partly reflected in the emergence of
claims that a new extreme right has emerged, variously labelled radical
right-wing populists, radical right populists, the post-industrial extreme right, or even ethno-liberals (Betz, 1994; Kitschelt, 1998; Ignazi,
1992, 1997; Griffin, 2000), but it is also reflected in developments
within the more anti-systemic variant of neo-fascism that is the radical
right.[3]

This chapter focuses on both the 'radical right', whose rejection
of the 'system' extends to a refusal to participate in the electoral
process, and the vision of the so-called 'extreme right', which accepts
electoral participation but which is nevertheless often classified

amongst post-war fascism not only by its political opponents but also by a number of academics.[4] Analysis of French and Belgian radical right ideologies reveals a number of distinctive, though competing, forms of third way. This is followed by the argument that recent successes by the French extreme right have been a product of a greater degree of fluidity in its ideological composition.

WHICH NEO-FASCISM?

Before turning to examine radical right variants of neo-fascism, we need to identify precisely which variants we are concerned with. Here we face a problem: namely, the absence of any agreement on subgroup divisions. Griffin, for example, distinguishes between the following: 'Nostalgic Fascism/ Neo-Nazism' (for example, the Italian Social Movement (MSI), Mosley's Union Movement); 'Mimetic Fascism/ Neo-Nazism' (for example, the British Movement, the Belgian *Vlaams Blok*); and 'Neo-fascism', which he further subdivides into: 'Revolutionary nationalists', who propose a 'third position' fascism, such as the French student movement *Groupe Union Défense* (GUD); 'Crypto-fascists', who offer a 'latent ultra-nationalism' (for example, the German National Democratic Party (NPD), the German Republikaner Party (REP) and the Austrian Freedom Party (FPÖ)); Holocaust-deniers or 'Revisionists'; and 'Conservative revolutionaries' (for example, the French and Italian New Right) (Griffin, 1991: 162–6; see also Eatwell, 1996).[5]

Writing about France, Rossi divides neo-fascism into: exclusivist nationalists (for example, *L'Œuvre française* (OF)); ethno-differentialist revolutionary nationalism (for example, *Troisième voie* (TV), the *Groupement de Recherche et d'Etudes pour la Civilisation Européenne* (GRECE), the *Groupe Union Défense* (GUD), *Nouvelle Résistance* (NR) and the Belgian *Parti Communautaire National-européen* (PCN)); supremacist racialist nationalism (for example, the *Fédération d'Action Nationale et Européenne* (FANE) and the *Faisceaux Nationalistes Européens-Parti Nationaliste Français et Européen* (FNE-PNFE)) (Rossi, 1995: 97).

Camus, on the other hand, regards the elements united by Rossi under the umbrella term of ethno-differentialist revolutionary nationalism as separate, and distinguishes between the 'nouvelle droite' (GRECE), solidarism (for example, TV) and national revolutionaries (for example, NR), dividing the remainder into neo-fascists, neo-Nazis and Holocaust-deniers (Camus, 1998; see also Camus and Monzat, 1992).

Given the high degree of interaction in terms of personnel, and the overlaps in ideology, Rossi's taxonomy seems most appropriate for outlining the various threads of the radical right. Regarding the ethno-differentialist nationalist revolutionaries, for example, groupings such as GUD, the more wide-ranging political movements stemming from a tradition labelled, alternatively, 'solidarist', 'tercerist', 'national revolutionary' or even 'national communist', as well as the so-called French 'new right', whose main element is GRECE, have a high degree of ideological continuity. The discourses of solidarist movements and that of GUD are very similar (see Jeunes contre le racisme en Europe (JRE), n.d.: 5). In turn, these are also quite closely linked with the ideas of GRECE, or certainly with those ideas propounded in the early 1960s by such people as Dominic Venner, which eventually fed into the formation of GRECE (see Boutin, 1996), as well as cultural movements such as *Terre et Peuple* (see Flood, 2000). Indeed, Christian Bouchet, the leader of the national revolutionary movement, *Unité Radicale* (UR), argues that the ideology of UR and of historical solidarist groups, such as the *Groupe Action Jeunesse* (GAJ), the *Mouvement National Révolutionnaire* (MNR) and TV is 'the same thing', and suggests that terms such as 'solidarisme', 'tercerisme' and 'national-bolchevisme' describe the same national revolutionary ideology. He also claims 'an uninterrupted organisational continuity from GAJ to UR via the MNR, Troisième Voie and Nouvelle Résistance'.[6]

Adopting Rossi's taxonomy, in this chapter we describe the third way discourse of two of the ideological formations he identifies – 'ethno-differentialist revolutionary nationalism' and 'exclusivist nationalism' – on the premise that supremacist racialist nationalism adds little or nothing to the third way discourse of inter-war fascism. The former will be investigated through an analysis of a number of the French groupings mentioned above, together with the national-communitarianism associated with the work of Belgian radical right activist, Jean Thiriart.[7] The latter will be investigated through an analysis of the French groups, the OF and *Jeune Nation* (henceforth JN).[8]

As we shall see, there exist a number of commonalities between these two groupings. The differences between them emanate from what appear minor, but are in fact significantly contrasting, perspectives on the role of the nation-state in the contemporary world. These similarities and differences will be shown through a focus on the following themes: the rejection of capitalism and communism; anti-

Semitism; anti-colonialism; anti-materialism and the cult of action; the critique of liberal democracy; revolution; and Europeanism versus exclusivist nationalism.

A Third Way Between Capitalism and Communism: Ethnic Rootedness

The crisis proclaimed by neo-fascists is that of a generalised ethnic decline or degeneration whose markers are the triumph of global capitalism, the decline of the nation-state, decolonisation, political corruption, the disempowerment of the 'people' by liberal democracy, and so on. All of these result from the 'fact' that the people of Europe are being squeezed by the rampant materialism of both capitalism and communism.

In the face of this materialism, neo-fascists propose an anti-materialist, or spiritual third way based in ethnic identity. A crucial difference within neo-fascism, however, consists in competing definitions of the roots of this ethnic identity. Exclusivist nationalists, as the name implies, limit rootedness to the characteristics of the French nation. National revolutionaries, on the other hand, locate it in an ethnicity that transcends the nation, incorporating regional and European identities.

The primary signifier in OF discourse is 'integral nationalism' (OF, 1973a).[9] Thus Pierre Sidos argued that 'outside the national framework there is no salvation, nothing serious, nothing useful' (Sidos, 1966; see also Sidos, 1967e). The 'General Proposition' passed at the first Congress of the OF in 1970 called for the installation of 'a nationalist State with all speed' (OF, 1970a, Domestic Policy, point 1). This nationalism proclaims 'a natural community', articulating links with all those rooted in the French nation through blood, a common Celtic ancestry and productive activity. These constitute links in a 'historic chain': 'We are French and our existence only has sense in the framework of our nation . . . Our history begins with the first Celts who implanted themselves on our land' (Le Goff, 1968). Correspondingly, the exclusivist nationalist emphasis on 'Frenchness' led them to call for the uniting of the different elements that make up the francophone family in Europe, suggesting a privileged status to people from the communities concerned (Cantelaube, 1967f; *Le Soleil*, 2–8 August 1967; Plumyène and Lasierra, 1963: 109). The OF affirmed and supported 'the right of separated French people to rejoin the national community' (Cantelaube, 1967a; OF, 1970a, Foreign Policy, point 1), a position it would reaffirm at its second Congress in 1975 (OF, 1975a, point 2). This position is still held by the OF today (see Maillard, 1998a). JN also argue that the nation is rooted in 'natural communities: the Family which brings him up, Work, which nourishes him and the Nation which protects him' (Jeune Nation (JN), n.d.A; see also Benedetti, n.d.A; 2001a). Such a vision is explicitly opposed to the liberal nationalism that underpins republican France (Benedetti, n.d.A; Jeune Nation (JN), n.d.A, section on 'La Patrie, c'est la terre et les morts, c'est le sol').

National revolutionaries also devote much attention to the nation. Like exclusivist nationalists, they focus on the community and reject individualism, claiming to be 'animated by the principles of life in the service of the collectivity' (Malliarakis, 1985: 457), this latter involving elements rooted in blood and soil. However, whilst elements of extreme nationalism can be found in both the national revolutionaries and exclusivist nationalists, the position of the nation in their discourse differs.

The nation acts as the nodal point of exclusivist nationalist discourse. Indeed, from their inception, this exclusivism marked out OF from other fascisms that gave space to the idea of a reunified European 'white race' (see Plumyène and Lasierra, 1963: 206–8). The OF, however, ridiculed the very idea that such a thing as a European identity existed. Conlon, for example, argued that 'giving a national meaning to the word Europe is only pure imagination' (Conlon, 1970; see also Perroux, 1974a). A logical corollary of this anti-Europeanism was a severe hostility to the, then, European Community (see Le Coeur, 1970b; Perroux, 1971, 1972), although this did not prevent Cantelaube from declaring that the OF would form 'economic, military and political alliances with states on the continent which have a nationalist regime, in order to arrive at the union of Europe' (Cantelaube, 1967a). Conlon, too, envisaged France adopting 'a useful and necessary opening' towards Europe, but one which 'does not alter our national independence for that' (Conlon, 1970; OF, 1970a, Foreign Policy, point 3).

The same is true in the discourse of the JN, which rejects the idea that action within the European or regional levels is concomitant with nationalism – our revolutionary fight cannot constitute for itself an alternative homeland, whether it be regional or European. The nation is the only possible social framework for us' (JN, n.d.B) – and is therefore profoundly anti-European Union, and opposed to any form of European federation (Benedetti, 1996). As for the regionalist dimension to neo-fascist action, they argue that whilst 'cultural regionalism is indispensable, for it roots the individual in his earth and in his soil', political regionalism cuts man off 'from his natural domain of expression, the homeland' (Benedetti, n.d.B; n.d.C).

National revolutionaries, on the other hand, specify the nation as only one – albeit a key – focus of action. For them, the third way is a European way; the defence of the race and the nation, and the rejection of globalisation, does not necessitate anti-Europeanism. For states to stand up to the West (that is, the USA), they must join together within Europe, not reject it. Moreover, the peoples of Europe are seen as forming a homogeneous race.

National revolutionary groupings thus support a strong Europe, able to stand up against the superpowers. Although UR rejects the EU as 'the merchant's Europe', it calls instead for the union of the nations of Europe 'in an Empire including Russia'. Only this 'can give Europeans the chance to resist as a political force and as an homogeneous ethnic bloc' (UR, n.d.C; see also Unité Radicale (UR), n.d.A).[10] The PCN also agrees on the need for a European dimension to nationalist revolutionary action, arguing that it is 'no longer possible to rely on France, Germany or Italy alone' (PCN, n.d.B). Although critical of the current form taken by the EU (Parti Communautaire National-européean (PCN), n.d.A), it sees it as having the potential to be transformed in a revolutionary nationalist direction, constructing a European state dedicated to the struggle against American imperialism (Thiriart, n.d.A) and creating an empire from Dublin to Vladivostock (Thiriart, n.d.B).

Exclusivist nationalists are explicit about their difference from national revolutionaries. Their anti-Europeanism and anti-regionalism (in the political sense) fed into a rejection of the position of national revolutionary discourse as early as the 1960s, following the collapse of the *Algérie Française* movement (see, for example, OF, 1967a). The European focus of national revolutionaries, on the other hand, sometimes extends to a relative hostility to nationalism. For example, the PCN condemns 'Left and Right nationalism which divide Europe and are thus consciously or not anti-European', and rejects 'micro-regional nationalisms which are chimerical and noxious to the European cause', although it does favour 'regionalist movements which are capable of getting integrated within the framework of the European Nation' (Thiriart, n.d.B). Nevertheless, the PCN treats Europe as if it were itself a nation, envisaging Europe as 'a unitary nation, a common country' (Parti Communautaire National-européean (PCN), n.d.A).

Whether nationalist or Europeanist, however, neo-fascists all argue that this ethnic rootedness offers an anti-materialist third way between capitalism and communism. The logical corollary of the chain of equivalence articulating their ethnicism is an opposition to those forces deemed to have brought about the crisis of the nation, and thus threaten ethnic identity: capitalism, communism, Zionism (the source of both of the former) and the immigrant. Let us consider each in turn.

Anti-communism

All neo-fascist groups are highly critical of Marxism and communism. Sidos, for example, argued that 'the most fearful enemy of the nationalists, today and tomorrow, internally and externally, remains Marxism in general, and communism in particular' (Sidos, 1967c). The OF claimed that France was increasingly threatened by 'Sovietisation' (see, for example, Sidos, 1967b; Le Coulon, 1970a), a process that extended through to the very practices of the right, de Gaulle and Giscard being described as 'leftists of the right' (Cantelaube, 1967b; Sidos, 1967b; on Giscard, see *Le Soleil*, 15 March 1975). This led to repeated calls for the banning of Marxist organisations in France (see Saint-Julien, 1967a, point 2) and the denunciation of the threat posed worldwide by Soviet expansionism, which sought to spread 'methodically around the globe' (Cantelaube, 1967c). The OF thus declared their support for organisations in countries 'under the yoke of communism' in their struggle to remove the Marxist regime (Cantelaube, 1967a).

The *raison d'être* of the GUD has always been fighting against the left in general, although it has more specifically targeted communists. GUD is notorious for its violent actions against left-wing student organisations (Jeunes contre le racisme en Europe (JRE), n.d.: 8). A joint tract signed by GUD, Jeune Résistance and the Union des Cercles Résistance in 1996 declared that leftist groups active in the universities deserved 'a good punch in the gob' (Haimart, 1998).

Anti-capitalism

Neo-fascists, however, also reject the mainstream political right. This involves a strong critique of capitalism. For exclusivist nationalism, capitalism is 'fundamentally anonymous and countryless', and thus at odds with any communal order (Sidos, 1969). JN criticises the 'internationalist and globalist merchants who today monopolise

Power', whose 'only and unique ambition is to install a new world order able to embrace the widest possible mass of consumers' (Benedetti, 2001a).

UR rejects economic globalisation for causing 'dislocations and unemployment' (Unité Radicale (UR), n.d.A, point 4). They declare: 'The enemy is the system, it is global capitalism!' (Besagne, n.d.). This is a process they link to the actions of 'large financial groups or lobbies', which impose 'decisions which are often contrary to our real interests and reduce our national independence to the meanest share' (UR, n.d.A, point 2). One element of the Cercles Résistance of UR, Résistance ouvrière, claims to be a revolutionary syndicalist labour organisation and calls for the construction of 'a classless society' by eradicating capitalism and commencing 'the construction of a society which abolishes the exploitation of man by man' (Résistance ouvrière, cited in UR, n.d.D).

The critique of global capitalism is closely tied to anti-Americanism (see, for example, Lehner, n.d.). Indeed, the OF often presented the two as synonymous. From the start, the OF adopted a hostile stance regarding America: Jean-Gilles Malliarakis – future national revolutionary but in the 1960s writing for the OF newspaper, *Le Soleil* – criticised the expansion of US capitalism into French territory (Malliarakis, 1966). JN claims that Zionism and American imperialism 'have an economic and cultural form which is united in an expansionism which denies and kills national identities' (Benedetti, n.d.D). National revolutionary groups also roundly criticise the USA. Hence, for example, GUD's statement that Europe 'must refuse to be the 52nd state of America' and their demonstrations against Euro-Disney in 1992 and in 1994 on the theme: 'Welcome to the enemies of Europe, 1944–94: 50 years of American imperialism' (Jeunes contre le racsime en Europe (JRE), n.d.): 8, 17).

National revolutionaries strongly opposed the NATO intervention against Serbia over Kosovo, which they explicitly blamed on the US desire to dominate the globe (see, for example, Hauffen, n.d.). GUD groups in Strasbourg took part in a demonstration organised by Serbs in Strasbourg in March 1999. The Lille branch of GUD took part in 1999 in an anti-NATO demonstration held in Brussels and a demonstration in Lille against US action in Serbia. The Aix-en-Provence section of UR also intervened in university faculties on the theme of Serbia. Both Jeune Résistance and the GUD mobilised in the 'Front de la jeunesse' (FJ), which was very active in demonstrations against NATO and the US over Kosovo (see UR, n.d.E).

Anti-Semitism

Both national revolutionary and exclusivist nationalist groupings tie in this attempt at global domination with anti-Semitism. This has a number of aspects. First of all, one must note the coded manner of its anti-Semitism, utilising terms such as 'lobby', 'cosmopolitan', 'globalist', 'plutocracy', 'Zionism' or 'chameleon' to designate the Jew as enemy.[11] The critique of the international capitalist system is, for example, often a coded reference to the Jew, as NR's epithet, 'American-Zionist imperialism', indicates.[12] Anti-Zionism has a long history as a trope for anti-Semitism. Pierre Sidos explicitly sought to deny his anti-Semitism by arguing that he was against Zionist imperialism, not the presence of Jews in either the Middle East or France (Sidos, 1970). However, this use of the synonym 'anti-Zionist' was a covert form of anti-Semitism. Rejecting the idea that OF claimed any hierarchy of races, Sidos claimed that:

> Whatever we do and they [the Jews] do themselves, they will never have Celtic ancestors. If they are not the only members of the French community not descending from the old stock, the immense majority of them represent the exclusive particularity of demanding membership of two homelands, France being secondary (Sidos, 1967a).

Anti-Semitism can also be detected in repeated claims concerning the domination of the French economy, society and politics by Jews (Sidos, 1967a; see also Sidos, 1967d; Cantelaube, 1967d). It is on this point that we can see clear links with the anti-capitalism of the OF, for whom Jewry and capitalism were also synonymous, as Jews were held to control both Wall Street and American high finance (as well, of course, as lying behind international communism) (see Le Coeur, 1970a).[13]

Further, neo-fascists repeatedly denounce the State of Israel. The OF portrayed Israeli foreign policy as 'the abusive metropolis of Zionist ideology in France and in the world' (*Le Soleil*, 5–11 July 1967), whose 'bellicose and expansionist policy' was capable of provoking a third world war (Sidos, 1970). The period of the 1967 Arab–Israeli War, for example, saw a whole host of articles denouncing Israeli action (see, for example, Cantelaube, 1967e). Such anti-Zionist arguments were repeated during the 1973 Yom-Kippur War (see Sidos, 1973; Perroux, 1973a). Neo-fascists support – indeed, even have links with – Arab terrorism. National revolutionary movements, for example, have been known to support Arab terrorists such as Carlos.[14]

Finally, neo-fascists are propagators of historical revisionism – the denial of the Holocaust. National revolutionaries, for example, have condemned 'the repressive prevention of self-expression which hits revisionist historians' (UR, n.d.C).[15] JN has been strongly critical of the Pleven and Gayssot laws, which they hold responsible for preventing any sensible discussion of the extermination of the Jews during the Second World War (Benedetti, n.d.E).[16]

Anti-immigrant

A further threat to the ethnic basis to the community articulated by neo-fascism is the rejection of the immigrant, seen most clearly in the OF's call for 'stricter regulations' on 'an immigration which is inassimilable and has become too important' (OF, 1970a, point 8). Such measures included the idea that 'the unemployed and the professionally ill will automatically be returned to their country of origin', as would all those 'condemned by the French courts', together with tougher policies on naturalisation (OF, 1970a, points 8 and 9). At its second Congress, the OF called for the removal of citizenship from 'any French person who exercises political rights in a foreign country, who recognises links, of whatever nature, with a foreign nation or who shows by his acts or in any way that there are links between himself and a foreign nation' (OF, 1975a, point 4; see also Camus and Monzat, 1992: 289). Only French nationals should be allowed to 'exercise functions of leadership, command and responsibility' in the press and media (OF, 1975a, point 10).[17]

Like the OF, JN makes clear its rejection of 'non-French' identities. They describe anti-racism as a 'mental illness' and argue that 'poverty and misery are unacceptable when they affect an African'. Money is always found for overseas projects to alleviate poverty but we 'don't have the financial means necessary to struggle against the poverty which rages in our towns, to maintain the schools and the hospitals in our countryside' (Benedetti, n.d.F; see also Benedetti, n.d.G). The surreptitious racism of such statements is evident in their argument that: 'Everything which is still white, French patriotic, a lover of its land and its past no longer exists and no longer has any representation in the official France' (Benedetti, n.d.F). Immigrants are claimed to steal the bread of the 'poorest and most miserable French people' and behave like 'spoilt and badly brought up children'. Their sole objective is to combat authentic French people, the defenders of their heritage and their tradition (Benedetti, 2001a).

National revolutionaries connect anti-immigrant rhetoric with their critique of big capital, which is seen as responsible for the immigrant invasion. UR, for example, describes immigrants as 'like us, victims of the global liberal economic system' (UR, n.d.C). However, this makes them no less hostile to immigration. UR envisages the removal of immigrants in a series of stages culminating in a 'drastic and retro-active revision of the acquisition of French nationality', and a 'humane repatriation coordinated with countries of origin of immigrants pre-sent on our soil' (UR, n.d.C). In line with the arguments of the Nouvelle Droite (ND), this is presented as an anti-racist recognition of cultural difference. True racism, the ND also argues, is the attempt to integrate immigrants, undermining both cultures, that of host and of immigrant (see, for example, Bahzdid, 1998).

On the basis of the antagonisms sketched above, neo-fascists proclaim the framework of either the national or European commu-nity to be the foundation of a third way between communism and capitalism. This third way enables the crisis that such doctrines have allowed to beset the nation or Europe eventually to be overcome. For example, the exclusivist nationalists of the OF reject the distinction between left and right in favour of a national sentiment placed beyond different cleavages, above elections and outside of parties (OF tract, 'L'antiracisme, voilà l'ennemi!', in Rossi, 1995, Annex no. 4). The PCN explicitly proclaims itself a National Bolshevik party that ex-presses 'above all the political will to go beyond the cleavages of Left and Right' and offers 'a political alternative to the decadence of the contemporary world' (PCN, n.d.C). In a statement that recalls the Third Way politics of New Labour and the German SPD, the PCN proclaims itself the 'avant-garde of the Centre' (Parti Communautaire National-européean (PCN), n.d.A).

COMMUNITY AS AN ETHICAL IDEAL

In mainstream politics, appeals to the 'community' have often lent themselves to a conservative vision rooted in the maintenance of the status quo. However, the sense of crisis that underpins neo-fascism – which suggests that the community is being undermined by myriad threats (global capitalism, immigrants, Jews, communism) – is articu-lated around a voluntaristic vision of the historical process in which the threatened community is to be forged anew. Neo-fascism thus seeks to organise the collectivity around an ethics of combat, the taste for action, commitment and lived experience. For example, JN argues that the revolution implies the imposition of a will on historical events: 'Nothing is irredeemably inscribed in fate; there is no "sense of history" other than that imposed upon it by the thoughts and the will of men. When a people dies it only owes its fall to its own weaknesses and abandonments. Destiny and will are conjoined' (JN, n.d.B). This activist and militaristic conception of the community's ethical bonds contrasts starkly with traditional conservatism. We shall consider some of its key features.

Militarism and revolution

The deliberate creation of the ethnic community through historical intervention is reflected in a stress on militantism. UR claims that the 'main axis of our engagement' is 'the notion of the militant community'. Its heroes are 'men who have accepted prison and war wounds for their ideal' (UR, 1998b). Militantism often extends to the glorification of violence. Thiriart proclaimed that national revolutionaries needed to envisage as a working hypothesis the idea 'of an eventual insurrectional armed struggle against the American occupier', arguing that it is through the shedding of blood that unity is formed and the division from the enemy is best revealed (Thiriart, n.d.A). This glorification can also be seen in GUD's preference for violent action against the left rather than student electoral politics (Jeunes contre le racsime en Europe (JRE), n.d.: 9–12). Perhaps the clearest recent example of this glorification of violent intervention is the attempt to assassinate President Chirac by GUD activist and UR member (as well as member and former local election candidate of Mégret's MNR), Maxime Brunerie, on the grounds of his 'profound hatred of Jacques Chirac and of democracy' (Henley, 2002a). The stress on militant activity is also found in JN. They claim that history 'has always been written by small minorities', and positively cite the statement by José-Antonio Primo de Riveira that 'the revolution is the work of a minority which is inaccessible to discouragement' (Benedetti, n.d.H).[18] The militaristic aspect of JN's spiritual revolt against the forces of materialism can be seen in: their defence of 'a true army, reestablished in its function of state authority' (Benedetti, 1996);[19] their use of militaristic terminology in analysing the political system; and the homage paid to the *Organisation Armée Secrète* in devoting an entire issue to their struggle (Benedetti, 1997).

A further aspect of this militantism is the argument that the movement, as the agent of this re-birth of the national community, should adopt a hierarchical, authoritarian form of organisation, mirroring the form of community to come. This was clearly indicated by Sidos (see Sidos, 1975), and JN also claims that nationalists 'work under the sign of unity: unity of leadership, because in the last resort it is necessary that one person decides' (Benedetti, n.d.H). The PCN presents itself as 'a combat organism conceived under the sign of unity', which is 'integrated and hierarchised'. It conceives of itself as a sort of 'pre-state', mirroring in its organisation the organisation of the European state to come (Parti Communautaire National-européen (PCN), n.d.A).[20] This also explains why these groupings also tend to fetishise youth – linking them to the common emphasis on a 'new generation', 'new order', and on youth that, as noted in Chapter 1, is a recurrent feature of third way ideologies. The OF, for example, promoted a cult of youth in its claim that it would give 'French youth a patriotic and political education' (Cantelaube, 1967a), to which end it formed a 'Commission générale des jeunesses' (on which see OF, 1969).

The voluntarism of the neo-fascist renewal of the community explains why they proclaim that they are revolutionaries. National revolutionaries, for example, criticise consumer society and the bourgeois spirit. They call for a 'second Revolution' enabling the people to rediscover the nation – thus claiming a line of continuity with both the 1789 Revolution and with 1968 – although values such as the rights of man and the 'egalitarian myth' are denounced for weakening the quality of peoples (see Rossi, 1995: 112). National revolutionaries tend to give this proclaimed revolutionary character a more 'left-wing' flavour, although this should not be overemphasised – as is documented below, the OF declared itself the agent of a true 'French socialism'. National revolutionaries reference Che Guevara (Rossi, 1995: 125; UR, 1998a),[21] and have also cited nationalist statements made by former activists in the '68 movement as evidence of their proclaimed line of continuity (for example, Jacquemin, n.d.). If they draw from historical fascism, National revolutionaries often claim to draw upon the so-called 'revolutionary' wing of fascism, citing (amongst others) the Spanish national-syndicalist, Ramiro Ledesma Ramos; the left-wing 'national-bolshevism' of the NSDAP such as practiced by the Strasser brothers; the national-bolshevism of Ernst Niekisch; the German conservative revolutionaries of the inter-war period; the Hungarian fascist, Ferenc Szalasi (UR, n.d.F); the proclaimed authentically revolutionary Italian fascism of the 'movement' period (that is, before fascism came to power and made compromises with conservative forces such as big business and the Catholic Church);[22] as well as the so-called 'non-conformists' of the 1930s (on which see Bastow, 2001). National revolutionary groupings thus claim to belong to a true national socialism, a 'nationalism of the left'.

In the classic line of fascism, however, this revolutionary break, in revitalising the ethnic community, purports at the same time to restore it (see, for example, Julien, 1981: 44–5). This explains why they also cite figures associated with the reactionary right, such as Maurice Barrès (see Maillard, 1998a) as intellectual precursors. Thus neo-fascist movements define themselves in opposition to both left-wing socialism and right-wing conservatism, *and* they seek to fuse elements of both into their third way.

The critique of liberal democracy

The restoration of the national 'spirit' also requires an element of institutional reform. Neo-fascists are strongly critical of liberal de-mocracy, which is presented as the political edifice that has under-mined the authentic community that needs to be restored to health. It has undermined it both by having 'destroyed' the unifying cement of the French people – the sense of a shared destiny – by 'placing itself above the nation' (Benedetti, n.d.B) and by facilitating the domination of the people by big capital.

For the OF, liberal democracy involves domination of the political by the economic, of government by rootless capital (Le Coulon, 1970b). By big capital, of course, is meant the dominance of the French economy, politics and society by Jews. Arguing that the election of Valéry Giscard d'Estaing as President in 1974 did not represent a complete break with Gaullism due to the continued influence of 'Zionists', Perroux declared: 'In effect we hardly doubt that this Government serves the interests of the United States, of Germany and of Israel' (Perroux, 1974b). JN also see liberal democ-racy as enabling the domination of government by big capital and call for this domination to be reversed, with primacy given 'to the political in order to organise economic life' (Benedetti, n.d.I; see also Benedetti, n.d.K). Liberalism, argue JN, brings about 'the reign of materialism and the Money-King, the money which buys everything – politicians in the first place' (Benedetti, n.d.L), a fact largely brought about by the fiscal requirements of election campaigns (Benedetti, n.d.M, n.d.N).

Neo-fascist movements endlessly criticise the political mainstream for failing to defend the interests of the nation. This is extended to a trenchant rejection of party politics – 'denouncing elections and electoral campaigns amounts to denouncing political parties' (Benedetti, n.d.M). Contemporary political parties are described as no longer 'a gathering of men united around a common project of society' but as reduced these days to 'interest groups managed by technocrats defending their emoluments' (Benedetti, n.d.C). This denunciation extends – unlike the other elements examined here, including the OF[23] – to their continued hostility towards the Front national (Benedetti, n.d.H, n.d.O), which 'by participating in the institutional game . . . has adopted the stains of electoralism' (Benedetti, n.d.P; see also JN, 1999).

If liberal democracy is rejected, with what do neo-fascists suggest it should be replaced? Generally speaking, they advocate a strengthened state together with some form of corporatism or decentralised network that is in touch with the concrete life of the national community.

For OF, the state should be 'hierarchical, popular and nationalist' (Cantelaube, 1967a), standing above particular interests – especially economic and financial ones – and thus able to articulate the 'national' interest. It follows that OF economic policy subordinated economic concerns to those of the nation (Cantelaube, 1968). In so doing, it articulated a synthesis of elements emanating from both left and right – guaranteeing private property (see Sidos, 1967f; OF, 1970, Domestic Policy, point 5) and the defence of the independent middle classes via such things as the defence of savings (Sidos, 1967g) and of the traditional structure of French agriculture (Cantelaube, 1967a). At the same time it claimed to restore a 'French socialism', drawing on social Catholicism and the French revolutionary tradition of figures such as Proudhon (Sidos, 1969). The OF declared that it would return 'to the nation the means and the tools of production wrongfully held by financiers and countryless monopolies', and would seize and distribute 'apartments, premises, offices which are insufficiently occupied or in the hands of organisms or men who are countryless or without national interest' (Cantelaube, 1967a). It would achieve this, however, not through some kind of collectivism – the role of the state 'must be limited' (Le Goff, 1968) – but through the installation of a corporatist system. For OF, the national community found its concrete embodiment in the establishment of a corporatist system (Cantelaube, 1968; OF, 1975, points 15 and 16) based around regional and professional assemblies (Le Goff, 1968). This was deemed to reconcile 'patriots with the social and producers with the nation' (OF, 1970). Nevertheless, we should note the high degree of interventionism that such a doctrine left for the state in the areas of press and publishing (OF, 1975, point 10), measures aimed at increasing the birth-rate, such as the promotion of anti-abortion legislation (see Perroux, 1973b), and the maintenance of the moral order, such as a strong emphasis on law and order (OF, 1975, point 11).

National revolutionaries, too, denounce the operations of the state in the contemporary world and call instead for a strong state, impartial and above parties, which should also be organic (corporatist) and hierarchical, in order to overturn the dominance of economic over other forms of social and political participation. A strengthened state will, amongst other things, be economically interventionist, regulating the economy in the name of a policy of social justice. It will also reinforce the French moral order through a much more rigorous application of law and order (see, for example, Unité Radicale (UR), n.d.A, point 6). However, although the state is to develop major public services – education, health, broadcasting and planning – and place the economy in its service, this does not necessarily mean nationalisation of the entire economy, only state control of large (strategic) industry,[24] leaving the small and medium-sized businesses alone (see Thiriart, n.d.B).

THE THIRD WAY DISCOURSE OF THE FRENCH EXTREME RIGHT

An alternative third way vision to those outlined above is offered by the *Front national*. The electoral breakthrough of the party in the 1980s resulted from the attempt to break away from the third way label. In the 1980s, FN discourse was characterised as 'national-liberal', with a clear focus on the targeting of immigrants as a populist vehicle for gaining votes. This discourse was developed as a product of a number of factors that changed the ideological makeup of the FN. These factors included: entry into the FN of solidarists led by Jean-Pierre Stirbois and Michel Collinot in 1977, which led to the first real electoral breakthrough in 1983 at Dreux (Bergeron and Vilgier, 1985: 160; Camus, 1997: 50–1); entry into the party of elements of the 'nouvelle droite' that embraced economic liberalism; entry of elements from Catholic integralist circles, specifically those based around the movement *Chrétieneté-Solidarité*, expressing counter-revolutionary ideas rooted in the heritage of Barrès and Maurras; the assassination of the national-revolutionary and party number two,

François Duprat, in 1978, and the subsequent departure of a part of the national-revolutionary element from the FN; and the threat from the left displayed by the General Election victory of 1981 which cemented some degree of unity between the right and the extreme right. Thus, for example, middle-ranking elements from the right-wing Rassemblement pour la République (RPR) and the centre-right Union pour la Démocratie Française (UDF) jumped ship and joined the FN, as did elements based around the *Comités d'Action Républicain*. The 'national-liberal' strategy made it easier to oppose the state interventionism of the left and distinguished the FN from the right-wing Gaullist orthodoxy that gave the state a social interventionist role.

The FN's national-liberal strategy embraced the populist theme of anti-immigration, enabling the party to present itself as a party of the orthodox right, to resist attempts to present it as extremist, and to propose policies associated in many ways with the American 'new right'.

The key elements[25] of this strategy included: neo-liberal economic policies, such as privatisation, which aligned the FN with the new economic consensus shared by the major political parties but with an emphasis on the primacy of the nation in the form of a populist capitalism, 'handing over . . . nationalised companies to French people' (Mégret, 1990: 282); the assertion that France needed to reinforce a social order that had been threatened by governmental failures to maintain executive strength and by multiculturalism. Thus the FN extolled the moral virtues that stem from the family, the need for civic order and patriotic virtue, but that needed to be reinforced by a strong state. Hence, for example, the push to restore capital punishment and the traditional nature of the FN's policy on women in society, which was tied to a 'family' policy aimed at reversing the decline in the birth-rate (Fysh and Wolfreys, 1992; Wolfreys, 1993: 423), as well as calls for the expulsion of social groups deemed to threaten the very existence of France. A central feature of this was the critique of immigration. Though the FN denied that this could be construed as racist, suggesting, like the national revolutionaries noted earlier, that their arguments merely represented a claim for cultural 'difference', this nevertheless formed part of a wider discourse of what constituted 'good Frenchmen'. There were also demands for a popular input into the political decision-making process. Thus the FN presented itself as the champion of 'the people', who were excluded from power by the establishment, and called for greater use of referenda, for example. This return of power to the people also involved the question of Europe. The party was one of the leading critics of the European Union, calling for the abrogation of the Maastricht Treaty on the grounds that it 'has called our sovereignty into question' (FN, 1997: 367).

Taken as whole, the FN's national-liberal strategy broke from the idea that their political project promoted a 'third way' between capitalism and communism. This explains the hostility towards the FN in the 1980s by both national revolutionaries and exclusivist nationalists noted earlier. However, the articulation of 'liberal' elements around the defence of the nation mitigates against such an easy description of the FN's strategy. Indeed, Taguieff describes the FN in the 1980s as belonging to a form of third way thought that involves 'the redefinition of a national conservative right, more or less crossed with integral economic liberalism or Catholic integralism' (Taguieff, 1985: 1841).

In the 1990s, the FN incorporated further elements into its discourse, making clearer the third way character of the movement and its approximation to that of the radical right. This shift resulted from: the departure of a number of 'liberal' elements from the party following Le Pen's reference to the Holocaust as a 'mere detail' in history in 1987 and other public errors of judgement; the death of Stirbois in a car accident in 1988, which opened up the upper ranks of the party beneath Le Pen to elements from the 'nouvelle droite', such as Mégret; economic developments towards the end of the 1980s and through the early 1990s that undermined the claims of neo-liberalism to be the panacea to the West's economic ills, together with the increasing threat of US protectionist sanctions; the growing threat to particular interests such as farmers, fishermen, small-businessmen – traditional voters for the FN – stemming not just from changes in the global economy and the GATT negotiations but also from the reforms to the Common Agricultural Policy; the move towards a free-trade zone through the adoption of the Single Market and the fears generated by that policy; the collapse of communism in Eastern Europe, which meant that ties between the FN and the West were quite substantially weakened; and the increasing tendency for working-class elements to vote for the FN, thus increasing the numbers of voters who, as Mayer and Perrineau have noted, 'appear more in favour of state interventionism and social rights' than neo-liberal policies (Mayer and Perrineau, 1992: 131).

The impact of such changes was the introduction into FN discourse of new third way elements. First, an increasing anti-Americanism, revealed initially in the stance it took during the Gulf War of supporting Saddam Hussein and subsequently in its support for the Serbs in the conflict over Kosovo. Second, moves were made to reinforce economic protectionist policies (on which, see Bastow, 1997). Third, the party evolved towards what Camus sees as a policy of 'ethnic segregation' (Camus, 1997: 64). This culminated in the claim by Jean-Marie Le Pen that racial inequality was an 'incontrovertible fact' and more clearly linked the FN to the socio-genetic theories of the 'nouvelle droite' and other third way movements discussed earlier. Fourth, conspiracy theory took a higher profile in FN doctrine, with figures such as Monzat claiming 'the Front national is progressively effecting a synthesis and a modernisation of this vision of a world dominated by occult powers' (R. Monzat, cited in Camus, 1997: 65). Finally, the party developed its own union movements in fields such as transport, the police, prison officers, and so on, and from denigrating public sector strikes in Autumn 1995 had adopted a position supporting them by the following autumn. This final change was allied to a reworking of the FN's stance on the state, coming out in favour of more social intervention than in the heyday of its neo-liberalism in the 1980s (on which see Mégret, cited in Chombeau, 1996b).

This ideological shift led the FN to propose a third way strategy that had much more in common with a form of third way doctrine identified by Taguieff as that of an 'imperial Europeanism, rejecting "liberalism" as much (and sometime more) as "social-communism"' (Taguieff, 1985: 1841). This would explain the fact that the radical right groupings discussed earlier began to move closer to the FN as a result of such changes. In November 1996, Christian Bouchet's *Nouvelle Résistance* decided to put an end to hostilities with the FN. The OF, as we noted earlier, also organised a press conference in Orange to make official its support for the FN (see Chombeau, 1996a).

'OPEN' AND 'CLOSED' VARIANTS OF AN AUTHORITARIAN THIRD WAY?

If the FN has moved strikingly closer to the third way variants of neo-fascism noted earlier, their positions are not synonymous. Comparison reveals a significant difference that perhaps explains the success not just of the FN in France but more widely of what we noted earlier have been labelled radical right-wing populists, radical right populists, the post-industrial extreme right, or ethno-liberals (Betz, 1994; Kitschelt, 1998; Ignazi, 1992, 1997; Griffin, 2000).

The analysis of National Revolutionary and Exclusivist Nationalist variants of neo-fascism in France and Belgium revealed a highly complex, authoritarian variant of the third way theme. Like the FN, this seeks to overcome the antagonisms of contemporary society through the articulation of a populist discourse[26] that conceives 'the people' as an ethnic community under threat, and whose centrality and vital force they seek to restore. The contours of this community are traced through a logic of equivalence constructed between social actors such that the specificity of their social position is dissolved into a generalised expression of something essential underlying them all. They differ from the FN, however, in that the neo-fascist third way deploys an organic holism based around the notion of a closed community, drawing to an extent on biology (note the references to the white race, for example), but also on a proclaimed commonality of culture, religion and language. The centrality of this biological community leads it to operate as the horizon within which other conceptual terms are organised. Their anti-materialism is based on the myth of a spiritual ethos of the nation with its common linguistic, cultural and biological ancestry. Their rejection of capitalism, communism, Zionism and immigration is made on the basis of the threat these pose to the nation through their materialism and internationalism.

Consequently, national revolutionary and exclusivist nationalist's visions of politics are based on the need for the national community to be represented, arguing that liberal democracy not only disables the representation of the 'people' but threatens its very existence. The analysis of neo-fascism reminds us, therefore, that third way discourses do not always seek to be as inclusive as New Labour's Third Way and may seek to overcome binary divisions by appealing to new antagonisms in ways which are more hostile and threatening than those they originally sought to overcome.

The FN, by contrast, attempts to deal with the high degree of social complexity found in the contemporary West by a strategy of discursive ambiguity in which the elements of the FN's third way act as 'floating signifiers'.[27] They do this precisely because they seek election and therefore have to compromise with the system (see Bastow, 2002). This 'floating' character can be ascribed both to the national-liberal variant of the third way of the 1980s and to the more national revolutionary position developed later, and it underpins their electoral success since 1983 because it has enabled them to reach out to a multiplicity of different voters in France. Notwithstanding the break with Mégret in 1998 – a proponent of a much more explicit third way strategy (see Bastow, 2000) – the party has continued to utilise a third way discourse. For example, Le Pen's campaign slogan for the 2002 Presidential elections was 'Ni droite, ni gauche . . . Français'. It is this more nuanced variant of the third way strategy that underpinned the spectacular rise in support that enabled Le Pen to enter the second ballot of the Presidential elections in France that year, much to the horror of liberal Europe.[28] Whilst this ambiguity renders the nationalism of the FN more 'open' than that of neo-fascist movements, that is not to deny that it deploys a particularly nasty, xenophobic discourse, more worrying precisely because so many people appear attracted to it.

NOTES

1 Sternhell draws this formula from the work of Georges Valois, the founder of the first French fascist movement, the *Faisceau* (see Valois, 1926a, b and c). See the discussion of Valois in Chapter 1.

2 Indeed, there are legitimate debates concerning whether the term fascism can be applied to post-war movements or whether fascism is a discourse that only applies to the pre-1945 period.

3 The radical right, following Ferraresi, should be seen as the most radical section within the extreme right; that which accepts the use of illegal political means, including violence, in the political struggle against the system, and which totally rejects the 'whole process of modernisation and all the elements related to it (rationality, science and individualism)' (Ferraresi, 1996: 10–11).

4 We have a number of problems with the attempt to define parties such as the French *Front national* as purely 'fascist' (see Bastow, 2002). However, this issue does not prevent the incorporation of a discussion of the extreme right in this chapter.

5 It is worth noting that Griffin subsequently seems to have changed his mind regarding the classification of such parties as the Austrian Freedom Party as neo-fascist, although there is no space to deal with this issue here. See Griffin (2000).

6 E-mail correspondence from Bouchet, 3 June 2000.

7 Bouchet himself acknowledges the impact of the 'diliation thiriartienne' via Jeune Europe, the Organisation Lutte du Peuple, and Partisans Européens (E-mail correspondence from Bouchet, 3 June 2000). Moreover, these ties are shown by the fact that when NR split in the summer of 1996, due to dissatisfaction with its leadership, some NR defectors joined the (thiriartian) PCN. See JPR (1998).

8 The OF was founded in April 1968 by Pierre Sidos, former leader of *Jeune nation*, and director of the nationalist organ, *Le Soleil*. Denouncing the 'Zionist plot' and 'cosmopolitan bourgeoisie', the OF propagated a form of Catholic fascism based on the models of Franco, Salazar and Pétain, and drawing on the work of such pantheons of French fascism as Bardèche, Brasillach and Drieu la Rochelle, as well as social Catholicism. JN is an exclusivist nationalist grouping of much more recent vintage, which seems to be a break away from the OF and is based in Lyon.

9 The term 'integral nationalism' derives from the work of the extreme right thinker and activist of the latter part of the nineteenth and early twentieth century, Charles Maurras. By integral nationalism Maurras intended a nationalism that was both 'capable of being fully expressed only within the framework of the traditional institutions whose revival he advocated' and that admitted of no higher claims than the nation, seen as a 'prior condition of every social and individual good' (Pierce, 1966: 12–13).

10 On the French extreme right attitude to Europe in general, see Boutin (1996).

11 This coding is due to the Gayssot Law of 1990, which forbids incitement to racial hatred and the dissemination of Holocaust-denial propaganda.

12 See F. Lehner (n.d.), where the work of the anti-Semite, Emmanuel Ratier, is cited in support of the argument concerning globalisation.

13 National revolutionaries also link Jews to capitalism.

14 UR has claimed the terrorist, Carlos, as 'one of our own'. See Milan (1998).

15 General examples of anti-Semitism can be found in the regular feature in Jeune Résistance, 'Voyage en sionite'.

16 The numerous *hommages* to the revisionist Paul Rassinier in *Le Soleil* upon his death in 1967 (see, for example, Le Soleil, 20–26 September 1967) are testimony to the OF's position on the freedom to deny the Holocaust.

17 Clearly the main targets here were Jews but they were not the only social group that such a regulation would have hit.

18 See also Olivier Grimaldi's speech at the tomb of Robert Brasillach on the eve of the anniversary of his execution, in which he declared that 'our duty is to form nationalist elites with no complexes' (Grimaldi, 2001).

19 A similar defence of the French army, and critique of the French state's support of the army, was made back in the 1960s by the OF. See *Le Soleil*, 1 November 1966.

20 The parallels with the party-type developed by inter-war fascism should be clear.

21 On the use of such references by the radical right, see Bourseiller (1992: 20).

22 An argument first articulated in the post-war period by French neo-fascist, Maurice Bardèche. See Bardèche (1961).

23 Although the OF was extremely hostile to the FN during the 1980s and early 1990s (see the OF tract, August 1984, in Rossi, 1995, Annex no. 7), in 1996 it organised a press conference in Orange to make official its support for the FN and a number of OF activists campaigned for the FN in the 1997 general election. The most striking example of this was the candidacy of the OF militants, Thierry Maillard (Puy-de-Dôme) and Liliane Boury (Rhône) for the FN in the 1997 general election. Maillard explicitly stated that Le Pen's stated views on racial inequality in 1996 had persuaded him to move closer to the party. See Chombeau (1996a, 1997).

24 Note, for example, that the PCN calls for the 'nationalization of European based American companies and financial assets' (PCN, n.d.B).

25 See Bastow (1997 and 1998) for a more detailed discussion of these elements.

26 A populist discourse seeks to mobilise 'the people' as 'an antagonistic option against the ideology of the dominant bloc' (Laclau, 1979: 173).

27 Elements marked by an ambiguity which prevents them from being fully fixed (see Laclau, 1996a: 36).

28 Although this success was also partly due to protest voting against the mainstream parties.

CHAPTER 5
GREEN POLITICAL THEORY AND THE THIRD WAY

Green political parties have become increasingly successful actors in contemporary European politics. Several have recently been coalition partners in European governments. In Germany, the Greens (*Die Grünen*) managed to enter into the national parliament – by just crossing the 5 per cent threshold – only three years after various ecological and populist groups came together in 1980 to found the Green Party. Since then, excepting the post-unification election of 1990, they have performed extremely strongly in terms of electoral support. In the 1990s, several Red-Green coalitions were organised at Land level, between the Social Democratic Party (SPD) and the Greens in Lower Saxony and Hesen, and in Bremen there was even a so-called 'traffic-light'[1] coalition between SPD, Greens and the liberal Free Democratic Party (FDP). The 1998 German general elections were a triumph not just for the SPD of Gerhard Schröder but for the Greens, too, who became the junior coalition partner in the new government having received just under 7 per cent of the vote. In France, however, the ride has been less smooth. The massive success of green parties in the 1989 Euro elections (11 per cent of the vote and 8 seats) – won on a joint list between *Les Verts* and *Génération Ecologie* – seemed to hail an electoral breakthrough akin to that of the German Greens. But this was followed by dismal performances in the 1993 general elections and the 1994 European elections. However, the party, largely as a result of an electoral pact with the Parti Socialiste (PS), was a member of the ruling 'gauche plurielle' in power from 1997 to 2002.

The political links between greens and the traditional left, not just in

France and Germany but elsewhere in Europe, suggest that green political discourse belongs somewhere on the left of the political spectrum. This impression is reinforced by commentators such as Inglehart who, like others, refers to greens as part of what he terms the 'new politics' (Inglehart, 1977, 1990; see also Giddens, 2000: 132–42, 147). That view is underscored by the distinction Müller-Rommel makes between 'pure greens' and 'alternative greens', or Kitschelt's division between the 'left' and 'libertarians'. Each categorises greens and other parties concerned with the environment on the left.

However, these variants do not exhaust the range of green politics. Wissenburg, for example, points out that 'the sheer amount of "isms" used to describe green theories and people is remarkable'. He cites, amongst others, ecologism and environmentalism, 'grey', 'green' and 'Green', 'deep' and 'shallow' ecologism, anthropocentric, biocentric and ecocentric, ecofeminist, ecoterrorist forms of green politics (Wissenburg, 1997: 29). This suggests that ecologism is compatible with the broad field of ideologies and political platforms: liberalism, libertarianism, anarchism, social democracy, statist socialism, pluralistic socialism, conservatism, authoritarianism, fascism, communitarianism and feminism. Wissenburg even develops two of his own categories: 'political naturalism' (promoting a society organised around the rules of nature) and 'political agnosticism' (promoting no preferred political order) (Ibid.: 40). Moreover, some commentators argue that ecological politics constitutes a right-wing phenomenon and link greens to 'radical conservatism', even to fascism.

The argument set out in this chapter is that ecologism is best understood as a form of third way politics, that is, one that seeks to define a space beyond the established left and right antagonism. This is partly because many greens explicitly declare themselves to be 'neither left nor right' but also, more significantly, because the elements of green thought match the repertoire of third way discourse we outlined in Chapter 1. Third ways typically encompass a number of 'family resemblances': a stress on ethics and morality; a holistic focus on community; an optimism concerning the historic force of ideas; emergence during periods of social and political dislocation, and so on. As we shall see, each of these resemblances can be found in green discourses. What makes green third way discourses particularly interesting, however, is the division between radically different types of third way: on the one hand, a reformulation of an emancipatory politics of the left and, on the other, a more authoritarian politics of the right.

Michael Freeden ascribes the ideological breadth within green political thought to what he regards as the relative 'thinness' of its ideological core, by which is meant the claim that 'Green ideology does revolve around core concepts, though of a somewhat narrow range relative to the challenges other contemporary ideologies – functioning as socio-political agendas for public policy – have to meet' (Freeden, 1995: 5). Other political concepts that are 'central to progressive social and political discourse', such as liberty equality or rationality, 'are conspicuously lacking' within the core of green political thought (Ibid.: 5, 7). A further aspect of the thinness of green ideology highlighted by Freeden is 'the spread and lack of a unifying system of the ideological producers'; that is, green ideology 'lacks, for better or for worse, a Mill, Marx or Freud, a central intellectual agenda, or powerful philosophical or theoretical framework, from which to evolve or against which to focus sharply' (Ibid.: 24). The thinness of green ideology could be said to enhance the third way potential of green political thought by enabling elements to be appropriated from a wide range of political traditions. It also explains the surprising variety of third way positions that can be found in green thought.

In making this argument we shall not be analysing the entirety of the corpus of green ideological positions. That would be beyond the scope of a mere book chapter. Rather, we shall substantiate the claim articulated above through an analysis of the elements of green political discourses as they are found in the writings of what are variously called ecologists, 'deep' ecologists, 'radical' ecologists or 'social' ecologists. These examples do not exhaust the range of green ideological formations. Nor do they express exactly the same political vision. We demonstrate, however, that they all articulate a third way approach to politics as we have defined it.

Core Elements of Green Ideology

Freeden has argued that green political thought constitutes an authentic political ideology of its own, even if it consists 'of a somewhat narrow range relative to the challenges other contemporary ideologies . . . have to meet' (Freeden, 1995: 5). He suggests that the core elements of green ideology consist in the following:

1. Green ideology ascribes 'a crucial ontological as well as prescriptive status' to the relationship between human beings

and nature, in which the latter 'becomes an overriding factor in guiding human conduct'.

2. A recognition that nature is a finite resource, depletion of which cannot, in some cases, be reversed.
3. A number of variants of holism, conceived as 'the interdependence or harmony of all forms of life'.
4. An emphasis on the need to immediately set into effect 'qualitative human lifestyles' (Freeden, 1995: 5–6).

As we noted earlier, for Freeden it is the relative thinness of such core concepts compared with other political ideologies that partly explains the rich variety of green political forms (Freeden, 1995: 6). This thinness accounts for the emergence of fundamental differences amongst greens concerning humankind's relationship to nature, the role that technology may or may not play in the solution to the crisis, and the degree to which any intervention requires authoritarian means to bring it about – differences encapsulated in the different concepts mobilised by green thinkers. These differences will be more clearly outlined below.

Ecological crisis

Stavrakakis ascribes the emergence of contemporary green ideology to the combined dislocatory effects of two types of crisis: a crisis of nature and its representation, and a crisis of ideology and politics (Stavrakakis, 2000: 105).[2] On the one hand, the crisis of nature involves a dislocation of 'our (imaginary/symbolic) conceptions of nature by a feeling of environmental crisis', with environmental disasters such as Chernobyl gradually and cumulatively undermining the modern representation of science as the means for humankind's mastery and domination over nature. On the other hand, the crisis of ideology involves a dislocation of the radical left-wing ideological discourse of the post-war period (Stavrakakis, 2000: 107).[3] We shall turn to the dislocation of left-wing ideology later in this chapter. For the moment, we shall focus on the crisis of the representation of nature.

For Stavrakakis, the key aspect of the crisis of the representation of nature is primarily a crisis of science. Fundamentally, this is a crisis of the dominant paradigm setting out how humankind relates to nature and involves a shift from a Dominant Social Paradigm – which argued for humankind's right to dominate nature, 'this domination being fantasised as an operation with no hazards and no limits' – to a New Environmental Paradigm captured in the idea of 'sustainability'. This shift towards the awareness of an environmental crisis reveals 'limits to growth and economic expansion . . . to which the public is becoming sensitive' (Ibid.: 110). The environmental crisis is generated by a series of dislocatory events: environmental problems such as acid rain and toxic waste have been reinforced by frequent environmental disasters and the growing perception of global warming (Ibid.: 108–10).

The effect of this series of dislocations was to generate a sense that the world faced an imminent catastrophe. Greens typically argue that the world is faced with a crisis so great that it is often described in terms approaching apocalypse. In *Beyond the Limits*, for example, it is argued that:

> Human use of many essential resources and generation of many kinds of pollutants have already surpassed rates that are physically sustainable. Without significant reductions in material and energy flows, there will be in the coming decades an uncontrolled decline in per capita food output, energy use, and industrial production (cited in Dobson, 2000: 20).

According to greens, the problem is 'that there are natural limits to economic and population growth' due to the 'limited carrying capacity (for population), productive capacity (for resources of all types) and absorbent capacity (pollution)' of the Earth (Dobson, 2000: 15). The radical 'eco-centric' group, ECO (the Campaign for Political Ecology), for example, argues:

> It should be abundantly clear that the world cannot support an ever growing population of individuals with ever increasing material consumption. More efficient technology may buy time but cannot alone provide the ultimate solution (ECO, n.d.A).

The specification of an ecological crisis defines the discursive horizon of green ideologies and, as such, is presented as the 'objective' foundation of its own superior claims. For greens both announce the presence of the crisis and present their ideas and movements as the agency charged with the task of resolving it.

Voluntarism

The idea that there are limits to growth, beyond which the very existence of human life becomes questionable, is coupled with an anti-determinism that denies that this growth – and the crisis that it will produce – is inevitable. A shift in people's value systems and concomitant changes in behaviour, can bring an end to this crisis. Ecologists suggest that 'radical changes' can be made to our social habits and practices, enabling the formation of a 'sustainable society' (Dobson, 2000: 16). *Beyond the Limits* argues that:

> This decline is not inevitable. To avoid it two changes are necessary. The first is a comprehensive revision of policies and practices that perpetuate growth in material consumption and in population. The second is a rapid, drastic increase in the efficiency with which materials and energy are used' (cited in Dobson, 2000: 20).

Similarly, ECO argue that in the face of the ecological crisis there can be only two alternatives. If no action is taken then some form of disaster will take place: war, famine, disease, or pestilence. However, action can be taken to prevent such disasters, limiting growth 'by controlling population and consumption at sustainable levels'. This requires 'a fundamental change in personal and economic aspirations' (ECO, n.d.A).

Thus the crisis is generally agreed to be neither inevitable nor predetermined, and is generally portrayed as capable of reversal via some form of economic and political intervention, together with a change in people's lifestyles. However, although there is a general consensus that there is an environmental crisis, there are important differences over what is meant by 'sustainable development' and the means that might be used to bring about a sustainable society.

The original definition of the term sustainable development, which was popularised by the World Commission on Environment and Development, was: 'Development which meets the needs of the present without compromising the ability of future generations to meet their own needs' (ECO, n.d.B). However, as ECO notes, in practice the term 'means widely different things to different people' (Ibid.). For some ecologists, sustainability cannot be brought about through recourse to technological innovation. This 'merely shift[s] the problem around, often at the expense of more energy and material inputs and therefore more pollution' (Irvine and Ponton, 1988: 36). However, there are genuine disputes amongst greens over the general role of technology in a sustainable society. Dobson points out that some greens are more overtly hostile to technology than others (see Dobson, 2000: 86–7). Envisioning the nature of the solution to the crisis is made even trickier by the fact that for some greens – those Dobson labels environmentalists – technology is part of the solution. ECO, for example, argues that: 'We should all accept that some technologies bring considerable benefits without significant ecological harm. On the other hand, the ecological outcomes of many technologies are at best undesirable and potentially catastrophic' (Cripps, 1997). Consequently, though 'we must still act against inappropriate technology', some forms of technology can 'be made to serve the long term needs of mankind in an ecologically and socially acceptable manner' (ECO, n.d.A). Paradoxically, as Wissenburg notes, within the green paradigm a wide variety of positions are possible concerning the concept of 'limits to growth', including positions that don't really think that growth needs to be limited (Wissenburg, 1997: 39).

This division concerning the means whereby a sustainable society can be brought about is closely related to a further division concerning man's relationship to nature. There is a clear 'ecocentric–anthropocentric divide' within green political thought.

On the one hand, a number of analyses – those belonging to 'deep ecology' – deny that there is a sufficient ontological divide between humanity and the rest of nature 'to ground a value distinction between humanity and the rest of nature', whether this involves making human beings 'the sole object of value in the natural world', or merely the 'object of greatest value' (Humphreys, 2000: 249). For example, Sandy Irvine, arguing against the anthropocentric nature of much of the literature on sustainable development, claims that: 'The only way to avoid terrible consequences of ecological meltdown – a goal in the interests of all species, humans and non-humans – is to start putting the Earth first. Protection of the Earth's life-support systems, the conserver agenda, must become the overriding and all-pervading priority' (Irvine, n.d.). Such perspectives are claimed to be based on making the environment sustainable in order to maintain human enjoyment of the Earth, and thus not antithetical to human exploitation of the environment. As such, Irvine argues 'the programme of sustainable development is indeed the last refuge of humanism since it represents the final attempt to evade the limits to growth' (Ibid.).

On the other hand, anthropocentric arguments claim that there is something 'special' about humankind that generates greater priority for human interests. This argument focuses on humankind's ability to exercise reason (see Humphreys, 2000: 249). Thus, for example, Bookchin argues that: 'The entire conceptual framework of deep ecology is entirely a product of *human* agency – a fact that imparts to the human species a unique status in the natural world' (Bookchin, 1993: 47). He continues:

> To the extent that 'intrinsic worth' is something more than merely an agreeable intuition in modern ecological thought, it is an 'attribute' that human beings formulate in their minds and a 'right' that they may *decide to confer* on animals and other creatures. It does not exist apart from the operations of the human mind or humanity's social values (Bookchin, 1993: 48).

In turn, this divide over the relationship between humankind and nature feeds into divergent arguments about what nature is, with deep ecologists defending a more organic, sometimes mystical, vision of nature, whilst social ecologists, such as Bookchin, privilege the rational action of humankind as the highest form of nature (see Humphreys, 2000: 258).

The green community

The holistic stance of green political thought[4] – that is, their suggestion that there is a mutual interdependence between each of the concepts articulated by whatever form of green political thought expressed[5] – leads greens to place great emphasis on communality.[6] However, whilst all green political thought exhibits some form of holism, a plurality of different holistic systems are available to greens (see Freeden, 1995: 8): Green ideology is compatible with 'various types of organicism, interdependence and equilibrium as desired ends as well as prerequisites for viable life' (Ibid.: 7). Whilst all of them generate an emphasis on communality and duties to others, the form that that communality takes may differ substantially regarding the membership of the community, the status of the members, the intensity of the relationships within the community, and the time-span of the community (Ibid.: 11).

The membership of the green community to be forged depends on the definition of the 'enemy' to be overcome. In many forms of green thought, the identification of the 'enemy' – the force or those forces that have caused the crisis – is rather vague. The majority of green approaches operate a radical simplification of the social space through their assertion of crisis, articulating a chain of equivalence in which class, gender, ethnic differences, and so on, are downplayed in favour of a common opposition to the forces that have undermined the ecosphere. In general terms, this leads to an opposition between all those who seek an anti-materialist, anti-productivist lifestyle based around ecological sustainability (the friends) and all those who subscribe to a materialist, productivist and consumptivist lifestyle (the enemy). Within this general duality, however, there are substantial differences in terms of the elements constructed as 'friends' and those constructed as 'enemies'.

Dobson suggests that most greens make a utopian universal appeal on the basis that everybody should be concerned by environmental problems because 'Greens believe disagreement about the desirability of such things as a sustainable society to be irrational, suggesting that a lack of consensus about sustainability is something to be regretted' (Dobson, 1996: 136). Such an approach, however, undermines the erection of any clear boundary between who is part of the sustainable 'community' and who is not because everybody ought to agree with their position.

More radically democratic greens, however, seem to have a clear idea of who the 'enemy' is, who is part of the community and who isn't. Dobson himself, for example, is clear who the enemy is and who, therefore, belongs or should belong to the green community. He argues that a 'significant and influential proportion of society . . . has a material interest in prolonging the environmental crisis because there is money to be made from managing it' (Dobson, 2000: 146). The corollary of this is his identification of the green community as encompassing all those who are not only 'relatively "disengaged"' from society but are also 'already inclined towards the foundations of sustainable living' (Dobson, 2000: 154). Dobson argues that the increasing scarcity of resources will make it more likely that production costs will increase and make it harder to find the capital for this production. This will lead producers to seek to cut non-fixed costs (that is, wages) by transferring production out of the first world, whilst seeking to increase its capital income by generating more consumption. These two effects will be contradictory (increased unemployment in the West at the same time as promoting greater consumption) and greens should seek to mobilise those people squeezed by such changes. As Dobson puts it, it is 'the distance from the process of consumption and the degree of permanence of this isolation that currently determine the capacity of any given group in society for radical green social change' (Dobson, 2000: 155). The unemployed, third world poor, seasonal workers, those in other forms of poorly paid and insecure employment, and so on, form part of a wider set of those who are 'marginalized' from the process of production and consumption. These people may be mobilised, Dobson claims, on the grounds that the ecological situation 'structurally' prevents them from ever gaining access to the bright world of consumer society (Dobson, 2000: 158–60).

Similarly, the Green MEP and radical economist, Alain Lipietz, whose work has been very influential on the British left, argues that there is a viable ecological alternative to the neo-liberal models of post-Fordist development that were put into effect from the 1980s. The social basis for this alternative will be that of the oppressed, reviled and exploited people who are in revolt against alienation: women, workers affected by industrial restructuring or de-skilling technologies, unemployed and casual workers, young people of various ethnic groups in cities, small farmers burdened by debt or outside 'the system', and so on (Lipietz, 1995: xii–xiii).

These analysts, who tend to see green politics as belonging on the left, clearly see the enemy as capitalism.[7] However, precisely because they reject economistic approaches, these analyses offer a political reading of the coalition that must be waged against capitalism, rendering relatively fluid the parameters of the (sustainable) community to be formed.

It is this vagueness regarding the community that enables more ethnicist forms of community within the green framework, which argue that the community to be protected from rampant materialism is a spiritual one, rooted in blood and soil. Such ecofascist variants of the third way overlap with the French national revolutionary discourses examined in Chapter 4. These claim to be ecologist in so far as they seek to restore the natural balance between man and environment. UR calls for 'the defence of the countryside and traditional modes of exploiting land and sea, the defence of animal and vegetal diversity, the defence of traditional sports and ways of living' (Unité Radicale (UR), n.d.A; Larsen, 1998).[8] UR incorporates *Résistance Verte*, a national revolutionary green movement that coordinates diffusion of the propaganda of the 'Comité national contre les Mac Donald's' and that has been carrying out militant action against McDonald's in France for a number of years.[9] Similarly, the PCN explicitly calls itself an ecological party (Parti Communautaire National-européen (PCN), n.d.) and also has ties to *Europe-Ecologie*, a grouping that proclaims itself 'neither left nor right', denounces parliamentary democracy and the 'worn out and corrupted party-ocracy', and calls for 'radical, authentic honest ecological militants' to join in a united front gathering together 'all the enemies of the system, nationalist revolutionaries, communists, radical ecologists or authentic socialists' (Europe-Ecologie, n.d.).

Similar claims to those of French national revolutionaries are also made by a number of German neo-Nazi parties and movements, such as the *Freiheitliche Deutsche Arbeiterpartei* (FAP), and more electoral extreme right movements such as the *Deutsche Volksunion* (DVU) or *National-demokratische Partei Deutschlands* (NPD) (Biehl and Staudenmaier, 1995).

In addition, however, some commentators also claim that many of those movements that simply call themselves ecologists are, in fact, also fascists. Rather contentiously, a number of commentators claim that this is true of the activities of the former communist turned ecologist, Rudolf Bahro. Biehl argues that the ecologism of Rudolf Bahro represents an 'ecological spiritualism' that 'bears no small resemblance to the *Völkisch* Germanic spirituality of the 1920s' (Biehl and Staudenmaier, 1995: 48), whilst Dahl claims that 'it is not incorrect' to label Bahro an ecofascist (Dahl, 1999: 139).

As well as differences in the composition of the community to be revived, there are major differences within green political thought concerning the relationship between the members of the community. For some greens, organic holism implies an emphasis on egalitarian communities. For example, Dobson claims that the green support for equality and related criticism of hierarchy makes ecologism 'clearly left-wing' (Dobson, 2000: 27). This commitment to equality derives from an argument concerning the interdependence of all forms of nature. Political equality is derived from a view of nature as 'an interlocking system of interdependent objects (both sentient and non-sentient)', such that 'no part of the natural world is independent and therefore no part can lay claim to "superiority"' (Dobson, 2000: 24). Hence Goodin's description of the widespread support for participatory democracy among greens as 'arguably the central plank in the whole green theory of agency' (Goodin, 1992: 124).[10] Such arguments link into the support amongst many greens for the principle of workplace democracy. Carter points out that the majority of green political ideologies 'display a fondness for the worker co-operative'

(Carter, 1996: 56). He cites the 1983 programme of the German Greens, which declared that: 'Large combines are to be broken down into surveyable units which can be run democratically by those working in them' (Die Grünen, *Programme of the German Green Party* (1983) cited in Carter, 1996: 57), and that of the British Green Party in 1992: 'We support the formation and growth of co-operatives as a way of encouraging a democratic and non-hierarchical approach to work' (Green Party, *Manifesto for a Sustainable Society* (1992) cited in Carter, 1996: 57).[11] This view also supports Kemp and Wall's assertion that the principle of economic democracy is strongly supported by greens (P. Kemp and D. Wall, *A Green Manifesto for the 1990s* (Harmondsworth: Penguin, 1990), p. 80, cited in Carter, 1996: 58). Similarly, Colin Hines argues for a strategy of 'localisation', a 'set of inter-related and self-reinforcing policies that actively discriminate in favour of the local', whose 'end goal must be to increase the democratic involvement of citizens in the rebuilding of sustainable local economies' (Hines, n.d.).

As Freeden notes, an obvious connection can be made with anarchist thought and non-statist varieties of socialism regarding the conceptualisation of equality 'in so far as human organisation is retained only in participatory communal forms intended to eliminate invidious types of power' (Freeden, 1995: 12). This tapping of the socialist heritage is often explicitly made. Lipietz, for example, argues that greens 'are heirs of a Left which is without a heritage' (Lipietz, 1995: xii) and outlines ecological values that clearly draw on traditional socialist themes:

> *Solidarity*: rejecting the exclusion of certain individuals of a social category or group of countries.
> *Autonomy*: giving individuals greater control of their activities in the factory, countryside and home and communities greater control of their region.
> *Democracy*: sounding out the opinions and aspirations of all on the range of problems concerning their existence, and seeking a peaceful and negotiated solution to contradictions which emerge.
> *Ecological responsibility*: limiting needs and always choosing the means to fulfil them which take account of the interests of life on the planet and the rights of future generations (Ibid.: 7).

However, this egalitarian vision is not the only one concomitant with green holism. The organicist conception may take the form outlined above of an emphasis on mutual responsibility through emancipatory socialism but it can also privilege more hierarchical approaches to communal relations (see Freeden, 1995: 15–16). As Dobson has shown, in terms of equality it is just as easy – indeed, possibly easier – to argue that the equivalence of man and the rest of nature means that human society should be organised along hierarchical lines as it is to suggest that this underpins a commitment to equality, as nature tends to be organised hierarchically (Dobson, 2000: 28).

To further complicate the picture a number of other ideological elements seem to connect green ideology to the right. Ecocentric variants of green politics have been known to draw upon an extreme right ideological heritage of green thought that can be traced back to Romanticism,[12] although this is not to suggest that all ecocentric forms of green ideology do so.[13] As Dobson admits, it is not so easy to declare ecologism 'unequivocally' left-wing because of its naturalism, which is more clearly of the right (Dobson, 2000: 28). The very naturalism that underpins the commitment to both democracy and political equality clearly enables greens to link into themes stemming from the traditional right, such as birth control and the defence of tradition. Moreover, as a number of commentators have noted, not only is the green commitment to democracy purely contingent but the ecological imperative brought about by the belief that, if catastrophe is to be avoided, a sustainable society needs to be introduced immediately, implies for some greens that any means necessary, whether authoritarian or otherwise, are acceptable as long as they bring such a society about (see Saward, 1993; Passmore, 1993; and Barry, 1996). That is, greens, as Saward argues, tend to operate around the 'simple binary choice' between the acceptance of ecological principles or social destruction; there can be no halfway house. This essentialism means that there is effectively no real choice, but rather an imperative that 'usually contains a number of elements, variously economic, political, social, geographical, religious and so on' (Saward, 1993: 65). As such, Saward argues that the characteristics of political ecology, as set out by people like Porritt – 'low consumption', 'labour-intensive production', and so on – or by the German greens, are not consistent with direct democracy, which cannot operate if the outcomes are already proscribed in advance (Ibid.: 66). In sum, he states:

> [A]t best direct democracy can only be at or near the bottom of value-lists of greens. A commitment to democracy must clash

with core green values which, if taken on board, limit the range of acceptable policy outcomes beyond those self-binding constraints that democracy logically requires (Saward, 1993: 68).[14]

Critics of the green commitment to democracy cite individuals such as Bahro and Ophuls as evidence of the potential authoritarian consequences of green politics (see Saward, 1993: 64, 67; Mills, 1996: 97–8; Barry, 1999: 195–201). These 'ecoauthoritarians', to use Mike Mills' term, argue that because ecological goals are seen as essential, they are prepared to accept the possibility that the means to achieve them might not necessarily be democratic (Mills, 1996: 97). Indeed, for ecoauthoritarianism, Barry argues, democracy is part of the problem, as it is 'ill-suited to dealing with social problems which demand immediate and widespread social change', and also 'represents the unleashing of desires, or demands that cannot be satisfied and which have to be authoritatively restrained' (Barry, 1999: 196). Thus Ophuls argues:

> The steady-state society will not only be more authoritarian and less democratic than the industrial societies of today . . . but it will also in all likelihood be much more oligarchic as well, with only those possessing the ecological and other competencies necessary to make prudent decisions allowed full participation in the political process (Ophuls, 1977: 163).

This indicates that although one can find greens who are genuinely radical democrats – what Mills refers to as 'ecoradicals' (Mills, 1996) – green political ideology can take authoritarian forms.

In addition, we might point to the traditional vision of sexual relations held by many within the ecological movement as a result of the assignment of female status to the Earth. This reinforces the traditional views of femininity that 'have consigned women to an inferior status because they are held to be subordinate qualities' (Dobson, 2000: 26). Moreover, one of the more unsavoury (from the perspective of the left) aspects of the green vision of the sustainable society is their call for a reduction in the world's population. The UK Green Party in its early years had a clear position on the necessity of curbing population growth, a manifesto of the late 1980s suggesting a reduction in the UK's population to 30 million would be a major contributing factor in reducing overall impact on the environment. Although they have focused on this issue less in more recent years, their 1999 *Manifesto for a Sustainable Society* continued to state that 'growth in human numbers is probably the greatest long-term threat to achieving ecological stability either locally or throughout the world' (cited in Dobson, 2000: 81).

ECO, too, argues that 'though there are many "solutions" to the carrying capacity "equation", limiting population will always be a key factor'. They suggest that a 'large human population with consequent overcrowding increases the probability of large scale conflict, disease and starvation' and 'also decreases the scope for responding to "natural" disasters' as well as conflicting 'with the interests of many other species' (ECO, n.d.A; see also ECO, n.d.C). Such positions raise contentious questions regarding how the Earth's population might be reduced. Furthermore, there are discussions within the green movement about just how much population migration should be allowed (see Dobson, 2000: 81–3). Stevens, for example, argues that:

> The 'solution' of regarding all people as global citizens entitled to live anywhere and to use resources from anywhere (within theoretical global sustainability constraints) should be rejected as an answer because it is inherently unecological, denying the importance of place and community. The humanitarian and ecological answer would seem to be to make hugely increased efforts to aid poorer countries to raise living standards for their people and to improve medical, educational and welfare provision, alongside good systems of justice – thus reducing the impetus for them to seek greener pastures elsewhere (Stevens, n.d.).

LEFT AND RIGHT IN GREEN DISCOURSE

The above outline of the core elements of green discourse indicates that its various sub-divisions simply reproduce modern divisions between left and right. Thus many commentators frame green political discourse within those categories.

In terms of the left, a number of commentators see green ideology as a new variant of the ideology of the left. Some of these were mentioned in the opening section of this chapter, notably the work of Inglehart. Similarly, if we return to Stavrakakis's analysis of green ideology discussed earlier, we can note the second dislocation that he sees as feeding into the emergence of green ideology is a crisis within the ideology of the left. Stavrakakis points out that 'there is no necessary link between the development of so-called "environmental conscious-ness" and Green politics *per se*, or the construction of a Green political ideology', and suggests that a green political ideology only emerged because a crisis in the left created 'the need for a rearticulation of radical politics' (Stavrakakis, 2000: 112–13).

Such arguments are rather problematic. It is true that the disloca-tions that fed into the crisis of the left fed into the emergence of a green left-wing variant. For example, the crisis of the state, brought about by concerns over the domineering tendencies of state bureaucracies and by the failures of economic management in the 1970s, the spiralling costs of the health service, and so on, clearly fed into the decentralising tendency within green political thought. The crisis of social and political identity, featuring a fragmentation of formerly dominant identities such as class, and the emergence of new ones, such as ethnicity, as an effect of post-war European migration patterns can also be seen at work in the emergence of green politics. In addition, a crisis of materialism, related to the search for new values in a world in which commodification has spread from the economic realm to embrace all aspects of social life, is a signal factor in the development of green ideology.

However, merely to emphasise the impact on the left ideological space of this series of dislocatory events is to assume in advance that green politics is left wing, and that the dislocations affected only the left, not the right. This is clearly wrong on both counts. Dislocations such as the crisis of the nation-state brought about by economic recession, the impact of globalisation, and so on, the crisis of the post-war form of liberal democratic politics and the crisis of identities, whilst they did play a major role in the crisis of tradi-tional left-wing ideologies from the 1970s on (see Martell, 1992), also impacted upon other ideological forms. Post-war right-wing ideologies were also predicated on some form of materialist ethic of production and consumption, privileged the state and supported traditional forms of social identity. Consequently, these dislocations also fed into a crisis of the predominant post-war variants of the right, whether of the Christian Democrat variety, that of the Conservatives in the UK, or that of continental European forms. It is fair to say that, for the most part, these dislocations resulted in a neo-liberalisation of the mainstream right wing. However, they also opened up a political space for right-wing anti-materialist variants of long-standing. This explains why, as we have already noted in the discussion of community above, one can identify green ideological variants that seem to have little to do with the egalitarian discourse of the left.

It is for just such reasons that several commentators, most notably from a more orthodox left position, have argued that green politics is a right-wing phenomenon. Thus, Göran Dahl points to calls by some European green parties for a 'third way' located 'beyond left and right', as well as the existence of 'some real "Ecofascists"', and suggests that their arguments claim that: 'Nature possesses the highest value of all, and in order to save it, it would probably be a good idea to have dictatorship that guarantees the ongoing care of Nature' (Dahl, 1999: 138). People are wrong to associate green issues with 'leftist' attitudes, claims Dahl, as, historically, 'environmentalism is an old conservative issue, and the ecologists in the fascist and Nazi movements and regimes were not without influence'. Thus, as was noted earlier, Dahl labels Bahro an ecofascist (Dahl, 1999: 139).

Biehl and Staudenmaier (1995) provide a more nuanced version of this view, accepting that the left version of green political thought (presumably the anarchist version propagated by activists like Bookchin) exists alongside a right-wing, fascist version rooted in the Romantic, naturalist and *Völkisch* ecologism of the Nazi era. Other perspectives link green political discourse into conservative thought in more general terms. Thus, for example, Weston states:

> Clearly the green analysis of environmental and social issues is within the broad framework of right-wing ideology and philosophy. The belief in 'natural' limits to human achievement, the denial of class divisions and the Romantic view of 'nature' all have their roots in the conservative and liberal political divisions (cited in Dobson, 2000: 28)

From a slightly different perspective, the academic John Gray has claimed that there are deep affinities between green and conservative thought. This is so in terms of their 'multi-generational' perspective, their rejection of the sovereign subject and their prudence in the face of new technologies or social practices (see Dobson, 2000: 28–9, 174–5; Gray, 1993).[15] He notes, for example, the similarity between green thinking and 'the Burkean idea of the social contract, not as an agreement among anonymous ephemeral individuals, but as a compact between the generations of the living, the dead and those as yet unborn', and their shared scepticism about progress (Gray, 1993: 124).

A GREEN THIRD WAY

The tendency to locate green thought on either the left or the right of the political spectrum fits ill with the argument that green politics is a form of third way politics. It seems to suggest that – despite greens' insistence on rejecting left and right – such categories must necessarily inform our reading of green ideology. We would suggest that arguments linking green politics both to the left *and* to the right are more accurate in two senses. First, like New Labour and other third way discourses, green political ideology draws on elements of left and right ideological heritages. Second, that ideology can take both authoritarian and radical democratic forms. In both cases, however, they propose third ways between capitalism and communism, reflecting the fact that third way politics is not homogeneous and can assume a number of different guises.

This argument fits in with a number of assessments of New Labour's Third Way, which have emphasised the plurality of possible approaches within the 'paradigm'. For example, Pels (2002) has argued that this diversity most clearly takes the form of a distinction between a more collectivist or community-oriented variant in tension with a more individualistic and market-oriented variant within the broader ideological envelope of a 'liberal socialism'.[16] This repeats an older division between left and right *within* the discourse of the third way itself. Concerning green discourse, however, this plurality can also be seen in terms of a dualism between an authoritarian version of collectivism, and a more democratic collectivism.

This suggestion is not made simply because a number of green commentators and political parties have declared that green politics is neither left nor right, although they have done so. For example, according to Spretnak and Capra: 'In calling for an ecological, non-violent, nonexploitative society, the Greens (*Die Grünen*) transcend the linear span of left-to-right' (Spretnak and Capra, 1985: 3). Similarly, *Les Verts* in France, up until the pact with the PS, also claimed to be neither left nor right. This was the reason why, in the 1980s, for example, under then leader Antoine Waechter, it refused to endorse either of the two candidates in the second ballot after the first ballot of the 1988 Presidential elections. In addition to this, however, we claim that green politics of the types examined here are forms of third way politics because the ideological categories of greens noted in the course of this chapter can be clearly located within the repertoire of third way discourse outlined in Chapter 1. Let us take each of these in turn.

As we noted in Chapter 1, third way discourses tend to come to prominence during periods of crisis in which traditional ideas of left and right no longer seem to apply. It is precisely because they have no roots in the order that has been dislocated that third way activists stress their novelty, and lay claim to offer a way out from the problems caused by decaying doctrines. As we have seen, green politics is rooted in the proclamation that there is a crisis threatening the very existence of humanity on the planet and that the only solution to this crisis is the implementation of a sustainable economy.

The diagnosis of this crisis feeds into the second commonality with the repertoire of third way discourse. For ecologists, as we noted earlier, the ecological crisis is fed by all of the other ideological alternatives available, which are each predicated on some form of materialist ethic of production and consumption. As Dobson notes, this widespread rejection amongst greens of the left and right labels stems from the idea that, from an ecological perspective, 'the similarities between communism and capitalism can be made to seem greater than their differences' (Dobson, 2000: 26–7). This similarity relates to a common materialism. Thus Porritt notes:

> Both [capitalism and communism] are dedicated to industrial growth, to the expansion of the means of production, to a materialistic ethic as the best means of meeting people's needs, and to unimpeded technological development. Both rely on increasing centralisation and large-scale bureaucratic control and co-ordination. From a viewpoint of narrow scientific rationalism, both insist that the planet is there to be conquered, that big is self-evidently beautiful, and that what cannot be measured is of no importance (Porritt, 1984: 44).

The solution to this crisis rooted in materialism is a 'spiritual' or ethical revolution. Hence, ECO's argument that 'unbridled materialism must be replaced by values based on moderation and restraint' and that 'material wealth and consumption should be seen in a context of sufficiency and optimisation rather than moreism and maximisation' (ECO, n.d.A). Green discourse, then, seeks to bring about a new form of ethics – born from a complete re-working of the relationship between humankind and nature, as well as a stress on the ethical demand of our relationship as humans living in a community – and challenges our commitment to material wealth on this basis. This ethical focus means that, like other forms of third way, green ideology is also voluntaristic.

As we noted earlier, greens believe that the catastrophe that uninter-rupted growth in the levels of production and consumption is leading to is not inevitable; that economic and political intervention together with lifestyle changes can reverse the process.

The core values of culture, community, solidarity and responsibility that stem from this ethical aspect of third way thinking have been noted at varying points in this chapter, whether they take the form of an egalitarian, decentralised community or that of the ethnic, spiritual community united in common attachments of blood and soil.

Green politics can also be seen to incorporate the elitism noted in the third way repertoire. This takes different forms, of course, depending on whether the green ideology in question takes the egalitarian, decentra-lised form or the authoritarian one. In terms of the former, one finds an emphasis on a 'new' – in this case 'postmaterialist' – generation, as the work of Inglehart has focused upon (see Inglehart, 1977, 1990). Such arguments clearly display an optimism about the historical force of ideas and the mission of 'intellectual' politicians. In terms of the latter, the hierarchical, organicist forms of community advocated obviously lend themselves to the notion that an elite exists that symbolises the form of society to come and has the will to bring it about.

Finally, all third way visions strongly criticise contemporary forms of liberal democracy for being based on a too abstract individualism and not paying sufficient attention to intermediary forms of associa-tion. This is clearly seen in both new liberalism and a variety of inter-war French third way visions, and can even be seen – whatever the faults in practice – in the rhetoric of New Labour, with its talk of decentralisation. Our discussion of the forms of green political thought that seek either to reform liberal democracy in the direction of direct democracy – through economic and workplace democracy, cooperatives, and so on – or at least to enhance the democratic aspect of liberal democracy through some form of decentralisation clearly involve the introduction of some form of intermediary association between state and citizen. Ecoauthoritarians, of course, seek to reform liberal democracy in a different direction, as do those strands of the green movement labelled ecofascist, although they too root the criti-cism of the liberal democratic system in an absence of links between the political system and 'natural' communities, such as the region and the family (this latter being embodied in the idea that voters with large families should have more votes, for example).

Whatever form green political discourse takes – authoritarian or radical democratic – it tends towards a third way politics because it seeks to carve out a distinctive space that is beyond the established antagonism between left and right. Indeed, for greens the principal antagonism is between the defenders and the destroyers of nature. Of course, a range of possible green positions can be articulated from within this framework. Notwithstanding differences in intellectual heritage, however, these forms of green third way share family resemblances both between each other and with other forms of third way thought.

What does the analysis of green thought show us about third way thinking in general? Two, related, points are perhaps worth making. First, we have seen several examples of third way movements in this book. Green political thought can be seen as a microcosm of this larger ideological whole through the very variety of third way positions that are locatable within the green ideological framework. Second, the very fact that green ideology offers such a variety of possible third way positions signals the fact that these positions are not mutually exclusive; the family resemblance between diverse green movements – the degree of discursive overlap – facilitates a transition from one position to another. This offers grounds both for optimism and pessimism because it opens up the possibility that New Labour's Third Way has the potential to be developed in a much more radically democratic way than it has hitherto shown through an extension of its decentralising and empowering tendencies, whilst at the same time it reveals the potential for it to adopt a much more authoritarian posture, emphasising, on the contrary, the more anti-democratic aspects which critics have pointed to.[17] It is to the analysis of what a more radical democratic third way might look like that we shall now turn.

NOTES

1 Political parties in Germany are assigned colours (red for the SPD, amber for the Liberals, green for the Grünen, and so on), hence the 'traffic-light'.

2 Stavrakakis understands by dislocation Laclau's definition; that is, as 'the moment of failure and subversion of a system of representation' (Stavrakakis, 2000: 105). See Laclau (1990: 39–45).

3 The parameters of the ideological dislocation involved in the emergence of green thought are wider than those identified by Stavrakakis, who relates green thought to the left only. We shall return to this point later in the chapter.

4 'Mental (or semantic) holism is the doctrine that the identity of a belief content (or the meaning of a sentence that expresses it) is determined by its place in the web of beliefs or sentences comprising a whole theory or group of theories' ('Holism' in Craig (1998)).

5 Freeden notes that it is possible to assert that Bookchin excludes holism from his version of green discourse, but argues that this would be incorrect (Freeden, 1995: 18).

6 On the political importance of community, see Finlayson (2002a) and Little (2002a).

7 Lipietz himself uses the term productivism – the whole set of socio-economic structures and mentalities which push people to "produce for the sake of producing", with no care for the real needs of people or the sustainability of the production regime' (Lipietz, 1995: 26) – but argues that this term means to greens exactly what the term capitalism does to reds (Lipietz, 1995: 27).

8 This ecologism is tied to their wider critique of capitalism and the USA, proclaiming that 'the ecological militant is a wholly political fighter, for whom it is imperative . . . to fight capitalism and its consumerist logic' (Séveno, 1998: 3; Relano, n.d.).

9 For details of UR's hostility towards McDonald's, see Ghezzo (1998: 5) and UR (n.d.B).

10 For a consideration of green arguments in favour of institutional decentralisation see de Geus (1996: 194).

11 Nevertheless, Carter is quick to point out that the green case for workplace democracy is not as clear-cut as greens imagine (see especially Carter, 1996: 68–72).

12 The reaction against Enlightenment rationalism that stressed the importance of non-rational (and even irrational) aspects of human nature that, although not entirely the province of right-wing thought, is associated with conservative thinkers such as Burke, Herder and de Maistre.

13 Robyn Eckersley's ecocentric vision of green politics, for example, clearly articulates a form of politics that seeks to extend liberalism, not reject it (see Eckersley, 1992: 173–8; also Eckersley, 1996a, 1996b).

14 See also Dobson, 'Ecologism', in R. Eatwell and T. Wright (eds), *Contemporary Political Ideologies* (London: Pinter, 1993: 234), cited in Mills, 1996: 101.

15 For an interesting discussion of the difference between conservative greens and green conservatives see Freeden (1995: 13).

16 Personalism 'is the name given to a number of philosophies which correlate the conceptions of personality and value, which conceive of personality as a unique entity in every human being which has a movement towards value and is the source of our knowledge of value' (Coates, 1949: 9). It is generally traced back to the thought and action of the founder of the French journal, *Esprit*, Emmanuel Mounier (see, for example, Mounier, 1952), and can clearly be seen as a third way discourse (see Bastow, 2001).

17 Examples of the latter, of course, would include the more recent shift in the Labour government's attitude to the integration of ethnic minorities within the UK, and its attitude to asylum and immigration.

CONCLUSION
RADICAL POLITICS AND
THE THIRD WAY

Contemporary proponents of a Third Way in social democracy make the puzzling claim to occupy the 'radical centre'. In so doing, they exhibit the paradoxical desire to move beyond the antagonistic oppositions of left and right, and yet remain in some way oppositional. But can radical politics be conceived in terms of a third way? Surely, abandoning oppositions means abandoning the antagonism that makes radical politics what it is? In this concluding chapter, we return to these questions and, in light of the earlier chapters, we consider the possibility that the notion of a third way may yet offer up radical opportunities for those committed to a democratic and pluralist politics. For it to do so, however, we argue that it is necessary for third way politics to re-engage antagonisms, not simply as a return to old forms of politics but as a way of opening up to new kinds of struggle and conflict. In short, it is necessary for proponents of a third way to abandon any notion of moving 'beyond politics' altogether, to accept the irreducible character of antagonism and the role of power and conflict in social life. Certainly this will suggest a politics that is different from the ideas of contemporary social democracy. Nevertheless, it will allow us to imagine a third way that goes beyond old antagonisms in order to embrace and engage new ones.

THIRD WAYS: POSSIBILITIES AND PROBLEMS

Our survey of third ways in this book was premised on the notion that these ideologies are distinguished, or distinguish themselves, by invoking a politics that transcends the received antagonisms of left and right. We have seen some of the various ways in which this move is made: third ways between principles of individual liberty and social justice, between East and West, or capitalism and communism. Clearly, there is a broad range of third ways. We have noted how, whilst seeking to transcend left and right, third ways typically stem from within that distinction: thus there are left-of-centre third ways, radical right third ways, and so on. Perhaps, then, third way discourse is rather mundane and of little relevance since it appears in so many forms and doesn't fully accomplish the transcendence it boasts. Perhaps, as Anthony Giddens remarks, the very notion of the third way is of little substantive interest in itself.

Such views, we believe, are mistaken. As we noted in the Introduction and Chapter 1, and have indicated throughout our discussion of different ideological formations, the semantic structure of the third way is itself part of the politics it promotes. Third ways, however they are constructed, direct us to the exhaustion of dominant forms of ideological thought and make explicit the failure of ideologies to fully hegemonise the field of dislocated subjects and social antagonisms. However, in looking 'beyond' antagonism, third ways run the danger of seeking to eradicate antagonism altogether. Let us consider the possibilities signalled by third way discourses and the problems these raise.

We argued in Chapter 1 that third ways can be closely associated with periods of intense social dislocation. Under such conditions, the ideological parameters, themselves always in flux to some extent, are confronted with circumstances they seem radically unable to explain. Under such conditions, it is highly plausible that dominant political ideologies will eventually succeed in accommodating change and adapt themselves to new circumstances without radically altering their principles. This, indeed, is what the history of mainstream ideologies suggests. Another approach, however, is to proclaim a 'crisis' in the modes by which we understand social and political life and to use this crisis to launch a programme of change based on principles that both transcend and absorb key aspects of the ideological field. This strategy, we have argued, characterises the discourse of the third way.

From the perspective of the study of political ideologies, third ways illuminate the essentially unfixed character of ideological systems and the manner in which any fixity at all is achieved through the contingent hegemonisation of differences around certain principles. Third ways unpick the relatively settled arrangement of ideas, beliefs, models of social, economic and political institutions and reassemble them in order to form new ideological systems. There is in the articulation of third ways, then, an implicit recognition of the contingent character of political ideologies and the horizons these set for social and political action. For in re-ordering once antagonistic principles, third ways seek to reconfigure the choices and decisions that are practically available. To recognise this peculiar feature of third ways is, at some level, to accept that our ideas and beliefs, our principles and the institutions we seek to uphold them, are in part constitutive of society. To accept these ideas is to begin creating the society third ways promote.

This discursive character accounts for the emphasis we have noted on ethics: subjective belief is fundamental to third way discourses. Third ways pin their hopes on individual subjects recognising for themselves the need to transcend the stale and alienating materialism of earlier systems of belief. These, it is often argued, fail to grasp the internal motivation that ought to drive political ideology, preferring instead to view social order as the outcome of impersonal forces such as the dialectical 'laws of history' or the 'hidden hand' of human rationality. Third ways, by contrast, address individuals as social subjects, not as atomistic individuals or passive bearers of class interests, and as conscious agents of a better society to come. Whether it be as citizens of the ethnic community, the anti-fascist liberal order or the ecologically aware society, third ways give priority to an active belief-in-common over a passive resignation.

These characteristic features of third ways – which, we must emphasise, are played out in starkly different ways in different ideologies – underscore some of its positive political characteristics. Third ways acknowledge the possibility for reassembling political ideas and practices in novel ways, for refashioning the hierarchies of principles and values that other systems of belief appear to set in stone. They do this with an emphasis on developing new types of ethical subjectivity, on forging social order from within the authentic experience of social subjects themselves.

However, this opening to the contingency of ideological structures and the active role of subjects is often strikingly limited by a further appeal to essentialist principles aimed at grounding the third way in some kind of 'necessity'. This essentialism is most visible in the notions of 'community' that we have argued are key to third way discourses. Third ways typically point to notions of communal solidarity not on the basis of rational choices of individuals but on a spiritual bond that ties people together at a pre-rational level. This bond – expressed in terms of ethnic or national identity, a common link to nature, or a shared sense of 'risk' in a global society, for example – is typically presented as forming a necessary part of subjective identity. That is, it is a bond that is not open to contest but precedes the subject as a natural, or nature-like, condition. Essentialist principles, however, effectively close down the space for rearticulating ideological elements. Indeed, some notions of community achieve this closure retroactively by positing the community as an already-given identity, not one that is itself forged contingently (see Finlayson, 1998). The third way is thus conceived as a return to an authentic community lost in the empty decadence of the modern age. Such ideas are found in third ways emanating from the right, such as fascism or neo-fascism, whilst the centre and left tend to regard their communities as historically novel, nevertheless also positing an underlying necessity as the source of a common bond, for instance in notions of globalisation or 'nature'. The effect, however, is the same: the unifying principle of community is conceived as fundamentally incontestable.

It is this tendency towards essentialist closure that makes the third way appeal to move beyond the antagonisms of left and right tend towards a claim to move beyond *all* antagonisms. This explains a common orientation towards various levels of authoritarianism. At the core of many third ways is the appeal to a mythical order in which social difference is, fundamentally, harmonised. In fascist totalitarianism, this mythical ideal invokes a total identity in which individual difference is almost eliminated by the unity of the nation. Socialist, social democratic or green ideologies certainly do not invoke this specific ideal, yet their third ways also eliminate social differences at some fundamental level even if they accept that people will disagree, possibly quite sharply, over this or that issue. On the basis of this basic unity, third ways have tended to justify hierarchical notions of political action and social order. It is because the essential unity of society has been grasped as the ethical basis of social order that its institutional form does not need to be open to contest. The economic plan, the party, the social reformer, and so on, are too often conceived as being beyond reproach and any difference in opinion over their functioning is assumed to be neutralised by the wider ethical unity that legitimises them. Thus whilst third ways may be more or less democratic in their organisation, the limits of democracy are often placed around the conditions that give rise to the community itself.

Third ways, then, typically promise both a genuine, radical change and yet often limit this change within an essentialist discourse that restricts political conflict (that is, contest over the boundaries and needs of the community) by disguising its own contingency. But does this, admittedly sweeping, characterisation limit the radical potential of third way discourses? Is it conceivable that radical democratic theory might itself be understood as a third way type of discourse? This is a question that demands more attention than can be given here, yet it is possible to map out how an answer might be given in the affirmative.

The Third Way and the Left

For all its evident weaknesses, the Third Way in social democracy signals a sense of exhaustion by those on the left with the traditional ideas, conflicts and achievements signified by the notion of being 'on the left' in modern politics. Whilst today many may wince at the idea of the centre-left Third Way as the road to renewal, nevertheless there is a large constituency in Europe that senses, and has sensed for some time, the declining appeal of a politics of opposition. What is this politics and what are the intellectual and practical foundations of its decline?

For much of the twentieth century, being on the left meant a number of related things: an attachment to social and political change as a form of progressive improvement of individual and social life; the formal and substantial achievement of equality amongst individuals in industrial societies; the reorganisation of wealth and power in favour of the poor; and the democratisation of state and society. In these broad commitments the left stood in opposition to conservatives of authoritarian and liberal hues who sought either to turn back the achievements of modernisation and progress, or at very least to limit them and their effects. To be sure, the 'left' signified wildly diverse, sometimes contradictory, aims and aspirations but its goals placed it in opposition to the present order, looking forward to a society of greater co-operation, material well-being and individual and collective fulfilment. Socialists, social democrats, communists, syndicalists, anarchists, radical liberals, feminists: all saw in the advances of the previous one hundred years the as yet unfulfilled opportunity to surpass various forms of oppression and inequalities. To be on the left signalled an awareness that social improvements were still unfinished, that modern society could bring emancipation in a way that could never be imagined in pre-modern society.

In the course of the twentieth century, however, the cluster of assumptions that gave the left its oppositional, forward-looking politics have either dwindled or eroded altogether. This was partly the result of the fact that the left in power – social democracy in Europe, Communist socialism in Eastern Europe – proved to be of debatable success. As is well known, neither Eastern nor Western versions of socialism proved as radically emancipatory as they were (and still are) claimed to be. In the Soviet Union, Stalin's reign suggested massive industrial advance could only be achieved by the loss of individual political liberty, by state suppression and international aggression; in Europe, the left's achievements were premised on a form of state-led expansion built on techniques learned during wartime and a fortuitous economic boom, neither of which proved to be of enduring success. Some of the foundational assumptions of left-wing and radical politics, therefore, were gradually exhausted by the very success of the left in the twentieth century. For many on the left, these assumptions and the practical means of achieving them (that is, the state) became the object of opposition itself.

The growing sense of disillusionment with the left in practice, which fed into the emergence of the so-called 'New Left' in the 1960s, coalesced around a further series of emergent dislocations that came to challenge the general patterns of ideological antagonism in Europe. First, there was the related emergence of mass culture and the penetration of capitalist relations of production under Fordism, which reduced our sense of a rationality underpinning the 'real' world still more from that already figured in the crisis of modernity at the end of the nineteenth century, transforming society into a vast market 'in which more and more of the products of human labour were turned into commodities' (Laclau and Mouffe, 2001: 161; see also Lash, 1990: 38–9). This commodification of social life both instrumentalised social relations – thus producing, for some, a soulless social world void of any ethical framework – and increasingly broke down the distinction between the economic and the cultural realm, making it difficult to discern reality from its representation, introducing 'chaos, flimsiness, and instability in our experience of reality itself' (Lash, 1990: 15; see also Smart, 1992: 189). In turn, this fostered a generalised distrust of 'grand narratives' with a concomitant rejection of the feasibility of the modernist project to bring about the emancipation of humanity from poverty, ignorance, prejudice and the absence of enjoyment (Lyotard, 1984).

Second, a number of changes have undermined the regulatory role of the state that was so central for post-war social democracy. In the first place, the national capital that had been so important for the economy from the inter-war period onward, declined as effective units of production and, at the same time, the regulatory power of the nation-state diminished. This has been paralleled by the rise of the global market and of global corporations, exacerbating the declining power of nation-states to intervene in economic affairs (see Held, 1995; Held, et al., 1999: ch.1), as well as the emergence of regional economic and political institutions and agencies, such as the European Union, which have usurped both the power and the authority of nation-states in an increasing number of domains.

Third, the emergence of the phenomenon of global warming, together with events such as Chernobyl, undermined belief in the mastery and control of science over nature and encouraged many to believe that unfettered economic production and consumption were having a catastrophic effect on the natural world. This increasingly called into question the whole premise of uninterrupted economic growth, which the left required in order to fund the expansion of the welfare state apparatus.

Fourth, a number of changes have fed into a general weakening of the political authority of the liberal democratic systems of the post-war period with which social democracy was increasingly bound. Mass-based interest groups (primarily the trade unions) have declined at the same time as social movements and 'networks' based on region, race or gender, or on single-issue politics, and peripheral, sub- and supra-national movements have emerged. These latter groupings form part of a so-called 'new politics' more inclined to bypass the political institutions of the liberal-democratic order such as developed in the post-war period (see Inglehart, 1977: 3).

Political authority has been further weakened by major changes in the experience of social and political identity, which have led a number of commentators to talk of a 'crisis' of identity (see Woodward, 1997: 15). The social identities around which political conflicts coalesce have fragmented and pluralised.

The changes in the economy noted above have disrupted class identities, such that class is no longer the primordial force it once was (on which see Crook, et al., 1992: 110–12). This is not necessarily to suggest that class has ceased to exist as a mode of political identification and social cleavage but that, as Laclau notes, social class in contemporary societies has been displaced not only in the sense of class as a function of economic organisation and of processes of production but in its sense as a 'master' category, as Marxists deploy the concept, as a determinant of all the other social relations. For Laclau, not only is class struggle not inevitable, it is no longer possible to argue that social emancipation lies in the hands of one class (see Laclau, 1990: 40). At the same time, new struggles have emerged in contemporary society to express resistance against new forms of subordination – ecological struggles, urban struggles, and so on – on a multiplicity of different sites, struggling against inequalities and claiming new rights (Laclau, 1990: 161). Struggles over race and sexuality, the environment, abortion, and so on, and the new social movements of the 1970s and '80s did not replace class politics, but they came to rival the focus upon questions of distribution and scarcity that mainstream parties had traditionally mobilised. Ultimately, all of these transformations in identity have meant that we increasingly feel less like members of a homogeneous political community, making it difficult for all political parties to mobilise the 'people'. Although the left was never entirely based around the mobilising of the working class in the post-war period, the declining salience of class, together with the emergence of social groups mobilised around social issues such as feminism and racism, increasingly problematised the nature of the 'people' that the left claimed to represent.

Taken together, these changes have called into question the traditional assumptions of social democracy. It is this questioning that New Labour's Third Way addresses by its 'modernisation' programme. To what extent, however, can we square this social democratic Third Way with a radical democratic politics? Is this third way discourse not intrinsically centrist, even mildly conservative? It is to this question we now turn.

THE RADICAL DEMOCRATIC IMAGINARY

Earlier we noted Bobbio's claim that what he labels the 'inclusive middle' is inevitably centrist, which seems to indicate its incompatibility with any radical democratic politics (Bobbio, 1996: 7–9). Indeed, one of the leading proponents of radical democratic politics, Chantal Mouffe, reiterates the point. Mouffe, whose analysis draws upon Bobbio (Mouffe, 2000: 123), has explicitly rejected New Labour's Third Way, arguing:

> Relations of power and their constitutive role in society are obliterated [by New Labour] and the conflicts that they entail

reduced to a simple competition of interests that can be harmonized through dialogue. This is the typical liberal perspective that envisages democracy as a competition among elites, making adversary forces invisible and reducing politics to an exchange of arguments and the negotiation of compromises (Ibid.: 110–11).

For Mouffe, the Third Way 'sacrilises' consensus, making it the basis (and goal) of any democratic politics. This leads to an emphasis on shared identity rather than difference, agreement rather than conflict, and she counterposes it to a pluralism entailing 'the recognition and the legitimation of conflict and the refusal to suppress it through the imposition of an authoritarian order' (Ibid).

> A counter-hegemonic strategy is precisely what is precluded by the idea of a radical centrism which denies the existence of antagonisms and the need for political frontiers and which proclaims that 'flexibility' is a modern social democratic aim. To believe that one can accommodate the aims of the big corporations with those of the weaker sectors is already to have capitulated to their power (Mouffe, 2000: 120).

We agree with Mouffe's argument that the Third Way sacrilises consensus – as Little has noted, the works of theorists like John Keane, John Gray and Benjamin Barber, who envisage civil society as 'the sphere where diversity can flourish' and in which social consensus can be established, 'could be (and often are) incorporated into the political analysis of the "Third Way" or "radical centre"' (Little, 2002c: 111–12) – and that the emphasis on consensus evades antagonism. Moreover, we agree that such a criticism holds true for many other forms of third way discourse that, as we noted earlier, affect an essentialist closure through the articulation of a 'natural' community that is to be restored. The question is, however, whether this critique holds for *all* forms of third way. Here we would disagree with both Mouffe and Bobbio. Indeed, we believe that radical democracy can itself be posed as a form of third way. Let us sketch Laclau and Mouffe's vision of the 'radical democratic imaginary' and then go on to outline its third way character.

In the final chapter of *Hegemony and Socialist Strategy*, Laclau and Mouffe make the following claim: 'Every radical democratic politics should avoid the two extremes represented by the totalitarian myth of the Ideal City, and the positivist pragmatism of reformists without a project' (2001: 190). By this they mean that a radical politics of the left needs to steer a route between the twin efforts to wholly eradicate politics either by totally organising society and removing the possibility for social conflict, or by abandoning any radical aspirations and simply administering to social demands in a pragmatic and piecemeal way. The first, totalitarian option represents the strategy of Soviet communism, the second that of social democratic reformism: both, however, shared the rationalist assumption that social antagonisms could be eradicated once economic power relations were handed over to a socialist(-inspired) administration. Of course, both communism and reformist social democracy regarded each other with antipathy – indeed they constituted antagonistic visions of the left project – yet both functioned on the assumption that the rational management of the economy would enable political differences to subside, making politics itself merely a matter of neutral administration.

For Laclau and Mouffe, the rationalist assumptions underlying these visions must be abandoned by the left. Socialism cannot be grounded in the idea of achieving a harmonious social order in which all differences are reconciled and no serious conflict emerges. Such a view is hopelessly utopian and is premised on the essentialist notion that society can be objectively understood in its totality and that social division is ultimately a failure to recognise the rational order underlying appearances. Socialism, in this sense, is the inheritor of the legacy of the Enlightenment's view that beneath the surface of conflict and instability of human life lay a rational structure intelligible to reason. Such a view, however, has oppressive political implications in as much as the idea of a 'true' understanding of society legitimises the coercion of those unwilling to recognise the validity of such claims, this being the kind of logic informing Rousseau's chilling suggestion that those who do not obey the General Will must be 'forced to be free'. The effect of this logic is to imagine a society in which individual differences can be harmonised and politics ceases to be a contest in which starkly opposed visions are contested. Instead, politics becomes a form of benign management, the co-ordination of differences in an essentially reconciled community.

Thus Soviet communism was premised on the belief that the eradication of class differences and a totalitarian organisation of economy and society in which state and citizenry were 'merged' through the party could unify social differences. In a slightly different way, post-war social democracy was guided by a sense that capitalism could be rationally managed in such a way that open class conflict could be minimised and wealth redistribution and state-provided public services would suppress the aspiration to disrupt the social order in any radical way. Both visions proved misguided: Soviet communism failed both to uphold basic human and political rights and, to assuage this loss of political freedom, to generate the material equality (not to say abundance) that socialism requires. Social democracy, on the other hand, misrecognised an economic boom for its own superior management of capitalism. Once growth in post-war economies stopped rising, class and other conflicts broke out and proved the era of 'consensus' a transient phenomenon. In short, both failed to recognise the impossibility of fully eradicating politics in favour of rational administration.

Laclau and Mouffe argue for a radical left project that rejects the essentialist assumptions of the socialist tradition and openly incorporates the view that power and conflict can never be erased. In their view, as we have seen, antagonism is a constitutive dimension of social identity. The idea of a fully reconciled society without antagonism is simply mythical, for it is only through defining ourselves in terms of aspirations that seem to be 'blocked' that we come to have a stable identity at all. In this sense, society is intrinsically political – that is, defining and contesting the limits of social existence is what society is about. Thus the political is an ontological condition of the social; it is the way society comes to be a meaningful order. To seek to eradicate political conflict, or even to radically minimise it, is to refute the very condition of being social: that is, it is self-negating. It is this aspect, the attempt to transcend all divisions and promote an illusory consensus that Mouffe, quite rightly, rejects about the Third Way of New Labour. Moreover, this illusion is also that which drove the great left projects of the twentieth century but which also underscores their ultimate failings. Gripped by the notion that the economy constitutes a privileged site of social antagonism whose resolution would lead to the resolution of all major conflicts, socialists ended up either displacing conflict and division onto other sites such as the welfare state or the party, marginalising it or suppressing it altogether.

But how can antagonism be incorporated into a left project, and with what effects? For Laclau and Mouffe, abandoning essentialism means displacing socialism in favour of what they call the 'radical democratic imaginary'. This is a vision of a social order that can never be fully reconciled, in which there are no universally privileged sites of conflict and which aspires to deepen democracy in a pluralistic way.

This vision is clearly different from the image of a community of self-governing workers that the left has tended to promote as its core view of society. Indeed, it is not a vision of a definite society at all so much as an abstract horizon against which a variety of social orders may be envisaged. Thus Laclau and Mouffe state that whilst 'it is necessary to put an end to capitalist relations of production, which are at the root of numerous relations of subordination', 'socialism is *one* of the components of a project for radical democracy, not vice versa' (2001: 178). Radical democracy can incorporate various types of project, socialist or otherwise, but none can exhaust it or function as its necessary core, for that would contradict the idea of there being no privileged site of antagonism. Workers' democracy, for instance, might give workers more control over their factories but it cannot necessarily solve conflicts that occur outside the relations of production – for example, questions of consumption, or race and gender discrimination. If these conflicts are to be recognised as genuinely autonomous and therefore irreducible to relations of production, then the horizon against which they are defined by the left must be a radical democratic one, not that of socialism.

Laclau and Mouffe seek to promote radical democracy as a hegemonic conception of the left project. That is, they aim to develop a space in which a variety of social antagonisms irreducible to economic conflicts can be seen as potentially equal – and therefore unifiable – without subordinating them by appealing to some fixed reference point. For this reason, they define radical democracy as part of the tradition of the 'democratic revolution' that began with the American and French revolutions of the late eighteenth century. These revolutions involved the rejection of Divine Right as the unconditional principle of political order; thereafter democracy has stood for the unfixity of political relations, a regulated instability in social orders whereby all elements are potentially open to contest and change. Against this backdrop, radical democracy promotes a further deepening of the democratic moment, an extension of the democratic contestability to wider areas of state and society than liberal democrats have hitherto admitted. In later work, Mouffe has written of two elements of modernity: the epistemological project of the Enlightenment and the democratic project. Radical democracy rejects the first but develops the second in a new, mildly 'postmodern' way (that is, open to a plurality of social and political identities formed around agendas of anti-racism, anti-sexism, and so on) (see Mouffe, 1993). Likewise, Laclau has called into question the classic notions of 'emancipation' in order to assert the idea of multiple varieties of emancipation (Laclau, 1996a).

In elaborating the philosophical premises of their vision of 'radical and pluralist democracy', Laclau and Mouffe both assert the ineradicable necessity of antagonism in social life and recognise that no single antagonism can present itself as the a priori essence of all the others. Thus we must accept that any social order will be riven with multiple antagonisms as a consequence of a whole series of dislocations, and yet none can be plausibly identified as bearing some universal essence and therefore having any natural superiority over the others. This point has rightly been identified as a direct challenge to the Marxist tradition that has claimed the variety of dislocated identities must be led by the working class, for their conflict has deeper roots in the foundations of society than any other social agent. For Laclau and Mouffe, however, the rejection of any foundation to society means that this claim simply cannot stand. As a consequence, the division between left and right becomes 'blurred': 'Say we try to define an ultimate content of the left which underlies all the contexts in which the word has been used: we shall never find one which does not present exceptions' (Laclau and Mouffe, 2001: 179).

The only answer, in their view, is to accept that what constitutes 'the left' is not a 'unified discourse' (Ibid.: 191) but a constantly shifting 'balance of forces' organised around democratic struggles over the meaning and relation between liberty and equality. In modernity, democratic struggles have involved competing conceptions of the meaning and application of equality and liberty in society. Whilst the right has fastened on to economic liberty and the left to social equality as the key elements of their traditions, a radical democratic project has to balance the two. Aligning the left simply with equality is to ignore the importance of struggles for democratic recognition and autonomy, especially amongst contemporary social movements. Different groups demand different conceptions of freedom (economic, religious, sexual, and so on): liberty cannot therefore be uniform, for that would imply that one account of freedom serves everyone. A pluralist democracy must be open to competing definitions of liberty. Yet the left cannot abandon equality in its economic sense and must temper it with an acceptance of the equal worth of other groups.

A left hegemonic project, then, can only ever be a 'compromise', a contingent and 'unstable equilibrium' of diverse, sometimes contradictory, demands that find their equivalence in the promotion of radical democracy. But Laclau and Mouffe are keen to point out that this project must not simply be a form of oppositionalism, a crude gathering of 'anti-system demands' that seek merely to subvert the present order. Rather, a left hegemonic project must combine a 'strategy of opposition' with a 'strategy of construction of a new order'. The negative moment must be combined with a positive one in which specific institutional arrangements are defended (Ibid.: 189). Inevitably, however, this means that certain compromises have to be made, that some demands for liberty and equality go unheard so that others may predominate.

A RADICAL DEMOCRATIC THIRD WAY?

The radical democratic imaginary is not a commitment to a specific institutional form of politics but a theoretical expression of the terms within which a politics of the left can be articulated without appealing to essentialist categories. In our view, its organising principles, as we have sketched them, develop an agenda for a type of third way politics comparable with the discursive repertoire we set up in Chapter 1.

Laclau and Mouffe's recommendation to avoid the twin extremes of utopian revolutionism and reformist pragmatism positions them between the left and right poles on the radical left. We may think of this position as consonant with Hendrik de Man's 'revolutionary revisionism' in so far as, like de Man, they renounce the fantasy of the proletariat becoming the 'universal class' emancipating humanity as they free themselves but they do not see this as a renunciation of radicalism in general. Laclau and Mouffe's third way imagines a broad space between the multiplicity of contemporary antagonisms and the need for an overarching project, between a reformism recognising the autonomy of different struggles and a radicalism opposing efforts to halt change.

The politics they propose is not one of an absolute Otherness or what Laclau calls the 'particularism' of so-called 'identity politics' (see Laclau, 1996a). This would fall into the trap of advocating an 'essentialism of the elements' in which differences are accorded an essential primacy over collective identity. It is the absence of any final closure, the irreducible tension between identity and difference, that frames a radical third way politics. The strategy of Laclau and Mouffe might be termed a form of third way politics without a *telos*, a kind of endless 'thirding' involving a tension between a logic of equivalence – the search for consensus between antagonistic social groups – and a logic of difference, the acceptance that this consensus will always already exclude the 'Other'. It is precisely this endless process of inclusion/exclusion that radical democracy seeks to institutionalise.[1]

Radical democracy also implies a distinctive ethics. Having renounced objectivist and rationalistic forms of reasoning that look to universal foundations to theorise political order, Laclau and Mouffe follow other third ways in emphasising that social order is constructed *between* subjects. However, unlike other third ways they highlight the ineradicable place of power and exclusion in this (ongoing) construction. Although the thrust of their anti-essentialism is to reject the idea of ethical discourses as having any logical primacy (see Mouffe, 2000: 134–5), radical democracy nevertheless opens up space for what Mouffe calls a 'democratic ethics' to govern the conduct of antagonistic differences. However, this is not the ethics of a community whose borders are settled but more like an 'ethics of dis-harmony', where the potential for conflict and violence are permanently visible markers (Ibid.: 137–40). Mouffe regards this ethics as indissociable from politics. In her view, it is best encapsulated in the idea of an 'agonistic' democratic community; that is, a democracy of adversaries who recognise their opposition to each other but do not seek to suppress that opposition. Instead of prioritising consensus, an agonistic democracy institutionalises conflict, limiting violent antagonisms and transforming them as much as possible into conflicts between 'adversaries' (Ibid.: 98–105). Recognising antagonists as adversaries legitimises them as political opponents but refuses to exclude them from the political game altogether. Thus the democratic order can be conceived as fundamentally pluralist, difference being interwoven into the very idea of community.

Interestingly, Mouffe's emphasis on conflict and pluralism aligns her with the associative democracy proposed by Paul Hirst – an explicit advocate of a third way whose work she has endorsed (see Hirst, 1994; Hirst and Bader, 2001; Mouffe, 1993: 98–100). Hirst's associationalism fits well with the radical democratic denial that there can be no firm guarantee that the plurality of communities located within civil society can be articulated around any unifying principle because it opens up new sites of conflict for communities to interact and undermines any effort for a singular community to be mobilised as the ultimate container of all others. Like the radical democracy espoused by Laclau and Mouffe, contemporary associationalists claim that current liberal democratic thought and practice are insufficiently responsive to the growing diversity in values and lifestyles within Western populations. The associationalist response is a call for the reordering of the scale and direction of liberal democratic practices such that smaller organisational forms can generate a closer proximity of the public to the decisions of government, so that power flows 'upwards' from below rather than vice versa. From a radical democratic perspective, the essential advantage of associative democracy is its practical reconfiguration of power in a pluralistic manner.

Associative democracy involves the decentralisation of public services to a plurality of self-governing associations that are voluntarily generated and democratically accountable to their members (see Warren, 2001; Hirst, 1994, 1997; Carter, 2002; Cohen and Rogers, 1995). By dispersing power from the centre, central state powers require only a minimal degree of consensus over their functions; the actual provision of public services does not require total 'national agreement' and can therefore be delivered in a variety of ways from a number of sources. By 'publicizing the private sphere', Hirst's model removes the possibility of a single public sector being the site of conflict between competing parties and interest groups. Associative principles thus frame democracy as a practice responsive to the inherently diverse and potentially antagonistic nature of human communities, and provide a promising institutional form to an ethics of democracy (see Little and Martin, 2002). Other contemporary third ways on the left similarly recognise the partial and contestable nature of social order.[2]

Of course, what we have outlined here is only the briefest of sketches of a radical democratic third way. Yet it serves to underline the point we have tried to make throughout this volume. The appeal to a third way ought not to be dismissed, least of all by the left. Third way discourse marks out a terrain of political struggle in which the exhaustion of received antagonistic ideologies is announced and the promise of a new ethics and new types of communal order can be imagined. Whilst many on the left fairly criticise the Third Way of New Labour and other European social democrats, this terrain remains a challenge to be confronted but it is also a promising source for radical change.

In an age when the utopian ideal of 'total emancipation' has lost its currency, the left should not organise exclusively around simple, all-embracing oppositional dichotomies such as 'anti-globalisation', nor even anti-capitalism. No single struggle can hegemonise all the others without suppressing pluralism and autonomy. Rather, the struggles these movements articulate need to be recognised as different but, at various levels, potentially equivalent. The horizon of radical democracy offers a way to express this recognition. Only a left politics that embraces difference and antagonism without idolising the myth of collective unity and consensus can succeed. This, indeed, is the promise of third way discourse.

NOTES

1 Like other third ways, Laclau and Mouffe's also appropriates elements from ideologies widely thought to be antagonistic to the left. For example, Mouffe has returned to the ideas of Carl Schmitt to support her defence of an agonistic theory of democracy. Although Schmitt was a conservative critic of liberal democracy in the inter-war period – and lent his support to the Nazi movement – his political philosophy is acknowledged by Mouffe (and others) as both original and adaptable to a radical democratic project, in particular his characterisation of the political in terms of the friend/enemy distinction. Whilst, for Schmitt, this notion suggested the impossibility of democracy, for Mouffe it implies the intrinsic limits of democratic inclusion and the necessity for an ongoing process of inclusion/exclusion. See Mouffe (1993: ch. 8 and 2000: ch. 2).

2 Such a rationale underpins the politics of the Dadaist and anarcho-communist political activist, Raoul Haussmann. Dadaism believed that reality was a chaotic, disordered flux and criticised the belief in the supremacy of human reason. As such, Dadaists sought to transcend binary opposites – Self-Other; identity and difference – that limited meaning. They accepted the arbitrariness of language and presented human history 'as a conflict between the human urge to create fixed forms and the flux that perpetually sweeps them away, leaving things much as they had ever been' (Sheppard, 2000: 182). Thus Dadaism could be seen as a quintessential third way position, explaining, in part, the general support by Dadaists for anarchism or anarcho-communism (see Sheppard, 2000: 305).

BIBLIOGRAPHY

Anderson, P. (2000) 'Renewals', *New Left Review* (II), no. 1: 5–24.

Bagnoli, P. (1984) *Piero Gobetti: Cultura e politica in un liberale del Novecento*. Florence: Passigli.

Bagnoli, P. (1996) 'L'idea liberalsocialista', in P. Bagnoli, *Rosselli, Gobetti e la rivoluzione democratica*. Florence: La Nuova Italia.

Bahzdid [no first name] (1998) 'Du racisme et de "l'inégalité" des races', *Résistance!*, 2 (December 1997– January 1998): 6–10.

Bardèche, M. (1961) *Qu'est-ce que le fascisme?* Paris: Les Sept Couleurs.

Barry, A., Osborne, T. and Rose, N. (eds) (1996) *Foucault and Political Reason: Liberalism, Neo-Liberalism and Rationalities of Government*. London: UCL Press.

Barry, J. (1996) 'Sustainability, Political Judgement and Citizenship: connecting green politics and democracy', in Doherty and de Geus (eds) (1996).

Barry, J. (1999) *Rethinking Green Politics: nature, virtue and progress*. London: Sage.

Bastow, S. (1997) 'Front national economic policy: from neo-liberalism to protectionism?', *Modern and Contemporary France*, vol. 5, no. 1: 61–72.

Bastow, S. (1998) 'The Radicalization of Front national Discourse: a Politics of the Third Way?', *Patterns of Prejudice*, vol. 32, no. 3: 55–68.

Bastow, S. (2000) 'Le Mouvement national républicain: Moderate Right-wing Party or Party of the Extreme Right?', *Patterns of Prejudice*, vol. 34, no. 2: 3–18.

Bastow, S. (2001) 'Third way discourse in inter-war France', *Journal of Political Ideologies*, vol. 6, no. 2: 169–90.

Bastow, S. (2002) 'Ideology and Social Movements: the case of the FN', in A. Finlayson and J. Valentine (eds) (2002) *Politics and Post-Structuralism: An Introduction*. Edinburgh: Edinburgh University Press.

Bastow, S., Martin, J. and Pels, D. (eds) (2002a) *Third Way Ideologies*, Special Issue of the *Journal of Political Ideologies*, vol. 7, no. 3.

Bastow, S., Martin, J. and Pels, D. (2002b) 'Introduction: third ways in political ideology', *Third Way Ideologies*, Special Issue of the *Journal of Political Ideologies*, vol. 7, no. 3.

Béland, D., Vergniolle de Chantal, F. and Waddan, A. (2002) 'Third way social policy: Clinton's legacy', *Policy and Politics*, vol. 30, no. 1: 19–30.

Bell, D. (1988) *The End of Ideology: On the Exhaustion of Political Ideas in the Fifties*. Cambridge, MA: Harvard University Press.

Bellamy, R. (1985) 'Liberalism and historicism: Benedetto Croce and the political role of idealism in modern Italy, c. 1890–1952', in A. Moulakis (ed.) *The Promise of History*. Berlin/New York: De Gruyter.

Bellamy, R. (1991) 'Between economic and ethical liberalism: Benedetto Croce and the dilemmas of liberal politics', *History of the Human Sciences*, 4.

Bellamy, R. (1992) *Liberalism and Modern Society: An Historical Argument*. Cambridge: Polity.

Bellamy, R. (2001) 'Two views of Italy's failed revolution', *Journal of Modern Italian Studies*, 6.

Benedetti, J.-Y. (1996) 'Maastricht, c'est la mort, la nation c'est la vie', editorial, *Jeune Nation*, no. 19 (January).

Benedetti, J.-Y. (1997) 'OAS: les raisons d'un échec', editorial, *Jeune Nation*, no. 29 (February).

Benedetti, J.-Y. (2001) 'Speech at the Fête Jeanne d'Arc', 13 May 2001, at http://www.jeune-nation.com/.

Benedetti, J.-Y. (n.d.A) 'La réalité nationale', editorial, *Jeune Nation*, no. 25, at http://www.jeune-nation.com/.

Benedetti, J.-Y. (n.d.B) 'La nation est l'addition de ses régions', editorial, *Jeune Nation*, no. 10.

Benedetti, J.-Y. (n.d.C) 'France: ton avenir est le nôtre', editorial, *Jeune Nation*, no. 32.

Benedetti, J.-Y. (n.d.D) 'Un seul ennemi: Le mondialisme', editorial, *Jeune Nation*, no. 11.

Benedetti, J.-Y. (n.d.E) 'Jamais Israel', editorial, *Jeune Nation*, no. 23.

Benedetti, J.-Y. (n.d.F) 'Une seule allégeance: la France', editorial, *Jeune Nation*, no. 36.

Benedetti, J.-Y. (n.d.G) 'La fierté français', editorial, *Jeune Nation*, no. 8.

Benedetti, J.-Y. (n.d.H) 'Le Front national et nous', editorial, *Jeune Nation*, no. 26.

Benedetti, J.-Y. (n.d.I) 'Les feux de la sagesse', editorial, *Jeune Nation*, no. 17.

Benedetti, J.-Y. (n.d.K) 'Un monde nouveau', editorial, *Jeune Nation*, no. 1.

Benedetti, J.-Y. (n.d.L) 'Démocratie: le peuple en esclavage', editorial, *Jeune Nation*, no. 21.

Benedetti, J.-Y. (n.d.M) 'Une insulte à l'intelligence', editorial, *Jeune Nation*, no. 28.

Benedetti, J.-Y. (n.d.N) 'Démocratie: la règne de l'argent', editorial, *Jeune Nation*, no. 31.

Benedetti, J.-Y. (n.d.O) 'La crise du Front national et nous', editorial, *Jeune Nation*, no. 35.

Benedetti, J.-Y. (n.d.P) 'Pour un manifeste nationaliste', editorial, *Jeune Nation*, no. 37.

Bergeron, F. and Vilgier, P. (1985) *De Le Pen à Le Pen*. Bouère: Editions Dominique Martin Morin.

Berman, M. (1983) *All That is Solid Melts into Air: The Experience of Modernity*. London: Verso.

Besagne, Y. (n.d.) 'Megret? Oui, mais encore?', *Résistance!*, vol. 10.

Betz, H.-G. (1994) *Radical Right-Wing Populism in Western Europe*. London: St Martin's Press.

Bevir, M. (1999) *The Logic of the History of Ideas*. Cambridge: Cambridge University Press.

Bevir, M. (2000) 'New Labour: a study in ideology', *The British Journal of Politics and International Relations*, vol. 2, no. 3: 277–301.

Biehl, J. and Staudenmaier, P. (1995) *Ecofascism: lessons from the German experience*. Edinburgh: AK Press.

Blair, T. (1993) 'New Community, New Individualism', 10th Arnold Goodman Charity Lecture, reprinted in Blair (1996a) *New Britain*: 215–22.

Blair, T. (1994) 'New Labour, New Britain', Speech to Labour Party Conference, reprinted in Blair (1996a) *New Britain*: 35–50.

Blair, T. (1995a) 'The Young Country', Speech to 1995 Labour Party Conference, reprinted in Blair (1996a) *New Britain*: 62–72.

Blair, T. (1995b) 'The Radical Coalition', Speech to Fabian Society, reprinted in Blair (1996a) *New Britain*: 4–21.

Blair, T. (1996a) *New Britain: My Vision of a Young Country*. London: Fourth Estate.

Blair, T. (1996b) 'The Stakeholder Economy', Speech to Singapore Business Community, reprinted in Blair (1996a) *New Britain*: 291–6.

Blair, T. (1996c) *'Faith in the City* – Ten Years On', Speech in Southwark Cathedral, reprinted in Blair (1996a) *New Britain*: 297–309.

Blair, T. (1998) *The Third Way: New Politics for the New Century*. London: Fabian Society.

Blair, T. (2001) 'Third Way, Phase Two', *Prospect*, March: 10–13.

Blair, T. and Schröder, G. (1999) *Europe: the third way/Die Neue Mitte*. London: Labour Party.

Blumenberg, H. (1983) *The Legitimacy of the Modern Age*. Cambridge, MA and London: MIT Press.

Bobbio, N. (1986) *Italia fedele: Il mondo di Gobetti*. Florence: Passigli.

Bobbio, N. (1995) *Ideological Profile of Twentieth-Century Italy*. Princeton, NJ: Princeton University Press.

Bobbio, N. (1996) *Left and Right*. Cambridge: Polity.

Bookchin, M. (1993) 'Deep Ecology, Anarchosyndicalism, and the Future of Anarchist Thought', in *Deep Ecology and Anarchism*. London: Freedom Press.

Bosetti, G. (ed.) (1989) *Socialismo liberale. Il dialogo con Norberto Bobbio oggi*. Trento: Nuova Stampa Mondadori.

Bourdrel, P. (1970) *La Cagoule: 30 ans de complots*. Paris: Editions Alban Michel.

Bourgeois, L. (1998) *Solidarité*. Paris: Presses Universitaires de Septentrion.

Bourseiller, C. (1992) *Extrême-droite: l'Enquête*. Paris: Editions François Bourin.

Boutin, C. (1996) 'L'extrême-droite au-delà du nationalisme, 1958–1996', *Revue Française d'Histoire des Idées Politiques*, vol. 3, no. 1: 113–60.

Brendon, P. (2000) *The Dark Valley: A Panorama of the 1930s*. London: Jonathan Cape.

Burrin, P. (1986) *La dérive fasciste: Déat, Doriot, Bergery 1933–1945*. Paris: Seuil.

Callinicos, A. (2001) *Against the Third Way*. Cambridge: Polity.

Calogero, G. (1940) 'Primo manifesto del liberalsocialismo', in G. Calogero (1972) *Difesa del liberalsocialismo*: 199–220.

Calogero, G. (1941) 'Secondo manifesto del liberalsocialismo', in G. Calogero (1972) *Difesa del liberalsocialismo*: 221–6.

Calogero, G. (1943) 'Le "precisazioni" programmatiche del Partito d'Azione', in G. Calogero (1972) *Difesa del liberalsocialismo*: 227–8.

Calogero, G. (1944a) 'Ricordi del movimento liberalsocialista', in G. Calogero (1972) *Difesa del liberalsocialismo*: 189–98.

Calogero, G. (1944b) 'La democrazia al bivio e la terza via', in G. Calogero (1972) *Difesa del liberalsocialismo*: 71–96.

Calogero, G. (1944c) 'Socialismo liberale e liberalsocialismo', in G. Calogero (1972) *Difesa del liberalsocialismo*: 67–70.

Calogero, G. (1972) *Difesa del liberalsocialismo ed altri saggi*, eds M. Schiavone and D. Cofrancesco. Milan: Marzorati.

Camus, J.-Y. (1997) *Le Front national*. Paris: Editions Olivier Laurens.

Camus, J.-Y. (1998) *L'extrême droite aujourd'hui*. Toulouse: Editions Milan.

Camus, J.-Y. and Monzat, R. (1992) *Les droites radicales en France*. Lyon: Presses Universitaires de Lyon.

Cantelaube, A. (1967a) 'Positions', *Le Soleil*, 22–28 November.

Cantelaube, A. (1967b) 'On en parle', *Le Soleil*, 13–19 September.

Cantelaube, A. (1967c) 'Politique Internationale', *Le Soleil*, 26 July–1 August.

Cantelaube, A. (1967d) 'Positions', *Le Soleil*, 19–25 July.

Cantelaube, A. (1967e) 'Positions', *Le Soleil*, 27 September–3 October.

Cantelaube, A. (1967f) 'Positions', *Le Soleil*, 18–24 October.

Cantelaube, A. (1968) 'On en parle', *Le Soleil*, 10–16 July.

Carter, A. (2002) 'Associative Democracy' in A. Carter and G. Stokes (eds) (2002) *Democratic Theory Today: Challenges for the 21st Century*. Cambridge: Polity.

Carter, C. (1996) 'Worker Co-Operatives and Green Political Theory', in Doherty and de Geus (eds) (1996).

Chombeau, C. (1996a) 'Plusieurs groupuscules d'extrême droite se rapprochent du Front national', *Le Monde*, 12 November.

Chombeau, C. (1996b) 'Le syndicalisme officiel n'est plus légitime', *Le Monde*, 24 October.

Chombeau, C. (1997) 'Un ancien dirigeant OAS parmi les candidats du FN', *Le Monde*, 30 April.

Clarke, P. (1978) *Liberals and Social Democrats*. Oxford: Oxford University Press.

Coates, J. B. (1949) *The Crisis of the Human Person: Some Personalist Interpretations*. London: Longmans.

Cohen, J. and Rogers, J. (1995) *Associations and Democracy*. London/New York: Verso.

Cole, G. D. H. (1972) *Self Government in Industry*. London: Hutchinson.

Conlon, J.-Y. (1970) 'Quelle Europe?', *Le Soleil*, 22 May–5 June.

Cowling, M. and Martin, J. (eds) (2002) *Marx's Eighteenth Brumaire: (Post)Modern Interpretations*. London: Pluto.

Craig, E. (ed.) (1998) *Routledge Encyclopaedia of Philisophy*, at http://www.rep.routledge.co.m/views/home.html.

Cripps, H. (1997) 'An Ecologically Rational Approach to Technology', Supplement to the newsletter of the Campaign for Political Ecology, Issue 12 (Spring) at http://eco.gn.apc.org/ ev12supp.html.

Croce, B. (1946) *Ethics and Politics*. London: Bradford and Dickens.

Crook, S., Pakulski, J. and Waters, M. (1992) *Postmodernisation: change in advanced society*. London: Sage.

Dahl, G. (1999) *Radical Conservatism and the Future of Politics*. London: Sage.

Daly, G. (1999) 'Marxism and Postmodernity' in A. Gamble, D. Marsh and T. Tant (eds) *Marxism and Social Science*. Basingstoke: Macmillan.

de Geus, M. (1996) 'The Ecological Restructuring of the State', in Doherty and de Geus (1996).

de Jouvenel, B. (1928) *L'Économie dirigée*. Paris: Librairie Valois.

de Man, H. (1929), *Au-delà du socialisme*, 2nd edn. Paris: Alcan.

de Man, H. (1932) *Réflections sur l'économie dirigée*. Paris: L'Eglantine.

Déat, M. (1922a) 'La définition du socialisme d'après E. Durkheim', *La Vie Socialiste*, 14 January.

Déat, M. (1922b) 'Matérialisme historique et science sociale', *La Vie Socialiste*, 30 September: 1–2.

Déat, M. (1927a) 'Bolchevisme et socialisme', *La Vie Socialiste*, 15 January: 8–10.

Déat, M. (1928a) 'Notes pour l'action', *La Vie Socialiste*, 21 July: 8–12.

Déat, M. (1928b) 'Notes pour l'action', *La Vie Socialiste*, 28 July: 3–10.

Déat, M. (1929a) 'Religion et Régime social', *La Vie Socialiste*, 12 January: 7.

Déat, M. (1929b) 'Morale de classe et culture humaine', *Le Populaire*, 10 June: 1–2.

Déat, M. (1929c) 'Socialistes et Jacobins', *La Vie Socialiste*, 8 June: 8–10.

Déat, M. (1929d) 'Puissance de la logique', *Le Populaire*, 26 June: 1–2.

Déat, M. (1929e) 'La séparation du capitalisme et de l'Etat', *Le Populaire*, 31 August: 2.

Déat, M. (1929f) 'Pouvoir politique et puissance économique', *La Vie Socialiste*, 7 December: 9–10.

Déat, M. (1930) *Perspectives socialistes*. Paris: Librairie Valois.

Derrida, J. (1978) 'Structure, Sign and Play in the Discourse of the Human Sciences' in J. Derrida, *Writing and Difference*. London: Routledge.

Dobson, A. (1996) 'Democratising Green Theory: preconditions and principles', in Doherty and de Geus (1996).

Dobson, A. (2000) *Green Political Thought: An Introduction*, 3rd edn. London: Routledge.

Doherty, B. and de Geus, M. (eds) (1996) *Democracy and Green Political Thought: Sustainability, Rights and Citizenship*. London: Routledge.

Donzelot, J. (1984) *L'invention du social*. Paris: Fayard.

Dorémus, A. (1992) 'Esquisse pour une mise en perspective des rapports entre Carl Schmitt et le regime Hitlérian', in Dupeux (1992).

Driver, S. and Martell, L. (1998) *New Labour: Politics after Thatcherism*. Cambridge: Polity.

Driver, S. and Martell, L. (2000) 'Left, Right and the third way', *Policy and Politics*, vol. 28, no. 2: 147–61.

Dupeux, L. (ed.) (1992) *La Révolution Conservatrice Allemande sous la République Weimar*. Paris: Editions Kimé.

Eatwell, R. (1996) 'Towards a new model of generic fascism', *Journal of Theoretical Politics*, vol. 4, no. 2: 161–194.

Eckersley, R. (1992) *Environmentalism and Political Theory*. London: UCL Press.

Eckersley, R. (1996a) 'Liberal Democracy and the Rights of Nature: the Struggle for Inclusion', in F. Mathews (ed.), *Ecology and Democracy*, special issue of *Environmental Politics*, vol. 4, no. 4.

Eckersley, R. (1996b) 'Greening Liberal Democracy: the rights discourse revisited', in Doherty and de Geus (1996).

ECO (n.d.A) *Core Principles*, at http://eco.gn.apc.org/.

ECO (n.d.B), 'Sustainable Development', at http://eco.gn.apc.org/.

ECO (n.d.C), 'Population, Environment and Development: Seeking Common Ground', at http://eco.gn.apc.org/population.html

Europe-Ecologie (n.d.), *Manifesto of Europe-Ecologie*, at http://www.pcn-ncp.com/eco.htm.

Fairclough, N. (2000) *New Labour, New Language?* London: Routledge.

Ferraresi, A. (1996) *Threats to Democracy*. Princeton, NJ: Princeton University Press.

Finlayson, A. (1998) 'Ideology, discourse and nationalism', *Journal of Political Ideologies*, vol. 3, no. 1: 99–118.

Finlayson, A. (1999), 'Third Way Theory', *Political Quarterly*, vol. 70, no. 3 (July–September): 271–9.

Finlayson, A. (2000) 'New Labour: the culture of government and the government of culture', in T. Bewes and J. Gilbert (eds) (2000) *Cultural Capitalism: Politics after New Labour*. London: Lawrence and Wishart.

Finlayson, A. (2002a) 'The Horizon of Community', in A. Finlayson and J. Valentine (eds), *Politics and Post-structuralism: An Introduction*. Edinburgh: Edinburgh University Press.

Finlayson, A. (2002b) 'Elements of the Blairite Image of Leadership', *Parliamentary Affairs*, vol. 55, no. 3: 586–99.

Flood, C. (2000) 'The Cultural Struggle of the Extreme Right and the Case of Terre et Peuple', *Contemporary French Civilisation*, vol. 24, no. 2: 241–66.

Freeden, M. (1978) *The New Liberalism: An Ideology of Social Reform*. Oxford: Clarendon.

Freeden, M. (1986) *Liberalism Divided: A Study in British Political Thought 1914–1939*. Oxford: Oxford University Press.

Freeden, M. (1995) *Green Ideology: Concepts and Structures*. Oxford: OCEES.

Freeden, M. (1996) *Ideologies and Political Theory: A Conceptual Approach*. Oxford: Clarendon.

Freeden, M. (1999) 'The Ideology of New Labour', *The Political Quarterly*, vol. 70, no. 1: 42–51.

Front national (FN) (1997) *300 mesures pour la France*. Paris: Editions Nationale.

Fysh, P. and Wolfreys, J. (1992) 'Le Pen, the National Front and the Extreme Right in France', *Parliamentary Affairs*, vol. 45, no. 3: 309–26.

Gamble, A. (1988) *The Free Economy and the Strong State: The Politics of Thatcherism*. Basingstoke: Macmillan.

Gamble, A. and Wright, T. (eds) (1999) *The New Social Democracy*. Oxford: Blackwell.

Gentile, E. (1982) *Il mito dello stato nuovo dall'antigiolittismo al fascismo*. Rome-Bari: Laterza.

Ghezzo, M. (1998) 'Qu'est-ce qui se cache dans les hamburgers?', *Jeune Résistance*, no. 9 (janvier–février): 5.

Giddens, A. (1994) *Beyond Left and Right: The Future of Radical Politics*. Cambridge: Polity.

Giddens, A. (1998) *The Third Way: The Renewal of Social Democracy*. Cambridge: Polity.

Giddens, A. (2000) *The Third Way and its Critics*. Cambridge: Polity.

Giddens, A. (2002) *Where Now for New Labour?* Cambridge: Polity.

Giddens, A. (ed.) (2001) *The Global Third Way Debate*. Cambridge: Polity.

Gobetti, P. (1919a) 'Our Faith', in Gobetti (2000) *On Liberal Revolution*: 63–77.

Gobetti, P. (1919b) 'Towards a New Politics', in Gobetti (2000) *On Liberal Revolution*: 78–86.

Gobetti, P. (1922a) 'The Bourgeoisie', in Gobetti (2000) *On Liberal Revolution*: 86–92.

Gobetti, P. (1922b) 'Liberalism and the Workers', in Gobetti (2000) *On Liberal Revolution*: 125–6.

Gobetti, P. (1922c) 'A Teacher of Liberalism', in Gobetti (2000) *On Liberal Revolution*: 92–108.

Gobetti, P. (1924a) , 'Karl Marx', in Gobetti (2000) *On Liberal Revolution*: 22–4.

Gobetti, P. (1924b) 'A Problem of Freedom', in Gobetti (2000) *On Liberal Revolution*: 227–8.

Gobetti, P. (1924c) 'In Praise of the Guillotine', in Gobetti (2000) *On Liberal Revolution*: 212–15.

Gobetti, P. (1925) 'Our Protestantism', in Gobetti (2000) *On Liberal Revolution*: 137–40.

Gobetti, P. (1995) *La Rivoluzione liberale. Saggio sulla lotta politica in Italia*, ed. E. A. Perona. Turin: Einaudi. Originally published in 1924.

Gobetti, P. (2000) *On Liberal Revolution*, ed. N. Urbinati, trans. W. McCuaig. New Haven, CT and London: Yale University Press.

Goodin, R. (1992) *Green Political Theory*. Cambridge: Polity.

Gramsci, A. (1971) *Selection from the Prison Notebooks*, trans. Q. Hoare and G. Nowell-Smith. London: Lawrence and Wishart.

Gramsci, A. (1997) *L'Ordine Nuovo 1919–1920*. Turin: Einaudi.

Gray, J. (1993) 'An agenda for green conservatism', in J. Gray, *Beyond The New Right: Markets, Government And The Common Environment*. London: Routledge.

Griffin, R. (1991) *The Nature of Fascism*. London: Pinter.

Griffin, R. (1995) *Fascism*. Oxford: Oxford University Press.

Griffin, R. (1998) *International Fascism: theories, causes and the new consensus*. London: Arnold.

Griffin, R. (2000) 'Interregnum or endgame? The radical right in the "post-fascist" era', *Journal of Political Ideologies*, vol. 5, no. 2: 163–78.

Grimaldi, O. (2001) Speech at the tomb of Robert Brasillach on 3 February 2001, at http://www.jeune-nation.com/03022001brassillach.htm.

Gundle, S. (2000) 'The "civic religion" of the Resistance in post-war Italy', *Modern Italy*, vol. 5, no. 2: 113–32.

Haimart, J. (1998) 'GUD, le retour', *Ras l'Front*, May.

Hall, S. and Jacques, M. (eds) (1989) *New Times: The Changing Face of Politics in the 1990s*. London: Lawrence and Wishart.

Hall, S. (1988) *The Hard Road to Renewal*. London: Verso.

Hattersley, R. (2001) 'It's no longer my party', *The Guardian*, 24 June.

Hauffen, K. (n.d.) 'Nous vivons une époque formidable: Le monde de demain', *Jeune Résistance*, no. 16.

Hay, C. (1994) 'Crisis and the Discursive Unification of the State', in P. Dunleavy and J. Stanyer (eds), *Contemporary Political Studies 1994*. Belfast: Political Studies Association, UK.

Hay, C. (1997) 'Blajorism: towards a one-vision polity', *Political Quarterly*, vol. 68, no. 1: 372–8.

Hay, C. (1999) *The Political Economy of New Labour: Labouring under false pretences?* Manchester: Manchester University Press.

Hayward, J. E. S. (1960) 'Solidarist Syndicalism: Durkheim and Duguit, *Sociological Review*, vol. 8: 17–36, 185–202.

Held, D. (1995) *Democracy and the Global Order*. Cambridge: Polity.

Held, D., McGrew, A., Goldblatt, D. and Perraton, J. (1999) *Global Transformations*. Cambridge, Polity.

Henley, J. (2002a) 'The quiet fanatic from the Kop', *The Guardian*, 16 July.

Herf, J. (1984) *Reactionary Modernism*. Cambridge: Cambridge University Press.

Hines, C. (n.d.) 'Localisation: A Global Manifesto', at http://eco.gn.apc.org/ColinHinesLocalization.html.

Hirst, P. (1994) *Associative Democracy*. Cambridge: Polity.

Hirst, P. (1997) *From Statism to Pluralism. Democracy, Civil Society and Global Politics*. London: UCL Press.

Hirst, P. and Bader, V. (eds) (2001) *Associative Democracy: The Real Third Way*. London: Frank Cass.

Hobhouse, L. T. (1994) *Liberalism and Other Writings*, ed. J. Meadowcroft. Cambridge: Cambridge University Press.

Hobsbawm, E. (1994) *Age of Extremes: The Short Twentieth Century, 1914–1991*. Harmondsworth: Penguin.

Horn, G.-R. (2001) 'From "Radical" to "Realistic": Hendrik de Man and the International Plan Conferences at Pontigny and Geneva, 1934–1937', *Contemporary European History*, vol. 10, no. 2: 239–65.

Howarth, D. (2000) *Discourse*. Buckingham: Open University Press.

Howarth, D., Norval, A. and Stavrakakis, Y. (eds) (2000) *Discourse Theory and Political Analysis*. Manchester: Manchester University Press.

Hughes, G. and Little, A. (1999) 'The Contradictions of New Labour's Communitarianism', *Imprints*, vol. 4, no. 1: 37–62.

Hughes, H. Stuart (1974) *Consciousness and Society*. St Albans: Paladin.

Humphreys, M. (2000) ' "Nature" in deep ecology and social ecology: contesting the core', *Journal of Political Ideologies*, vol. 5, no. 2: 247–68.

Ignazi, P. (1992) 'The Silent Counter-revolution. Hypotheses on the Emergence of Extreme Right-Wing Parties in Europe', *European Journal of Political Research*, vol. 22, no. 1: 3–34.

Ignazi, P. (1997) 'New Challenges: Postmaterialism and the Extreme-Right', in M. Rhodes et al., *Developments in West European Politics*. Basingstoke: Macmillan.

Inglehart, R. (1977) *The Silent Revolution: Changing Values and Political Styles Among Western Publics*. Princeton, NJ: Princeton University Press.

Inglehart, R. (1990) *Culture Shift in Advanced Society*. Princeton, NJ: Princeton University Press.

Irvine, S. (n.d.) 'Sustainable Development – The Last Refuge of Humanism?', ECO at http://eco.gn.apc.org/ sust_dev_humanism.html.

Irvine, S. and Ponton, A. (1988) *A Green Manifesto: Policies for a Green Future*. London: Macdonald Optima.

Jacobitti, E. E. (1981) *Revolutionary Humanism and Historicism in Modern Italy*. New Haven, CT: Yale University Press.

Jacquemin, A. (n.d.) 'De la bande à Baader au nationalisme', *Résistance!*, no. 8.

Jessop, B. (1994) 'Post-Fordism and the State' in A. Amin (ed.) (1994) *Post-Fordism: A Reader*. Oxford: Blackwell.

Jeune Nation (JN) (n.d.A) 'Doctrine', at http://www.jeune-nation.com/.

JN (n.d.B) 'Ce qu'il nous faut faire', editorial, *Jeune Nation*, no. 33.

Jeunes contre le racisme en Europe (JRE) (n.d.) 'L'Extrême droite dans les facs', at http://www.neuronnexion.fr/jre/j_broch_fafsfacs.htm.

Joll, J. (1976) *Europe Since 1870: An International History*, 2nd edn. Middlesex: Penguin.

JPR (1998) 'Antisemitism World Report, August 1998: France', at http://www.jpr.org.uk/antisem.

Julien, F. (1981) *Pour en finir avec la droite*. Paris: La Librairie Française.

Kenny, M. and Smith, M. J. (1997) '(Mis)Understanding Blair', *Political Quarterly*, vol. 68, no. 3: 220–30.

King, D. and Wickham-Jones, M. (1999) 'From Clinton to Blair: the Democratic (party) origins of welfare to work', *Political Quarterly*, vol. 70, no. 1: 62–74.

Kitschelt, H. (1998) *The Radical Right in Western Europe*. Michigan: University of Michigan Press.

Kumar, K. (1995) *From Post-Industrial to Post-Modern Society*. Oxford: Blackwell.

Laclau, E. (1979) *Politics and Ideology in Marxist Theory*. London: Verso.

Laclau, E. (1990) *New Reflections on the Revolution of Our Time*. London: Verso.

Laclau, E. (1996a) *Emancipation(s)*. London: Verso.

Laclau, E. (1996b) 'The Death and Resurrection of the Theory of Ideology', *Journal of Political Ideologies*, vol. 1, no. 3: 201–20.

Laclau, E. and Mouffe, C. (1990) 'Post-Marxism without Apologies' in E. Laclau (1990) *New Reflections*.

Laclau, E. and Mouffe, C. (2001) *Hegemony and Socialist Strategy: Towards a Radical Democratic Politics*, 2nd edn. London: Verso. First published in 1985.

Larrain, J. (1991) *Marxism and Ideology*. Aldershot: Gregg Revivals.

Larsen, F. (1998) 'Etes-vous prêts à avaler n'importe quoi ?', *Résistance!*, no. 2 (December–January): 11.

Lash, S. (1990) *Sociology of Postmodernism*. London: Routledge.

Lash, S. and Urry, J. (1987) *The End of Organized Capitalism*. Cambridge: Polity.

Laurat, L. (1931) *Économie planée contre économie enchaînée*. Paris: Librairie Valois.

Le Coeur, J.-Y. (1970a) 'Réflexions sur la monnaie', *Le Soleil*, mid-July–end August.

Le Coeur, J.-Y. (1970b) 'Le Marché Commun, An XIII', *Le Soleil*, 12–25 June.

Le Coulon, J.-Y. (1970a) 'Face à la tryannie marxiste', *Le Soleil*, mid-July–end August.

Le Coulon, J.-Y. (1970b) 'Briser le carcan capitaliste', *Le Soleil*, 26 June–9 July.

Le Goff', J.-C. (1968) 'Le Nationalisme', *Le Soleil*, 6–12 November.

Leadbeater, C. (1999) *Living On Thin Air: The New Economy*. London: Viking.

Lefort, C. (1986) *The Political Forms of Modern Society: Bureaucracy, Democracy, Totalitarianism*. Cambridge: Polity.

Lehner, F. (n.d.) 'L'ONU et consorts, creusets d'une conscience planetaire antinationale', *Résistance!*, no. 7.

Lepre, A. (1997) *L'anticomunismo e l'antifascismo in Italia*. Bologna: Il Mulino.

Levitas, R. (1996) 'The Concept of Social Exclusion and the New Durkheimian Hegemony', *Critical Social Policy*, vol. 16, no. 1: 5–20.

Levrat, J. (1992) 'Heidegger et le National-Socialisme', in Dupeux (1992).

Levy, C. (2000) 'Currents of Italian Syndicalism before 1926', *International Review of Social History*, 45.

Lichtheim, G. (1969) *The Origins of Socialism*. London: Weidenfeld and Nicholson.

Lipietz, A. (1995) *Green Hopes*. Cambridge: Polity.

Lister, R. (2001) 'New Labour: a study in ambiguity from a position of ambivalence', *Critical Social Policy*, vol. 21, no. 4: 425–47.

Little, A. (2002a) *The Politics of Community: Theory and Practice*. Edinburgh: Edinburgh University Press.

Little, A. (2002b) 'Community and Radical Democracy' in Bastow, et al. (2002a), *Third Way Ideologies*: 369–82.

Little, A. (2002c) 'Rethinking civil society: radical democratic politics and the legitimisation of unpaid activities', *Contemporary Politics*, vol. 8, no. 2: 103–15.

Little, A. and Martin, J. (2002) 'Conflict and Community: Radical Democracy and Associationalism', paper presented to the European Consortium for Political Research Joint Sessions, panel on 'Rescuing Democracy: the Lure of the Associative Elixir', University of Turin, 22–27 March.

Loubet del Bayle, J.-L. (1961) *Les Non-conformistes des années 30*. Paris: Seuil.

Lyotard, J.-F. (1984) *The Postmodern Condition*. Manchester: Manchester University Press.

Maillard, T. (1998a) 'France, francité, francisme: 3 exigeances nationalistes pour l'avenir', *Résistance!*, no. 4 (May–June): 8–9.

Malliarakis, J.-G. (1966) 'Indiscretions', *Le Soleil*, 13 December.

Malliarakis, J.-G. (1985) *Ni trusts, ni soviets*. Paris: Editions du Trident.

Mandelson, P. (2002) 'Introduction' to P. Mandelson, *The Blair Revolution Revisited*. London: Politico's.

Mandelson, P. and Liddle, R. (1996) *The Blair Revolution*. London: Politico's. Re-issued in 2002 as P. Mandelson, *The Blair Revolution Revisited*. London: Politico's.

Marion, P. (1933) *Socialisme et Nation*. Paris: Imprimerie du Centaur.

Marquand, D. (1988) *The Unprincipled Society*. London: Fontana.

Marquand, D. (1999a) *The Progressive Dilemma: From Lloyd George to Blair*, 2nd edn. London: Phoenix Giant.

Marquand, D. (1999b) 'Premature Obsequies: Social Democracy Comes in From the Cold' in Gamble and Wright (1999) *The New Social Democracy*.

Martell, L. (1992) 'New ideas of socialism', *Economy and Society*, vol. 21, no. 2: 15–72.

Martin, J. (1998) *Gramsci's Political Analysis: A Critical Introduction*. Basingstoke: Macmillan.

Martin, J. (2002) 'The political logic of discourse: a neo-Gramscian view', *History of European Ideas*, vol. 28, nos. 1–2: 21–31.

Mayer, N. and Perrineau, P. (1992) 'Why do they vote for Le Pen?', *European Journal of Political Research*, vol. 22.

Mégret, B. (1990) *La Flamme: les voies de la résistance*. Paris: Editions Robert Laffont.

Milan, D. (1998) 'Notre ami Carlos', *Résistance!*, no. 3 (March): 25.

Miliband, D. (ed.) (1994) *Reinventing the Left*. Cambridge: Polity.

Mills, M. (1996) 'Green Democracy: the search for an ethical solution', in Doherty and de Geus (1996).

Montagnon, B. (1929) *Grandeur et Servitude Socialistes*. Paris: Librairie Valois.

Morefield, J. (2002) 'Hegelian Organicism, British New Liberalism and the Return of the Family State', *History of Political Thought*, vol. XXIII, no. 1: 141–70.

Mosse, G. L. (1979) 'Towards a general theory of fascism', in G. L. Mosse,

International Fascism: New Thoughts and New Approaches. New York: Howard Fertig.

Mosse, G. L. (1999) *The Fascist Revolution*. New York: Howard Fertig.

Mouffe, C. (1993) *The Return of the Political*. London: Verso.

Mouffe, C. (2000) *The Democratic Paradox*. London: Verso.

Mounier, E. (1952) *Personalism*. London: Routledge and Kegan Paul.

Mura, V. (1994) 'Prefazione' to Bovero, et al. (eds) (1994) *I dilemmi del liberalsocialismo*. Rome: La Nuova Italia Scientifica.

Norval, A. (2000) 'Review Article: The Things We Do with Words – Contemporary Approaches to the Analysis of Ideology', *British Journal of Political Science*, vol. 30: 313–46.

Novak, M. (ed.) (1998) *Is There A Third Way? Essays on the Changing Direction of Socialist Thought*. London: IEA Health and Welfare Unit.

Novelli, C. (2000) *Il Partito d'Azione e gli italiani*. Milan: La Nuova Italia.

OF (1967) 'Indiscretions', *Le Soleil*, 16 May.

OF (1969) 'La Direction de l'OF a décidé la création d'une commission générale des jeunesses', *Le Soleil*, première semaine, November.

OF (1970) 'General Proposition of the 1st OF Congress', *Le Soleil*, 2–15 October.

OF (1973) 'Un outil d'action révolutionnaire', *Le Soleil*, 1 June.

OF (1975) Propositions of the 2nd OF Congress, *Le Soleil*, 1 July.

Ophuls, W. (1977) *Ecology and the Politics of Scarcity*. San Francisco: W. H. Freeman and Co.

Parti Communautaire National-européen (PCN) (n.d.A) 'Pourquoi le PCN?', at http://www.pcn-ncp.com/pourquoi.htm.

PCN (n.d.B) 'European Manifesto', at http://www.pcn-ncp.com/European-Manifesto.htm.

PCN (n.d.C) 'L'Alternative National-Communiste: Mythes et Réalités du National-bolchevisme', at http://www.pcn-ncp.com/alternNB.htm.

Passmore, J. (1993) 'Environmentalism', in A. Dobson and P. Pettit (eds) (1993) *A Companion to Contemporary Political Theory*. Cambridge: Cambridge University Press.

Payne, S. (1980) *Fascism: Comparison and Definition*. Madison: Univerisity of Wisconsin Press.

Pels, D. (1987) 'Hendrik de Man and the Ideology of Planism', *International Review of Social History*, vol. 32, no. 3: 206–29.

Pels, D. (2002) 'Socialism Between Fact and Value: From Tony Blair to Hendrik de Man and Back', in Bastow, et al. (2002a) *Third Way Ideologies*: 281–99.

Perroux, C. (1971) 'L'importante est de détruire la communauté européenne', *Le Soleil*, 1 August: 3–11.

Perroux, C. (1972) 'Non à l'Europe et à la reine d'Angleterre', *Le Soleil*, 22 April (Referendum Special): 3.

Perroux, C. (1973a) 'La guerre de Kippour ou la guerre pour qui?', *Le Soleil*, 1 November: 5–10.

Perroux, C. (1973b) 'Un projet pour le déperissement de la race française', dossier for *Le Soleil*, 1 November.

Perroux, C. (1974a) 'Les Neuf vont déparler d'une seule voix', *Le Soleil*, 15 December 1973–1 January 1974: 7.

Perroux, C. (1974b) 'VIe République ou IVe en pire?', *Le Soleil*, 1 July: 11.

Pierce, R. (1966) *Contemporary French Political Thought*. London: Oxford University Press.

Plumyène, J. and R. Lasierra (1963) *Les Fascismes français, 1923–1963*. Paris: Seuil.

Porritt, J. (1984) *Seeing Green*. Oxford: Blackwell.

Powell, M. (2000) 'New Labour and the third way in the British welfare state: a new and distinctive approach?', *Critical Social Policy*, vol. 20, no. 1: 39–60.

Pugliese, S. G. (1999) *Carlo Rosselli: Socialist Heretic and Antifascist Exile*. Cambridge, MA and London: Harvard University Press.

Raco, M. (2002) 'Risk, Fear and Control: Deconstructing the Discourses of New Labour's Economic Policy', *Space and Polity*, vol. 6, no. 1: 25–47.

Rawnsley, A. (2001) *Servants of the People: The Inside Story of New Labour*, rvsd edn. London: Penguin.

Relano, P. (n.d.) 'Ecologie: Ces industriels qui nous empoisonnent', *Jeune Résistance*, no. 16.

Revelli, M. (1994) 'Gobetti "liberal-comunista"?' in Bovera, et al. (1994) *I dilemmi di liberalsocialismo*: 63–84.

Roberts, D. D. (1981) 'Croce and Beyond: Italian Intellectuals and The First World War', *International History Review*, 3: 201–35.

Roberts, D. D. (1987) *Benedetto Croce and the Uses of Historicism*. Berkeley: University of California Press.

Roditi, G. (1934) 'Fascisme et "regime intermédiaire"', *L'Homme Nouveau*, September.

Rohkramer, T. (1999) 'Antimodernism, Reactionary Modernism and National Socialism. Technocratic Tendencies in Germany, 1890–1945', *Contemporary European History*, vol. 8, no. 1: 29–50.

Rorty, R. (1989) *Contingency, Irony and Solidarity*. Cambridge: Cambridge University Press.

Rorty, R. (1999) 'A World Without Substances or Essences' in R. Rorty, *Philosophy and Social Hope*. Harmondsworth: Penguin.

Rose, N. (1999a) *Powers of Freedom: Reframing Political Thought*. Cambridge: Cambridge University Press.

Rose, N. (1999b) 'Inventiveness in politics', *Economy and Society*, vol. 28, no. 3: 467–93.

Rose, N. (2000) 'Community, Citizenship, and the Third Way', *American Behavioural Scientist*, vol. 43, no. 9: 1395–1411.

Rosselli, C. (1933) 'Il neo-socialismo francese nel quadro internazionale', in C. Rosselli (1998) *Scritti dell'Esilio, Vol. I*, ed. C. Casucci. Turin: Einuadi.

Rosselli, C. (1994) *Liberal Socialism*, ed. N. Urbinati, trans. W. McCuaig. Princeton, NJ: Princeton University Press. English translation of Rosselli (1997).

Rosselli, C. (1997) *Socialismo liberale*, ed. J. Rosselli, intro. N. Bobbio. Turin: Einaudi. Originally published in 1930.

Rossi, E. (1995) *Jeunesse française des années 80–90: la tentation néo-fasciste*: Paris, Editions LGDJ.

Rusconi, G. E. (1995) *Resistenza e postfascismo*. Bologna: Il Mulino.

Saint-Julien, H. (1967a) 'Positions', *Le Soleil*, 25–31 October.

Sassoon, D. (1996) *One Hundred Years of Socialism: The West European Left in the Twentieth Century*. London: Fontana Press.

Sassoon, D. (1999a) 'Introduction: Convergence, continuity and change on the European left', in G. Kelly (ed.) *The New European Left*. London: Fabian Society.

Sassoon, D. (1999b) 'European Social Democracy and New Labour: Unity in Diversity?' in Gamble and Wright (1999) *The New Social Democracy*.

Saward, M. (1993) 'Green Democracy?', in A. Dobson and P. Lucardie (eds) (1993) *The Politics of Nature: Explorations of Green Political Theory*. London: Routledge.

Sbarberi, F. (1986) *Gramsci: un socialismo armonico*. Milan: Franco Angeli.

Sbarberi, F. (1999) *L'utopia della libertà eguale*. Turin: Bollati Boringhieri.

Schecter, D. (1990) 'Gramsci, Gentile and the Theory of the Ethical State in Italy', *History of Political Thought*, vol. 11, no. 3: 491–508.

Schecter, D. (1991) *Gramsci and the Theory of Industrial Democracy*. Aldershot: Avebury.

Schecter, D. (1994) *Radical Theories: Paths Beyond Marxism and Social Democracy*. Manchester: Manchester University Press.

Séveno, J. (1998) 'Pour une écologie radicale', *Jeune Résistance*, no. 8 (October–November): 3.

Shapiro, M. J. (1985–6) 'Metaphor in the Philosophy of the Social Sciences', *Culture and Critique*, vol. 2: 191–214.

Sheppard, R. (2000) *Modernism – Dada – Postmodernism*. Evanston, IL: Northwestern University Press.

Sidos, P. (1975) 'Interview', *Le Soleil*, October.

Sidos, P. (1966) 'On en parle', *Le Soleil*, 14 November.

Sidos, P. (1967a) 'On en parle', *Le Soleil*, 1–7 November.

Sidos, P. (1967b) 'On en parle', *Le Soleil*, 26 July–1 August.

Sidos, P. (1967c) 'On en parle', *Le Soleil*, 9 May.

Sidos, P. (1967d) 'On en parle', *Le Soleil*, 6 June.

Sidos, P. (1967e) 'On en parle', *Le Soleil*, 13 June.

Sidos, P. (1967f) 'On en parle', *Le Soleil*, 8–14 November.

Sidos, P. (1967g) 'On en parle', *Le Soleil*, 11 April.

Sidos, P. (1969) 'On en parle', *Le Soleil*, 12–25 February.

Sidos, P. (1970) 'Editorial', *Le Soleil*, 8–21 May.

Sidos, P. (1973) 'C'est la lutte finale qui commence', *Le Soleil*, 1 November: 2–4.

Smart, B. (1992) *Modern Conditions, Postmodern Controversies*. London: Routledge.

Smith, A. M. (1998) *Laclau and Mouffe: The Radical Democratic Imaginary*. London: Routledge.

Soucy, R. (1986) *French Fascism: The First Wave 1924–1933*. New Haven, CT: Yale University Press.

Soucy, R. (1995) *French Fascism: The Second Wave 1933–1939*. New Haven: Yale University Press.

Spretnak, C. and F. Capra (1985) *Green Politics*. London: Paladin.

Spriano, P. (1977) *Gramsci e Gobetti*. Turin: Einaudi.

Stavrakakis, Y. (2000) 'On the emergence of Green ideology: the dislocation factor in Green politics', in D. Howarth, et al. (2000).

Stern, F. (1961) *The Politics of Cultural Despair*. Berkeley: University of California Press.

Sternhell, Z. (1976) 'Fascist Ideology', in W. Laqueur (ed.), *Fascism: A Reader's Guide*. London: Pelican.

Sternhell, Z. (1983) *Ni droite, ni gauche*. Paris: Seuil.

Sternhell, Z. (2000) 'Fascism: reflections on the fate of ideas in twentieth century history', *Journal of Political Ideologies*, vol. 5, no. 2.

Stevens, V. (n.d.) 'Population and Immigration – the Hot Potato', ECO, at http://eco.gn.apc.org/immigration.html

Taguieff, P.-A. (1985) 'Les droites radicales en France: Nationalisme révolutionnaire et national-libéralisme', *Les Temps Modernes*, no. 465: 1783–1841.

Taylor, C. (1989) *Sources of the Self: The Making of the Modern Identity*. Cambridge: Cambridge University Press.

Telò, M. (1988) *Le New Deal européen: la pensée et la politique sociales-démocrates face à la crise des années trente*. Brussels: Editions de l'Université de Bruxelles.

Temple, M. (2000) 'New Labour's Third Way: pragmatism and governance', *The British Journal of Politics and International Relations*, vol. 2, no. 3: 302–25.

Thiriart, J. (n.d.A) 'L'Europe-Etat et l'Europe-Nation se feront contre les USA', at http://www.pcn-ncp.com/Europe.htm.

Thiriart, J. (n.d.B) 'Approche du communitarisme', at http://www.pcn-ncp.com/communautarisme.htm.

Thurlow, R. (1999) *Fascism*. Cambridge: Cambridge University Press.

Torfing, J. (1999) *New Theories of Discourse: Laclau, Mouffe and Žižek*. Oxford: Blackwell.

Toynbee, P. (2001) 'This is Blair's new road map, but it leads nowhere', *The Guardian*, 28 February.

UR (1998a) 'Hommage à Che Guevara', *Jeune Résistance*, no. 9 (January–February): 2.

UR (1998b) 'Crise du Front National', *Résistance!*, no. 7 (May–June): 6–7.

Unité Radicale (UR) (n.d.A) 'Le Programme d'Unité Radicale', at http://www.unite-radicale.com/ur2.htm.

UR, (n.d.B) 'Campagne contre les Mac Do', at http://www.unite-radicale.com/macdo.htm.

UR (n.d.C) 'Pourquoi Unité Radicale?', at http://www.unite-radicale.com/ur.htm.

UR (n.d.D) 'Front politique', at http://www.unite-radicale.com/fp.htm.

UR (n.d.E) 'Au commencement était l'action', *Jeune Résistance*, no. 15.

UR (n.d.F) 'Ferenc Szalasi, un fasciste de gauche', *Résistance!*, no. 6: 6–7.

Urbinati, N. (2000) 'Liberalism as a Theory of Conflict', introduction to P. Gobetti, *On Liberal Revolution* (2000): xv–lvi.

Valois, G. (1924) *La Révolution Nationale*. Paris: Nouvelle Librairie Nationale.

Valois, G. (1926a) 'Nationalisme et socialisme', *Nouveau siècle*, 25 January: 1.

Valois, G. (1926b) 'Nationalisme et socialisme – II', *Nouveau siècle*, 26 January: 1.

Valois, G. (1926c) 'Nationalisme et socialisme – III', *Nouveau siècle*, 27 January: 1.

Vanek, W. M. (1965) 'Piero Gobetti and the Crisis of the "Dopoguerra"', *The Journal of Modern History*, vol. 37: 1–17.

Vincent, A. (1992) *Modern Political Ideologies*. Oxford: Blackwell.

Vincent, A. (1998) 'New Ideologies for Old?', *Political Quarterly*, vol. 69, no. 1: 48–58.

Wallas, G. (1948) *Human Nature in Politics*. London: Constable.

Warren, M. E. (2001) *Associations and Democracy*. Princeton, NJ and Oxford: Princeton University Press.

White, S. (2001) 'The Ambiguities of the Third Way', in S. White (ed.) (2001) *New Labour: The Progressive Future?* Basingstoke: Palgrave.

Wissenburg, M. L. J. (1997) 'A taxonomy of green ideas', *Journal of Political Ideas*, vol. 2, no. 1: 29–50.

Wolfreys, J. (1993) 'An Iron Hand in a Velvet Glove: The Programme of the French National Front', *Parliamentary Affairs*, vol. 46, no. 3: 415–29.

Wood, E. M. (1998) *The Retreat from Class: A New 'True' Socialism*, rvsd edn. London: Verso. First published in 1986.

Woodward, K. (1997) 'Concepts of Identity and Difference', in K. Woodward (ed.), *Identity and Difference*. Milton Keynes: Open University.

Wright, T. (2001) 'Liberal Socialism: Then and Now' in N. Lawson and N. Sherlock (eds) *The Progressive Century*. Basingstoke: Palgrave.

INDEX

Novelli, C., 92 n21

Œuvre française (OF), 95, 96, 97, 100, 102, 103, 104, 106, 107, 108, 112, 115 n8, 116 n23
Ophuls, W., 130
organicism, 31–2, 37, 38, 79, 113, 124, 127, 128–9, 134
Organisation Armée Sécrète, 105

Parti Communautaire National-européen (PCN), 95, 104, 106, 116 n24, 126
Parti ouvrier belge, 35
Parti socialiste (PS), 117, 134
Partito d'Azione see Action Party
Pels, D., 134
Perrineau, P., 111
Perroux, C., 107
personalism, 31, 83, 138 n16
Plan Meidner, 45 n4
Planck, M., 27
planism, 34–5, 81
planned economy, 34
political ideology, 7, 14–20, 21–45, 59–60, 118, 140–1
populism, 62, 113, 116 n26
Porritt, J., 129, 135
post-Fordism, 65, 71 n4, 126
Powell, M., 61–2
pragmatism, 4, 5, 51, 62–3
Prezzolini, G., 76

Raco, M., 69
Ramos, R. L., 106
Rassemblement pour la République (RPR), 110
Rassinier, P., 115 n16
Résistance ouvrière, 101
Résistance Verte, 126
revolutionary liberalism, 75, 78
revolutionary nationalists (or 'national revolutionaries'), 19, 95, 97–116, 126
Roditi, G., 35
Rose, N., 55–6, 67
Rosselli, C., 73, 74, 79–82, 84, 86, 87–9, 91 n13
Rossi, E., 95, 96
Rousseau, J.-J., 148
Russian revolution (1917), 29, 33, 77

Salvemini, G., 76

Sassoon, D., 70
Saward, M., 129
Sbarberi, F., 86
Schmitt, C., 37, 155 n1
Schröder, G., 1, 117
Schrödinger, E., 27
Sidos, P., 97, 100, 102, 106, 115 n8
Smith, M. J., 61
social democracy, 1–4, 17, 45 n4, 46–71, 72, 118, 139, 146, 148, 149, 154; *see also* Geman Social Democratic Party; British Labour Party
social justice, 3, 5, 49, 54, 55, 60, 61, 63, 72, 73, 81, 83–4, 85, 109
socialism, 19, 24, 26, 32, 33–6, 59, 72–92, 128, 129
ethical, 34, 61
in Italy, 74, 78–9, 107
and revisionism, 33–4, 70, 80, 152
Soviet, 35, 82, 148
see also liberal socialism
solidarism (French), 30, 31–2, 109
Sombart, W., 37
Sorel, G., 27, 34
Spengler, O., 37
Spretnak, C., 134
Stalin, J., 144
state
and associationalism, 154
in inter-war period 29–38
and neo-fascism, 96, 109–12
and New Labour, 51–8, 65–6, 70
and socialism, 35–6, 143, 145
Staudenmaier, P., 133
Stavrakakis, Y., 120–1, 131–2, 137 n2–3
Sternhell, Z., 93, 114 n1
Stevens, V., 131
Stirbois, J.-P., 109
stock-market crash (1929), 28
Strasser, O. and G., 106
sustainable development, 122–3
syndicalism, 28, 34, 35, 38, 74, 106
Szalasi, F., 106

Taguieff, P.-A., 111, 112
Tawney, R. H., 72
Telò, M., 33, 35, 45 n4
Terre et Peuple, 96
Thatcher, M., 66
Thatcherism, 17, 57, 60, 62
Thiriart, J., 96, 105

179